STOCK MARKET PRIMER

Stock Market
Primer REVISED EDITION

Claude N. Rosenberg, Jr.

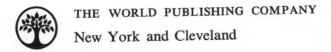

THE WORLD PUBLISHING COMPANY
New York and Cleveland

Published by The World Publishing Company
2231 West 110th Street, Cleveland, Ohio 44102
Published simultaneously in Canada by
Nelson, Foster & Scott Ltd.

First Printing—1969

Library of Congress Catalog Card Number: 75–88595
Printed in the United States of America

WORLD PUBLISHING
TIMES MIRROR

Investors, small and large,
who want to achieve real success in
the stock market and who realize
the wisdom of the philosophy:

The world belongs to those
who think and act with it,
who keep a finger on its pulse.

DEAN WILLIAM R. INGE

CONTENTS

7

From Writer to Reader

This book was originally published in 1962 at the "blue chip" price of $12.50. At that time—and since then in every year— I have heard from countless people who have read *Stock Market Primer* and who have told me that they consider it the most understandable and worthwhile book they have ever read on the subject of stocks and the market. Needless to say, I hope they are right —and I hope that you, too, find it meaningful.

The *Primer* is now fully revised. What encourages me most is that the revision entailed almost no change in basic approach. What seemed basic and important seven years ago still "holds water" today. This successful aging gives me more confidence than ever that the substance is there and that the reader can gain lasting benefit from its use.

* * *

The Stock Market! One very learned man I know calls it "The Greatest Dice Game in the World." "What," he asks, "makes Standard Oil of New Jersey worth two points less—or over $400 million less—today than it was yesterday? Has the company really changed by almost a half billion dollars in one day? And then what makes the same company worth three points more—or over $600 million more—next week?"

Indeed, these are good questions. And if you approach the market on this basis, it does appear to be a senior Las Vegas. Yet there is far more to the stock market than these day-to-day fluctuations. And, from the average investor's viewpoint, there is something of much greater importance. That is, what makes Standard Oil or Zenith Radio or XYZ Electronics Company worth double or triple or quadruple or ten times the value it was five or ten years ago?

15

The answer to this is relatively simple. After all, hindsight is *always* 20-20! The important thing is that we can learn from our hindsight.

Anyone connected with investment securities will agree that it is a very *in*exact science. Like many other pursuits, there is a certain amount of luck involved. But like many other pursuits, you can prepare yourself to do a better job than the next fellow and, in so doing, will achieve far superior results.

Is there an exact formula which will provide *you* with superior *results?* Is there a real formula for successful investing? Well, I know of one. And it results from a real life experience. It involves a man I know who, forty years ago, determined that he would retire forty years later with $100,000. Believe it or not, this man retired with $100,000. His ability to do this can be whipped into what I'm sure you'll agree is a true formula for successful investing. His ability to retire after forty years with $100,000 was due to four factors, as follows:

1. hard work
2. economical living
3. occasional saving

and, to the recent death of his uncle who left him $97,000.

Seriously, I don't know how many of you can depend on such a formula to provide you with *your* future. But I do know that there is a serious approach to the problem of investing money and achieving success. Boiling this serious formula down to two elements would look something like this:

Hindsight + Foresight = Success

The discussions to follow will give you the basic facts you need to know in buying stocks and bonds. They will give you the background and foundation for intelligent investing. In essence, they will attempt to fill the first part of our formula—hindsight. As to foresight, this is, of course, the *in*exact part of investing, but an important part of this book is devoted to providing you with the proper foresight—so that you will arrive at the right investment decisions in the future.

PART I

AN INTRODUCTION TO INVESTMENTS

CHAPTER 1

Investment Channels

Were I to give you a simple definition of the word "investment," it would read, "setting money to work to earn more money." Yet it seems that simple definitions are seldom enough and the case of investments is no exception. This is because there should be a few more words added to our simplification, namely that "any investment involves risk." And before you argue the point that certain investments do not involve any risk (i.e., savings accounts under $10,000, U. S. Government Bonds), let's take a look at the two basic risks which exist:

1. The risk that you might lose your capital (this is the ordinary risk that you take when you go into business, buy real estate, stocks, etc.).
2. The risk that your investment will not keep up with the purchasing value of the dollar.

The first of these risks is, of course, obvious and always has been. The second has become widely publicized in the United States in recent years. It involves the threat of that dreaded word *inflation* and the risk that $1.00 invested today will not buy the same $1.00 worth of goods and services in the future. Those of us in the investment business have done our best to warn people of the declining purchasing power of the dollar and how one should provide himself with a "hedge against inflation." The statistics, of course, bear us out. From 1939 to 1959, for example, the purchasing power of the dollar was more than cut in half; and the most recent ten years have witnessed another 20% deterioration.

Unfortunately, the people who suffered most from inflation were the conservatives—those who concentrated on safety and avoided the forms of investment that involve more risk. Those who preserved cash or who bought future protection through insurance, those who depended on social security or pensions—all were left behind by the increasing cost of living.

Before discussing the different types of investment and how they rank in risks and rewards, let me point out one more "risk" which we, in the U. S. especially, must meet. Some people might call it the risk of "not keeping up with the Jones' "; suffice it to say that our population simply enjoys living better and should not be denied such pleasures. Certainly it is easy to see that the standard of living in our country is increasing steadily and we must make our money work to keep us up with this progress. Luxuries turn into necessities as time flies by and we have to make our money grow to buy these new necessities. For example, twelve years ago, a television set was a luxury; today it is a necessity. As one philosopher so aptly put it: More and more we find ourselves pondering how to reconcile our *net income* with our *gross habits*.

WHERE TO INVEST?

Let's take a look at the various forms of investment and see where they fit in a discussion of risks. Following are the most obvious investment channels:

U. S. Government obligations (bonds, notes, bills, etc.)
Savings deposits in commercial banks
Savings deposits in savings and loan associations
Life insurance and annuities
Real estate mortgages
Real estate
Corporate securities (corporate bonds, preferred stocks and common stocks)

1. *U. S. Government Obligations*

Certainly U. S. Government securities do not carry the so-called "ordinary risk" described above. You should not have to worry about the government defaulting on its obligations (if you worry about this, then there just isn't any investment suitable for *you*). Without belaboring a detailed discussion of "governments," let's look at the two basic forms of government securities which are of interest to the average investor:

a. Government obligations which can fluctuate in market price;
b. Government obligations which are *not* traded and which do not, therefore, fluctuate in market price.

In the first category, you find all government securities *with the exception of savings bonds*. Treasury bills (which have a life of only 90 days), certificates of indebtedness (always come due within one year), treasury notes (1 to 5 year obligations) and treasury bonds (issued only for a term of 5 years or more) all sell after their issue on a supply and demand basis and are, thus, subject to changes in market price.

Savings bonds, on the other hand, are not transferable and cannot be sold. Instead, the holder must turn them in to the government if he wants cash and will be paid a fixed amount depending on how long the bonds have been held.

In either case, the investor knows that he will eventually get what he deserves and that his income from these securities is completely secure. Thus, government obligations fall into the category of investments without the ordinary risk of losing capital. What these fixed income securities lack is protection against the rising cost of living and thus they do carry the second risk mentioned. To illustrate this risk, the First National City Bank of New York's monthly bulletin published the following chart in its May issue of 1956:

The conclusion, of course, is that—accounting for taxes and the increased cost of living—savings bonds bought in any year from 1935–1946 would *not* have kept up with inflation. The experience of savings bonds purchased from 1947–1958 (after World War II) is better than the pre-War period. Rather than show another lengthy table, suffice it to say that those bonds maturing from 1957 through 1968 just barely kept abreast with the rising cost of living for even the lowest tax-bracket individual. And, as might be expected, a high-bracket taxpayer would have suffered a loss of purchasing power. Whatever small after-tax,

RETURN OF 1935-46 SAVINGS BOND ISSUES AFTER INCOME TAX AND "INFLATION TAX"

Bought For $75 In	Maturity Value Of $100 In	Initial (Lowest) Personal Income Tax Rate	Income Tax On $25 Interest	Maturity Value Less Income Tax	"Inflation Tax"— Increase In Cost of Living Index Over The 10 Years	Amount of "Inflation Tax"	Maturity Value Less Income Tax and "Inflation Tax"	Dollars of Original Investment Lost	Average Annual Rate Of Loss
1935	1945	23.0%	(a)	$100.00	35.9%	$26.42	$73.58	$1.42	0.19%
1936	1946	15.0	(a)	100.00	44.2	30.65	69.35	5.65	0.75
1937	1947	15.0	(a)	100.00	55.7	35.77	64.23	10.77	1.44
1938	1948	16.6	(a)	100.00	70.5	41.35	58.65	16.35	2.18
1939	1949	16.6	(a)	100.00	71.4	41.66	58.34	16.66	2.22
1940	1950	17.4	(a)	100.00	71.6	41.72	58.28	16.72	2.23
1941	1951	20.4	$5.10	94.90	76.5	41.13	53.77	21.23	2.83
1942	1952	22.2	5.55	94.45	61.2	35.86	58.59	16.41	2.19
1943	1953	22.2	5.55	94.45	51.3	32.02	62.43	12.57	1.68
1944	1954	20.0	5.00	95.00	47.7	30.68	64.32	10.68	1.42
1945	1955	20.0	5.00	95.00	43.5	28.80	66.20	8.80	1.17
1946	1956	20.0	5.00	95.00	34.0	24.10	70.90	4.10	0.55

(a) The interest on savings bonds bought from 1935–1940 was not subject to federal income tax.

Source: First National City Bank of New York, monthly letter, May 1956, page 57.

after-inflation gains did occur, however, would hardly be sufficient to provide the bond owners with much of an improved standard of living. With inflationary pressures building up again in the U. S., it is doubtful that savings bonds of the future will be any more suitable than in the past for real protection against living cost hikes.

2. *Savings Accounts in Commercial Banks*

Needless to say, here, too, we find an investment which lacks the ordinary risk (because of insurance with an agency of the federal government on savings accounts up to $15,000 in any one bank), but we assume the risk that our dollars will not keep up with the declining purchasing power. Savings accounts can only grow through compounding interest and the interest paid by banks has been well below that available from other investments.

3. *Savings Accounts in Savings and Loan Associations*

Here, again, we have a "static" investment and we take the chance that inflation may eat away at our dollars. Savings and loan deposits (also insured up to $15,000 by a federal agency) normally pay 1–1½% more than savings accounts in commercial banks, but it is questionable whether the return from such accounts is sufficient to overcome inflation over the years.

4. *Insurance*

While a discussion of the countless insurance plans available could fill many volumes, let me summarize a few points pertinent to this subject:

a. Insurance with the top companies carries no ordinary risk, because of the huge reserves set up for the policy holder.

b. Life insurance should be purchased as *protection*, not as investment. It should protect the family from death, but should not be counted on to accomplish much for you while you're living. (Life insurance has been aptly described as "a plan that keeps you poor all your life so you can *die rich*.")

c. Life insurance and annuities carry the very definite risk of not keeping up with the dollar. In both cases you are buying a guarantee of a specified number of today's dollars *for a future date*. As example, those people who bought annuities in 1939 and protected themselves with what looked like adequate income at that time found themselves far short of a living income fifteen or twenty years later.

d. Annuities, like life insurance, have their use as a protective device, but they constitute a very poor form of investment. For one thing, they provide no hedge against inflation. Secondly, they are an extremely low-yielding investment. Most annuity policies are written on the assumption that the insurance company will earn about 3% for the holder, which is far below par. Annuities are only a convenient savings medium and I frankly don't recommend them.* The advent of "variable annuities" (wherein future payments to the policy holder will *vary* according to the value of an investment portfolio managed by the insurance company) may overcome the weaknesses I have mentioned.

5. *Real Estate and Real Estate Mortgages*

Like insurance, real estate covers a broad field which is a study in itself. For the sake of our discussion, ownership of property (whether improved or unimproved) carries the ordinary risks of losing part of your capital, but well-chosen real estate should more than compensate for inflation. I happen to believe that real estate constitutes a wonderful investment vehicle. Just a few attributes of real estate ownership are:

a. Depreciation from a building provides certain tax advantages and enables the owner to receive a tax-free cash "throw-off" to pay off his investment; likewise, the fact that property taxes and interest payments are deductible items for income tax purposes is of sizable benefit to the property owner.

---

* The exception is if you live far beyond a normal life span. In 1960, for example, one of our country's largest insurance companies pointed proudly to the fact that certain (15) policy holders had collected over 2½ times their investment in annuities. These people were all between 99 and 102 years of age, however, and if I were you I wouldn't count on this kind of life span.

b. Rate of return (yield) is higher than on most corporate securities;

c. An investor can borrow more heavily to buy real estate, thereby affording considerable "leverage" (described later in Chapter 16);

d. There may be a limited supply of land and/or property in a given area. In a growing region, this creates a very favorable supply-demand relationship—and leads to increasing property values.

e. An owner can trade properties without incurring a capital gain tax.

Unfortunately, real estate is not generally available to the smaller investor (other than home ownership, that is) and it must, of course, be realized that real estate takes management. Faucets do leak, pipes will occasionally break and tenants often move. Furthermore, neighborhoods and property values do change and real estate, like the stock market (or, for that matter, anything in life) is not a "One-Way Street."

This discussion involves actual ownership of property and has excluded mortgages. Mortgages (especially second mortgages) can carry considerable ordinary risk and it is debatable whether they constitute completely adequate hedge against inflation, although certainly when they are bought at sizable discounts, the return is more than sufficient to account for any increased living costs.

6. *Corporate Securities*

Because Chapter 3 differentiates between the types of corporate securities, suffice it to say right here that:

Bonds and preferred stocks both carry the purchasing power risk, as they have not provided a hedge against inflation over the years. Common stocks generally have been successful for protection against the rising cost of living, although selection here is all-important.

CONCLUSIONS

Not everyone can afford to concentrate solely on ordinary risk investments such as real estate and common stocks. Later on, after we have discussed the stock market, growth stocks, etc., we will come to more conclusions on investing, but it is important to point out here that most everyone should *balance* his investments to include a certain portion of ordinary risk ventures and a certain portion into those which are safe from ordinary risks, even though they do carry the purchasing power risk. Emphasis, however, should decidedly be on equities—on *ownership* forms of investment such as real estate and common stocks. As a matter of fact, aside from the protection of life insurance, anyone other than the most conservative investor should think almost solely in terms of equities.

CHAPTER 2

Forms of Business Organization

Because this book is devoted almost exclusively to *corporate* securities, it seems only proper to distinguish a *corporation* from other forms of business organization.

There are three basic ways of going into business in our country —(1) by yourself (as sole proprietor); (2) in partnership with one or more associates; and (3) by forming a corporation. Let's take a look at these three:

Sole Proprietorship—Here you have the simplest way of going into business. No legal papers needed, no extra expenses, you have only yourself to blame if things go wrong and the world is all yours if you succeed. Tax consequences are the very simplest. Whatever you earn you simply report to Uncle Sam and pay the prevailing income tax on this amount.

Partnership—This, too, is easy to form. You and I can go into business together as partners with only a verbal agreement (but don't ever do it that way). Legal papers are relatively simple and, thus, these expenses are minimal. And there are no extra expenses in the way of state fees, etc. Taxes are also simple. You and I merely take our agreed portion of the year's profits and report that portion to Mr. Internal Revenue and pay our taxes.

Two distinct disadvantages exist in partnership, however. First of all, the death of any one partner automatically dissolves the partnership, necessitating a new partnership agreement being drawn. Of greater significance, though, is the fact that each partner assumes unlimited liability for debts incurred *in the business*. And I mean *unlimited personal liability*. For example, let's assume you and I go into partnership. I buy some heavy machinery and make other expenditures for our business that do not work out. In a short time, we're broke and we owe considerable money. Our creditors press us for the money and bring suit to get it. Nothing is left in the business, but they *can* sue us personally for these debts *because it's a partnership*. Frankly, partner, I haven't a dime. I put all my eggs into the business. Fortunately for our creditors, *you* have other assets. The court can take those assets away from you to pay *our* debts and there's no limit to how much they can take. They won't take the mattress out from under you, but almost. So you can see that a partnership is a business marriage. And I don't recommend becoming partners with "just anybody" any more than I do your marrying Lucy Vonderkronkle, whom you just met last night after consuming sixteen martinis at the local pub.

Corporation—Here we have a separate entity legally set up for business purposes. A corporation varies widely from a partnership. First of all, a corporation is not as easily set up (it can't possibly be done verbally or in a matter of minutes); it takes legal know-how and, naturally, involves the corresponding fees.

Of great importance is the liability limitation from being incorporated.* You simply can't lose any more money than what you put in. The company can go broke and owe millions, but the creditors can't get any more money from the stockholders. The obvious question then is: Why in the world doesn't everybody incorporate and protect themselves? The answer: *double taxation*. A stockholder is actually taxed twice in a corporation: first, in the form of a corporate income tax (maximum rate 52%) and, secondly, in the normal manner when the stockholder declares to the Internal Revenue how much dividends he received during the year. For example, let's assume you and I are considering the purchase of a business earning $100,000 a year and that we're both in the 50% tax bracket. If we go in as equal *partners*, each of us will report $50,000 in income from the business and Uncle

---

* Assuming stock is non-assessable and that's the only kind of stock under discussion in this book.

Sam will take $25,000, leaving $25,000 apiece (for a total of $50,000 net after taxes for both of us). If, instead, we incorporate, the $100,000 is going to be subject to the corporate tax (let's round it out to 50%), leaving us $50,000. Then (assuming all earnings are paid out in dividends) we have to declare our share of this—$25,000 each—and pay tax on it (in this case, $12,500 each). You can see that we are left with $12,500 each after taxes, for a total of $25,000—exactly half of what we would have retained as partners. The following table shows this rather clearly:

	PARTNERSHIP		CORPORATION	
Total Net Income	$100,000		$100,000	
Less Corporate Income Tax	none		50,000	
Balance available for owners	$100,000		$ 50,000	
	Your Share	My Share	Your Share	My Share
	$50,000	$50,000	$25,000	$25,000
Less Income Tax Paid Personally	25,000	25,000	12,500	12,500
Income Left After All Taxes	$25,000	$25,000	$12,500	$12,500

The discussion above is a broad generalization and gives you the major advantages and disadvantages of partnership vs. incorporation. It does not allow for the possibility of stockholders receiving salaries from their corporation (thereby minimizing the effect of double taxation), nor does it discuss new tax regulations (such as one which allows certain corporations to elect taxation as a partnership). In short, an attorney is the best judge in determining whether or not you should incorporate or form a partnership.

Now that we know more about corporations, we can go ahead and talk about the securities they issue.

CHAPTER 3

Corporate Securities

To commence business and to exist in business a corporation naturally needs capital. There are three basic means of getting this capital, namely through the sale of bonds, preferred stocks and/or common stock. Let's take a look at these three and see how they differ from one another:

Bonds—Bonds are issued in exchange for money loaned to a corporation (or to a federal government, state, city, etc.). The *lender* of money *becomes a bondholder and a creditor* of the company. As in any loan, the lender expects to receive a fixed rate of return on his money—called *interest*—and he expects to receive back the full amount of his loan at some future date, called the *maturity date*. Let me emphasize the fact that a bond-holder is a creditor of the company; he has *no ownership* and has nothing to say about the running of the business unless the company gets way behind in interest payments and is forced into bankruptcy or recapitalization. Therefore, a bondholder does not share in the success of a growing company, other than knowing that his interest is being better covered by earnings and through more assurance that he will get his original invest-ment back at maturity. Thus, bonds (unless convertible into common stock—discussed in Chapter 10) are bought for their fixed income; they do not provide a hedge against inflation because you will never get back more than a set amount at maturity. Incidentally, the *maturity date* serves to limit both the loss and gain in market price of a bond over the years. Assum-ing a bond is sound and that it will definitely pay off at maturity, this factor keeps a bond from going very far below its value at maturity or from rising very far above this price.

Preferred Stock—The term "preferred" makes this security sound glamourous and attractive. Nothing could be further from the truth! Although a preferred stock ranks ahead of common stock both as to payment of dividends and as to disposition of assets in the event a company goes out of business, a preferred stock is a "hybrid" security; it carries neither the extreme safety of a bond nor the chance for growth of a common stock. Like a bond, a preferred issue carries a fixed rate of annual payment (called a *dividend* in the case of a preferred, contrasted with *interest* paid on a bond) and this payment will *not* be increased.* No dividends can be paid on preferreds until all bond interest has been paid. Dividends are usually *cumulative*, meaning that the preferred stockholders are still entitled to omitted payments; that is, if preferred dividends are not earned and subsequently not paid, the corporation has to pay all those accrued dividends when its earnings do recover. Naturally, the corporation has to pay off all its accrued dividends (called "arrearages") before it can pay any dividends on the *common stock*.

Like bondholders, preferred stockholders generally have no voice in the management of the company (no voting power). Most bonds and preferreds have a *call price* (redemption price), which is the price at which the *company* can call the issues back in if it chooses. This call price limits any large gains in market price for bonds and preferreds. An investor is not going to pay 115 for an issue which has a call price of 105, because the day after he buys it at 115, the issue could be called at the 105 figure. The bond or preferred that has no call price does not have this disadvantage.

One of the big differences between bonds and preferred stocks is that the latter have *no maturity date*. At least a bondholder knows that he is entitled to a certain sum at maturity. The preferred stockholder has no assurance at all of getting his investment back. He has to depend on market conditions and could

---

* Unless it is a "participating" preferred, in which case the preferred holder, after receiving his stipulated regular dividend, then shares in the earnings available for the common stock.

conceivably hold his stock for 100 years and never see it back where it started. At least in a bond the investor knows that in 10, 20 or so-many years, he will have his money back. On the other hand, a preferred which is bought for its high yield at least guarantees its owner of that yield for as many years as he desires, with no "interference" from a maturity date.

Common Stock—Here you come to the actual ownership of a company. Whereas you are a lender of money as a bondholder and some in-between investor as a preferred stockholder, a common stockholder supplies permanent *equity capital* and owns the company. He has voting power, elects the board of directors and thereby indirectly controls management of the company. For this privilege, he has last claim on dividends and is low man on the totem pole in case the company goes broke and is forced to liquidate. On the other hand, the common stockholder is the one who benefits if the company is a success. As earnings increase, *he* is the one who gets higher dividends and he is the one whose corporate security goes up in market price.

CONCLUSIONS

Bonds represent a creditor's interest in a corporation. Bonds generally provide a high degree of safety—a fixed rate of return in good times and bad. Although corporate bonds are bought by some individuals, they are mainly bought by institutional investors (insurance companies, colleges, pension funds, etc.).

Preferred stocks represent a very limited form of ownership. They carry ownership risks with very little opportunity for appreciation of capital. Long unpaid preferred dividends are seldom settled satisfactorily and preferred stocks, because they have no maturity date and are not of the same quality as bonds, have greater price *in*stability than bonds and yet usually only provide slightly more yield. You're probably wondering who buys preferred stocks after this glum discussion. They are bought mainly by institutional investors, who want the higher return, and they are especially attractive to investing corporations, who get a tax advantage from receiving dividends from another corporation. Individuals, too, occasionally own preferred stocks, but I am generally opposed to this, except for an elderly person not interested in growth who needs that "last ounce" of current income. Why, for example, should an individual buy Pacific Gas and Electric preferred with a return around 6% when he can buy the common to yield only 2% less? Pacific Gas and Electric is a stable utility company; its common stock dividend is completely safe; as the company grows (and it is bound to, with the steadily rising population of California), earnings will, no doubt, rise and dividends will be increased over the years. Within a few years chances are that increased dividends will make up for the lower return now existing on the common and, over a longer period of time the PG&E common stockholder should end up with a far higher return on his investment. True it is that there is more market risk on the common, but for anyone who is looking more than a few years ahead for the benefits of his investment, give me the common stock!

Common stocks represent ownership. If it is growth of capital or a hedge against inflation you are seeking, here is where you are going to get it.

Now, before we learn to distinguish between attractive stocks and those we should leave alone, let's see how corporate securities are bought and sold.

PART II

HOW THE STOCK
MARKET FUNCTIONS

CHAPTER 4

How the Stock Market Works

One of the great advantages of owning corporate securities is that they are liquid. By that I don't mean you can drink them. Only that they can be sold on a moment's notice and converted into cash. Contrast that statement with trying to sell your business or a large piece of property. The best example of this liquidity is that provided by the New York Stock Exchange. Here we have as close to a "perfect market" as there is anywhere for investments.

Open five days a week from 10:00 a.m. to 3:30 p.m. (Eastern time), the New York Stock Exchange enables a buyer in Connecticut to get together with a seller in California in a matter of minutes. The New York exchange is essentially a communications system. Here you have one central market place connected with offices throughout the world by about a half a million miles of telephone and telegraph wire.

From the gallery, the exchange looks like a wild mass of confusion. But it's the most organized mass of confusion I know of. I'm sure a tobacco auction seems like confusion to all but the tobacco auctioneers and buyers, too. For those of you who have not seen the New York exchange, let's visualize it. Picture a floor about two-thirds the size of an ordinary football field. Around the floor are the countless telephone stations which connect the 1,366 stock exchange members with their offices. These are the brokers who are handling orders for their customers. Also stationed around the room are 19 "trading posts," each one manned by men called specialists. In early 1969, the exchange had 350 specialists on the floor.

Each specialist is assigned certain stocks. It is his business to see that a proper market is made in each and every one of these stocks. It is his job to take care of orders to buy and sell for brokers. And it is his job to buy and sell for his own account just to keep a good market at all times. In other words, the exchange expects there always to be a buyer of any stock within a close proximity of the last sale which took place in that stock. (Of course, the same rule goes for expecting to find a seller within close range of the last sale.) Now sometimes there will be no buyer (or seller) from the public and this is where the specialist must step in and bid to buy (or offer to sell) the stock for his own account. Needless to say, the specialist is closely regulated by the exchange and by the Securities and Exchange Commission (S.E.C.).

As to your broker, his privilege to buy and sell for you and to trade on the floor of the exchange comes about from owning a "seat" on the exchange. The number of seats available is limited and a new broker desiring one must buy it from a present holder, much the same as you buy a stock from another person. Also like individual stocks, these seats vary in price according to supply and demand. Over the past five years, for example, there has been a great variance in the price of New York Stock Exchange seats, as shown here:

	High Price	Low Price
1968	$515,000	$385,000
1967	450,000	220,000
1966	270,000	197,000
1965	250,000	190,000
1964	230,000	190,000

Aside from the high tariff to become a member of the exchange, a stock buyer can feel secure in knowing that his broker has substantial additional capital behind him. The exchange has to pass on any new members and has very high standards, including heavy capital requirements.

There are 2,736 men on the floor of the exchange, of which 952 are actual stock exchange members, 1,207 are member firm clerks and 577 are employees of the exchange itself. The clerks have to turn over orders to the specialists, while exchange members can make the choice to turn over orders to the specialists or attempt to transact the orders themselves.

Before seeing how an order is transacted on the exchange, let's distinguish between the various orders that can be placed by an investor to buy or sell stocks. The most common order placed is the *"market"* order, in which the investor is telling his broker to go ahead and transact the order *just as soon as he can* and *to buy it at the prevailing market* at that time. The broker is obligated to complete the order when he reaches the specialist's post, regardless of what the stock is selling for at that time (remember there may be considerable differences in price between the time a client places his order and the minute or so later when the broker reaches the post).

There is a distinction between a market order and an order giving *"market discretion."* In the latter situation, the client is also instructing the broker to complete an order to buy or sell but, in this case, the broker does not have to transact at the prevailing price. Instead, the broker is given the discretion to wait and attempt to get a better price for the customer. You might ask now why everyone doesn't use this order instead of a plain market order and the answer is that you take a chance in giving market discretion that the broker's judgment may prove incorrect. He may elect to wait to buy or sell instead of transacting the order right at the moment and his waiting may cost you money in the form of a higher price when you are buying or a lower price when you are selling. When you give a broker discretion, *he is not held* for his error of judgment. Of course, his discretion may prove correct and save you money, but there is no guarantee of this and you have to realize this when you place this order.

A third type of order placed is the *"limit"* order. In this case, you give your broker a price limit *that he cannot exceed* when buying the stock for you (or cannot lower in case you are selling the stock). For example, say you want to buy 100 shares of XYZ Company, which is currently selling at $10.00, but for which you are not willing to pay over $9.00. In this case, the broker is prohibited from paying any more than your designated limit of $9.00

for your intended purchase of 100 shares. When you put such a limit on a stock, you usually have to wait for the stock to reach that level and, therefore, most limit orders are put in for a period of time—and are called *"open"* limit orders. In the case of this XYZ purchase, you might instruct your broker to leave the order in for a week, two weeks, a month, or any period of your choice. In the meantime, of course, it is your privilege to change your limit price at any time; for example, you can raise the limit to 9½ or lower it to 8 or 8½ anytime—or you can cancel the order completely. After the designated period of the open order is over, it automatically expires, unless renewed by you. Of course, you may well place a limit order good only for one day, in which case it is called a *"day order."*

As to limit orders, I think there is one basic rule which should be stressed here. *Don't place a limit order only a fraction of a point away from the present price.* If you think a stock deserves to sell either far below or far above its going rate, then it may well pay you to wait for it to reach such a level, but when you are trying to save only a fraction of a point it's a bad gamble. Why? Because the very most you can save is the fraction you are trying to squeeze out, but you may lose a great deal by not transacting the order "at the market." For example, assume you are thinking of buying XYZ Company, whose stock is presently selling at $10.00. If you put your order in with a limit of, say 9¾, the very most you can save is ¼ of 1 point or 25 cents a share *if the stock declines to 9¾.* But say the stock does not decline to that level, what can it cost you? There's no limit! The stock may advance from 10 to 20 or 30 or upwards and you may "lose" a potential doubling or tripling of your money—and all for a measly 25 cents a share. The same thing, of course, goes for selling a stock that you own. If you think a stock is fully valued and that it should be sold, what can you gain by putting in an order a fraction above the market? Once again, a few pennies, and if the stock never reaches your fractionally higher level and commences to go down in price, you could lose many points—and this is out-of-pocket loss from not selling it at the market.

To illustrate the same point, it's a basic rule of investing or speculating that you should see a possibility for a good-sized gain from any venture before plunging. *Never risk a lot of dollars to make a few!*

It's a different philosophy if you feel in your own mind that a stock is overvalued now but that it represents a good buy at considerably lower levels. Here is where limit orders are most valuable, because you get yourself in line early to buy the stock where you think it represents a good buy. You give your broker your limit order and then it's there when the stock reaches that price. An advantage exists in that you are not influenced by your emotions at that time, whereas were you to wait for the stocks to get to that level, chances are the declining nature of the market would have an influence on you and you might well say to yourself, "I think it's going lower yet." And this is probably just the time you *should* be buying!

THE SPECIALIST'S BOOK AND
HOW ORDERS ARE HANDLED

Let's assume you want to buy 100 shares of XYZ Company and you instruct your broker to do so "at the market" for your account. Your broker writes out a tag with these instructions; this tag goes to his order department, which relays it to the floor of the exchange. The broker's partner on the floor receives the order and proceeds directly to the specialist's post where XYZ stock is traded. He asks the specialist what the going price is for XYZ. The very last sale price is easy to determine (and, as a matter of fact, is posted on an electric board at the post), but the *next* sale price is still a mystery. The specialist has a guide to what the next sale will be, because he keeps track of all limit orders for the brokers. Of course he can't keep them in his head, so he puts them down on paper, in what is known as the *specialist's book*.

The specialist keeps a separate book for each stock he follows and each page in the book keeps track of open orders at various prices. For example, let's set up the specialist's book on XYZ Company, as follows:

XYZ COMPANY

Orders To Buy	Broker Placing Order	Date Order Expires	Price of Stock	Orders To Sell	Broker Placing Order	Date Order Expires
100 shs.	Laurel	Feb. 26	9			
200 shs.	Hardy	Mar. 1	9			
100 shs.	Abbott	Mar. 15	9			
100 shs.	Costello	Feb. 12	9			
200 shs.	Lunt	Mar. 15	9⅛			
100 shs.	Fontanne	Feb. 13	9⅛			
100 shs.	Gilbert	Mar. 1	9¼			
100 shs.	Sullivan	Mar. 3	9¼			
500 shs.	Smythe	Mar. 5	9⅜			
	No orders—		9½	—No orders		
			9⅝			
			9¾	100 shs.	Chase	Mar. 20
				300 shs.	Sanborn	Mar. 1
			9⅞	100 shs.	Crosse	Mar. 3
			9⅞	200 shs.	Blackwell	Feb. 4

Your broker approaches the specialist and asks for a "quote," which is a request for the highest order to buy (the bid) and the lowest order to sell (the offer) which are open on the specialist's book. In this case, the quote would be "9⅜ at 9¾," which means that there is someone bidding 9⅜ and no higher, and someone offering stock for sale at 9¾ and no lower. As a matter of fact, your broker can also request the "size," meaning the number of shares wanting to buy at 9⅜ and the number for sale at 9¾. In this case, the size would be 500 and 400, meaning 500 shares bid for at 9⅜ and 400 shares offered at 9¾.

Now, if you have given your broker a market order, he is obligated to buy the stock at the lowest offering showing, which would be 9¾. Actually the specialist can help out your broker by "stopping" him at 9¾ (meaning that he will guarantee to sell him 100 shares at 9¾ if there is another purchase at 9¾ by someone else—after all, he is carrying open orders to sell 400 shares at 9¾). In this way, he allows your broker to step in and try to get you a lower price. Let's assume the specialist does "stop" your broker at 9¾. Then your broker will probably step in among the other brokers milling around the XYZ post and call out in a loud and clear voice, "9½ for 100 XYZ" (which means, "I'm willing to pay 9½ for 100 shares"). Chances are there are both potential buyers and sellers of XYZ in the crowd who have not entrusted their orders to the specialist. They haven't "tipped their hand" and are waiting to hear new orders for XYZ. When your broker bids 9½, he changes the quote from "9⅜ at 9¾" to "9½ at 9¾." Another broker hears the higher bid and decides he'll offer 100 shares for sale at 9⅝ (remember, if he waits for 9¾, he has to get in back of line behind Chase and Sanborn who are already on the Book for 9¾). Your broker is satisfied that he won't do much better than this and thus yells, "Take it," at the 9⅝ offerer and a sale has taken place.

Thus, the specialist has served his function of handling buy and sell orders and of seeing to it that a good market exists in his stock at all times.

This bidding and offering goes on all day in front of the post. The result is a continuous market which reflects the supply and demand for the stocks. You would be amazed how efficient the system is, especially if you have watched, as I have, thousands of shares of a particular stock bought or sold in a brief period of time without bringing about much of a change in the price of the stock.

RECORDING OF TRADES AND THE "TICKER TAPE"

Whenever a transaction takes place on the exchange it is recorded immediately and, within a minute, is sent over the wires and appears on the "ticker tape" in the office of every exchange member. Every stock has an abbreviated symbol and the transactions are shown as follows:

XYZ	GM	X
9⅝	2s 80	4s 45. 44¾

Our previous 100 share trade of XYZ is the first example; whenever a transaction involves 100 shares, no mention is made *of anything but the price.* When more than 100 shares are traded, though, the price of the stock is preceded by the volume; in GM (General Motors), the "2s" means "200 shares"; in X (U. S. Steel's symbol), the "4s 45" means that 400 shares traded in one block at the price of 45, then the "44¾" means that the 45 trade was followed by a 100 share transaction at 44¾.

There are other peculiarities to the ticker tape. I won't list them here—your broker can explain them simply if you are interested and have the time to spend in his office watching the tape. The main thing is that trends of the market and of individual stocks show up on the ticker tape—nothing is hidden from you.

ODD LOTS

Up to this time, we've been talking only about buying and selling stocks in 100 share lots—called round lots. Actually considerable business in stocks is not in round lots at all, but rather in less than 100 share units—called odd lots.

The exchange sets up specialists who deal exclusively in odd lots. You can imagine how difficult it would be to find a buyer for 39 or 62 or 3 shares of any given stock. So the exchange has four odd lot dealers who guarantee to sell or buy all the stock necessary to complete the odd lot orders. Their compensation is the odd lot "differential" or "fee." This fee, which is added on directly to the price of the stock, amounts to:

⅛ of a point (or 12½ cents) per share for a stock which sells under
   $54.875 (54⅞) on the exchange
¼ of a point (or 25 cents) per share for a stock which sells over
   $55.00 on the exchange

All odd lot transactions are filled from sales taking place on round lots. For example, if you are buying 10 shares of a stock selling around 50, the odd lot dealer in that stock waits for the next sale to take place in that stock and then sells you 10 shares at *that* price plus the odd lot fee of ⅛ of a point. So if the next sale is 50 you will buy the stock at 50⅛. If you are selling the same stock, instead of buying, then the ⅛ point will be deducted from the next sale price. In our example, you would thus receive 49⅞ for your 10 shares. The odd lot dealer makes his money from these ⅛ and ¼ point differentials, but he also stands a risk. Say that, all at once, six orders arrive at his post to sell 50, 30, 10, 85, and 25 shares of ABC stock. The dealer must buy all these odd lots (totalling 200 shares) at the next sale price of, say, 50—minus the ⅛ point differential. Thus, he owns 200 shares with a cost of 49⅞. Let's say the market is declining rapidly and, by the time he is able to sell the round lot of 200 shares in the open market, the price may well be 49 or 48½, in which case he has just lost a few hundred dollars.

The main thing is that the odd lot purchaser or seller is assured of a good market at all times for his securities—just another example of how the exchange is an excellent market place. *The odd lot fee is small and should never be a deterrent to a person's investing in the market in odd lots.*

COMMISSIONS

Naturally, the cost of acquiring or selling securities through your broker is important. Commission is figured on the *amount of money invested in each individual stock*. Following is the schedule of charges at present on the New York, the American, and other major stock exchanges.

On 100 Share Round Lots:

Money Involved	Commission
Under $100	As mutually agreed (usually 6%)
$100 to $399	2% of amount invested plus a flat $3.00
$400 to $2,399	1% of amount invested plus a flat $7.00
$2,400 to $4,999	½ of 1% of amount invested plus a flat $19.00
$5,000 and over	⅒ of 1% of amount invested plus a flat $39.00

On less-than-100 share trades, odd lots:

The same as above, less a flat $2.00

Thus, if a person is investing $4,000, his commission will vary according to how many stocks he buys. If he purchases 100 shares of a $20 stock ($2,000) and 50 shares of a $40 stock (also $2,000), there will be two separate commissions, as follows:

The 100 share round lot purchase commission will be 1% of $2,000, or $20.00, plus the flat $7.00, for a total of $27.00.

The 50 share odd lot purchase commission will also be 1% of $2,000, or $20.00, plus the flat $7.00, minus a flat $2.00, for a total of $25.00.

Commissions (figured as a percentage of the amount invested) will naturally vary with the amount of the purchase and can range as low as a very small fraction of 1% (commission on 100 shares of a $200 stock, or a $20,000 purchase, will be only $59.00, or less than $\frac{3}{10}$ of 1%) to as high as 6%. As an average, however, one can figure on a commission of 1–2% of the value of the transaction, which compares favorably with sales commissions on real estate (in most areas, 5–6% commissions are normal). In addition, I should mention the fact that the major exchanges recently instituted significant volume discounts—for orders exceeding 1,000 shares in a single transaction. To illustrate, the *second* 1,000 of an order to buy or sell 2,000 shares of a $20 stock would cost $140.00 vs. $270.00 on the first 1,000 shares.

SHORT SELLING

One of the interesting types of speculation in the stock market and one of the most difficult to comprehend is the "short sale." When a person *buys* a stock he does so with the hope the stock will go *up* in value so that when he sells it he makes a profit. When a person sells a stock "short," he is *selling something he doesn't now own* with the hope that he will make a profit by buying it back later at a lower price.

Now, don't think yourself dense if you are asking, "How in the world can a person sell something he *doesn't* own?" Let me give you a practical example.

I own a 1955 Chevrolet. You and I are talking one day and I tell you how I just turned down an offer to sell my car for $1,000.

It's only worth $500, but I'm sentimentally attached to the old buggy and I want to keep it. Well, it so happens that I'm going away tomorrow for a month and leaving my car here. The wheels start grinding in your mind: if you could only "borrow" my car for the month, find that fool who was willing to pay $1,000 for my car, sell it to him, and then plan to buy back a similar car for $500 before I return. The result would be a profit of $500 to you, like so:

$1,000 received by you when you sold my car
   500 paid out to put similar car back in my garage
$ 500 Net Profit to you

What you have done is sell my car "short." You don't own it, but you've sold it just the same with the idea of replacing it at a lower price at a future date.

Actually it's easier to sell short in stocks than in cars. How could you be sure the $500 1955 Chevrolet you put back in my garage would be the same exact color, have the same dented fenders, etc. as my original? You couldn't! But in stocks, it's easy. One 100 share certificate of General Motors is exactly the same as any other. And thus, if you think that the present market price of GM stock is too high and that it will go down, why not sell it now for $80 (your broker will arrange to borrow it for you to deliver to the buyer) and then simply buy it back when it goes lower, say to $60.

Short selling does serve a function. It allows one to speculate that the market is too high and thus has somewhat of a stabilizing influence. After all, if we had only buyers of stocks by a great majority, stocks would quickly become inflated and priced too high. And then we'd be in for a sharp drop some day. Since most investors are conscious of *buying* stocks, short sellers can at least have a restricting influence and keep stocks from becoming overly inflated. And remember that every short seller is a potential buyer later on and this buying when the market is sinking also becomes a stabilizing factor.

Actually, I don't recommend short selling for the average investor. For one thing, the risks are unlimited. There's no end to how much you can lose. If you sell a stock short at $10, who's to say it won't go to $100 or $1,000, in which cases you would lose 1,000% or 10,000% on your money, if you didn't buy back before.

This is exactly what enters the short seller's mind and it often panics him into buying back as quickly as possible when the market is rising. This sudden buying by short sellers (called "short covering") is one reason for occasional rapid upswings in various popular issues.

In contrast, if you *buy* a $10 stock, what is the worst that can happen? That the company will go bankrupt and the stock be worth nothing, in which case you've "only" lost your original investment (you've lost 100% of your money). And chances are that it will never go to zero; perhaps $2 or $3 or $5 is the lowest you can visualize, even under the worst circumstances.

A second disadvantage to short selling is that you have a minus return on your money to start with. Whereas when you *buy* a stock you receive dividends that give you a certain annual return on your money, in a short sale you have to *pay* out dividends as they are declared to the person from whom you borrowed the stock to make the short sale (you never come in contact with the person who owns the stock you are borrowing—your broker handles all of this for you, and generally there is no cost at all to the borrowing).

The third reason for avoiding short selling is psychological. If you have sold short and the market goes down, you're a hero. But, I can think of little worse than being short when the market is rising. Everyone you know either buys stocks or sells what they already own. Ninety-nine per cent of your friends are happy as a lark when the market is rising. To be losing money while all your friends are reaping the harvest is not easy. It would be tough to live with.

A fourth criticism of short selling involves taxes. No matter how long you wait to buy back a stock you have sold short, any gain from the transaction is considered by the Internal Revenue *to be a short term gain, and thus you can never benefit from the advantageous long term capital gain tax rate (see Chapter 28) in short selling.*

Short selling is thus for the real *speculator*, not the *investor*. And if you are one of those highly speculative individuals, remember that risk factor. And remember the old adage:

> *He who sells what isn't his'n*
> *Must eventually buy it back or go to prison.*

If you're short and the stock is rising, you're going to have to put up more money* right along—or eventually buy it back. So be sure you have ample cash around if you're going to be a short seller.

TWO "PROTECTION" ORDERS ON THE STOCK EXCHANGE

We've already discussed limit orders, but there are two other types of limit orders which should be mentioned briefly. These are the stop-sell and stop-buy orders.

Stop-sell: Suppose you own a stock which is now selling at $60. You think the stock may go considerably higher, but in case you are wrong you want to be sure you sell it at $55 on the way down. You can place a stop-sell order at $55 and, if the stock retreats *to that level*, your stock is automatically sold "at the market" after the $55 price is reached (since it becomes a "market order" there is no guarantee your stock will be sold at the $55 figure; you might receive 54½, 54¼ or even lower if numerous other stop-sell orders are touched off at the same time as yours). If the stock never retreats to $55 it won't be sold at all. The stop-sell order, therefore, gives you a way to limit your loss or protect your profit if the stock starts to decline.

Stop-buy: This order is intended mainly for the short seller. If a person sells a stock short at $60 and wants to be sure he loses no more than 5 or 6 points, he can place an open stop-buy at $65.

---

* Short selling requires original capital, too. In spite of the fact you receive money from your short sale right away, you are required to put up this amount out of your own pocket (or at least the existing margin requirement; i.e., in 1969, 80% of the total amount). Then, when you buy back the stock ("cover the short sale"), you can withdraw your cash plus the profit or minus the loss incurred from the short sale transaction.

Then, if and when the stock goes up to $65, his order automatically becomes an order to buy the stock "at the market."

The stop-buy order can also be used to buy stocks as they rise or as they break through "resistance points," etc. Some chartists utilize the stop-buy in this way to accumulate *stocks as they are rising*. The protection features of both the stop-sell and stop-buy orders make them sound very useful. Actually, these orders are most practical for the short-term speculator. They are really not too suitable for the long-term investor, who is not so concerned with day-to-day fluctuations and who is investing for large, long-range benefits. Stop orders tend to make an account too active (constantly in and out of the market) and, as I will point out in Chapter 30 on stock market "trading," I am convinced that considerable activity is to the definite detriment of the investor.

CHAPTER 5

Regional Stock Exchanges

Chapter 4 dealt with procedures on the New York Stock Exchange. While the New York Stock Exchange is by far the largest, I should mention that it is not the only central market place for securities. The American Stock Exchange is another and there are numerous regional exchanges throughout the country, including the Pacific Coast, Midwest, Philadelphia, Boston, Detroit, etc. Listing requirements are the strictest on the New York exchange, but these other markets serve an important function and the stocks traded on the other exchanges may well equal or even be superior in quality to many issues traded on the New York board.

None of the regional exchanges in the U. S. open before the New York exchange; the regionals all coincide their opening hours with that of the "big board." Because of differences in time, however, some exchanges are open after others have closed. The Pacific Coast exchange, for example, opens at 7 a.m. Pacific time, which is the same as the 10:00 a.m. Eastern time opening of the New York exchange, but the Pacific exchange does not close until 2:30 p.m. Pacific time (equivalent to 5:30 p.m. New York time) —or two hours after the close of the big board. Many times significant news will be released *after* the close of the *New York* exchange but *before* the close of the *Pacific*, and a great deal of activity will take place on the latter exchange. Assume, for example, that XYZ stock closed at 45 on the big board and that shortly after the 3:30 p.m. New York closing an important announcement affecting XYZ is made. Provided that XYZ stock is traded on the Pacific exchange too (many stocks are traded on more than one exchange) a person wanting to buy or sell XYZ can still do so on the Pacific because of the time differential. The theory, of course, is to make the purchase or sale before the news is widely spread, hoping to be ahead of those who hear later and are forced to act after you on the Pacific or have to wait until the New York opening the next day. I must point out here, however, that it may be dangerous to pay a big premium on the Pacific over what a stock closed in New York the same day (or, in the case of bad news, to sell well below what the last sale was in New York). This is because a great deal of "emotional action" takes place on the Pacific after the New York close: XYZ closes at 45 in the East; some good news suddenly appears and a few frantic people put in market orders to buy the stock; perhaps the first order results in a purchase at 45½, then the next at 46 or 46½, then 47 or so. Unless your order is the first or second you might pay a premium of a couple of points over the New York close. My experience has shown that, when frantic buying such as this appears on the Pacific after the New York close, the resulting prices are *usually inflated* and that actually a *person wanting to buy this stock in the limelight will be able to do so cheaper the next day in New York.* By the same token a person who engages in emotional selling on the Pacific at prices well below the close in New York the same day will generally realize a higher figure by doing so in New York the next day.

While we're on this discussion I should clear up one bit of confusion which exists in many investors' minds, namely why prices may vary so widely between the New York exchange and any of the regional exchanges in the same stock during the same day. For example, let's assume you are following the stock of Ampex Corporation, which is listed on both the New York and the Pacific Coast exchanges. You are anxious to know what happened to Ampex in today's market and rush to buy the evening newspaper. Frantically you turn to the financial section and look for Ampex in the long list of New York stocks and find the following:

Sls		High	Low	Close	N'Ch
146	AmpexCp	39	38	38	—½

Then you notice how the stock traded on the Pacific exchange:

2200 AmpexCp   38¾   38¼   38¼

Now perhaps the following legitimate questions come to your mind:

1. Why did Ampex close at 38 in New York and at 38¼ on the Pacific?

    A) The closing price on the NYSE was at or near 3:30 p.m. New York time (12:30 Pacific time) while the very last sale which took place in Ampex on the Pacific may have been either well before or well after the New York close. In other words, the Pacific close may have no relationship in time to the New York.

2. Did more volume occur on the Pacific than on the NYSE?

    A) No. The "146" on the NYSE means 14,600, whereas the 2200 on the Pacific really means 2200 shares traded.

3. Ampex never sold as high as 39 on the Pacific. Does that mean that a person could have bought it cheaper there than in New York?

    A) No. The volume of trading on the Pacific is small compared to New York. It happens that, at the time Ampex was selling at 39 in the East, there was no trading at all in the stock on the Coast.

CONCLUSIONS

Regional exchanges serve a vital function in our country. For one thing, they provide a good market for many stocks—most of which have a local following—that do not qualify or do not wish to qualify for listing on the American or New York stock exchanges. Regional exchanges are closely regulated; they have specialists and other conveniences and safeguards that are provided by the larger exchanges. In addition, they provide markets for many stocks that are also listed on the major exchanges. In this case though it is only fair to say that the great preponderance of trading exists in New York and thus the best market really exists there. Prices of stocks listed on both New York and a regional exchange are determined by the activity and trading *in New York*. Prices on the local exchanges are arrived at in sympathy with what is going on in the central marketplace—New York.

CHAPTER 6

The Unlisted
(Over-the-Counter) Market

Though listed stocks include most of our country's largest enterprises, listed securities *in number alone* are actually a small minority. Of approximately 55,000 securities traded in the U. S. today, only about 3,000 are listed on any exchange. The rest are *un*listed, or traded "over-the-counter" (please, not "*under*-the-counter"). The fact that a stock is unlisted does *not* mean that a good market doesn't exist for it. Take, for example, four top companies from the San Francisco Bay Area—Pacific Gas & Electric, Pacific Gas Transmission, Bank of America and Wells Fargo Bank. An active market exists in all four, yet PG&E is listed on the New York and Pacific Coast exchanges, PGT is listed only on the Pacific Coast, while Bank of America and Wells Fargo are traded over-the-counter (OTC).

Most of our country's top industrial concerns were originally traded OTC—and many experienced their greatest appreciation before being listed. Many blue chip companies are still unlisted. (Seven-Up, Tampax, American Express, etc.). Practically all banking and insurance companies are traded OTC (Chemical Bank, Connecticut General to name just two). All the bonds of our cities, counties, states (called municipal bonds) are unlisted, as are almost all U. S. Government securities. More than 75% of all corporation bonds and all mutual funds are OTC. And, of course, all new issues start out trading in the unlisted market.

The main differences between listed and unlisted markets are:

1. There is no one central market place OTC. Whereas an order to buy stock on the New York exchange goes directly

to that one spot, the OTC involves numerous dealers throughout the country who "make a market" in that stock.

2. There is generally a wider "spread" between the bid and ask price OTC than for a stock traded on an exchange (although there are many exceptions: i.e., the spread on Bank of America, unlisted, is normally narrower than that on Motorola, listed).

3. Large volume orders to buy or sell are more easily handled on the exchange.

4. There is no fixed commission rate in the unlisted market. Commission rates may run as low as the minimum New York Stock exchange rates or they may run considerably higher. Maximum OTC rate is 5% of the market value of the stock involved.

5. An investor cannot margin (borrow to buy) an unlisted stock through a broker (he can borrow from a bank on an unlisted stock, however).

6. Unlisted stocks do not fluctuate as much as listed on an *hour-by-hour basis.*

7. There is *no* odd lot fee in the over-the-counter market, there are no "stop" orders and short selling is impractical (in fact, it can seldom be accomplished by an individual).

Tracing through an actual transaction OTC might clarify a few things. Let's say you want to buy 100 shares of American Express stock. If the stock were *listed*, the order would go directly to the floor of the exchange and your broker would go through the procedure explained in Chapter 4 at the American Express post. But American Express is not *listed*. Therefore, your order will go to the OTC department of your broker (usually called the "trading department"). The OTC clerk receives the order and looks on the national quotation sheet, which shows which brokers throughout the country "make a market" in this stock. Let's assume there are four firms "trading" American Express. The clerk proceeds to get a quote from each of them, as follows:

Clerk asks, "How's American Express?"

Broker B answers: "71½ at 72½." (This means that B is willing to buy at least 100 shares of that stock at the bid price of 71½ and stands willing to sell at least 100 shares at 72½.)

Broker C gives his market as: 71¾ at 72½.

Broker D gives his market as: 71½ at 72¼.

Broker E gives his market as: 71¾ at 72¾.

The clerk has now checked the market and finds that the lowest offering is 72¼ by broker D. He calls D back immediately and, if he finds that his market has not changed, he tells D, "Buy 100 from you at 72¼." Actually, the clerk may try to get the stock a little cheaper by bidding 72, but he takes a chance that D may then change his offer. Assuming the clerk decides that 72¼ is a fair price, the transaction is completed and you will be billed at this price plus commission.

Certain firms make a business of "making a market" in OTC securities. They stand ready to buy and sell and naturally hope to make a good living from the spread which exists between the bid and ask. For example, if a broker can buy and sell the same number of shares without the market changing, he can make good money (in the American Express example, if broker D buys 100 shares from another firm at his bid price of 71½ and then sells your broker this 100 shares at 72¼, he makes himself $75). The difficulty is, of course, that these OTC dealers can't count on buying and selling the same number of shares each day—and the price is always fluctuating. Take the theoretical case of a firm making a market in Bank of America. Let's say he quotes the stock 65 bid, 65½ offered. In the course of the day he buys from other brokers 500 shares at 65, without selling any at the offer of 65½. The next day more selling comes in on Bank of America and the price drops to 63½ at 64 (that is, the other dealers in that stock have lowered their price to 63½ bid, 64 offered). This dealer naturally has to adjust his market to approximately the same level. Now another broker comes in and buys 500 shares at the current offer price of 64—this is the same 500 which the OTC dealer purchased only yesterday at 65 and thus he lost $1.00 per share on 500 shares, or $500. So you can see that "making a market" in OTC securities is risky business.

HOW DO UNLISTED SECURITIES
SHOW IN THE NEWSPAPER?

We'll see later on in Chapter 10 how stock prices show in the daily papers. Whereas nearly all the stocks listed on the various exchanges show in the paper every day, there would not be room for the many thousands of unlisted securities. Therefore, it is normal for the papers to show only the most widely traded unlisted issues and those which have a local following. Many papers will print quotations on 50–100 stocks total. *The Wall Street Journal* shows daily prices of a few hundred.

Now, suppose you own one of the many stocks which are not shown in your local newspaper or in *The Wall Street Journal* (or in a long list of weekly quotations shown in *Barron's*). How do you know where your stock is selling? Perhaps you're broke and you don't know it! Well, the only way to determine the stock's price is by asking your broker who can get you a quote at any time.

Let's assume, however, that your unlisted stock or stocks are printed *daily*. They will show like the following:

	Bid	Ask
American Express	71¾	72¼
Bank of America	63½	64

Preceding the over-the-counter prices there is usually a statement such as: "These quotations, supplied by the National Association of Securities Dealers, are bids and offers quoted by over-the-counter dealers to each other as of approximately 3 p.m. (Eastern time). The quotations do not include retail markup, markdown or commission, and do not represent actual transactions."

In other words, these prices are only a range and they do not tell you exact prices. Also notice that the prices are intended as of "approximately 3 p.m."; thus, the time of compilation can differ greatly from that for the prices shown on *listed* securities.

You can see that these over-the-counter quotations are not as accurate as quotations from the exchanges.

Also notice that these prices do not allow a column denoting the change in price from the previous day: there are no plus and minus signs to look at.* This is one reason many banks and insurance companies have preferred to keep their stocks unlisted. You can imagine the effect of large minus signs on people who have money on deposit in the Thriftiman's Bank, for example. After three or four days of —3, —2, —5, etc., a depositor might start thinking: "Say what's going on in that bank of mine? Maybe I better run down there and take my money out!" The same psychology applies to insurance policy holders. People simply don't notice the ups and downs of unlisted securities so much because the plus and minus signs are missing.

CONCLUSIONS

Some of the best money-making opportunities exist in the OTC market, because there are many not-so-recognized stocks which may become the blue chips of tomorrow. Many times you will find an OTC stock, which is not quite so well known, that is much more reasonably-priced in relation to its earnings, dividends, etc. than a comparable listed security. Then, if and when this OTC stock becomes better known, it may rise in price very rapidly, just because it is "catching up" and beginning to sell on the same basis as better known, comparable stocks.

There are certain securities in the OTC market which do not have a "good market." In certain stocks, you have little assurance that you will be able to find a buyer when you want to sell. If you are considering investment in this type stock (which, incidentally, is the exception) you should realize the risk you are taking in sacrificing marketability or liquidity.

For the most part, however, you can feel sure that you have reasonable marketability in unlisted stocks. One general rule might

---

* Actually, the recent trend is towards showing plus and minus signs for OTC stocks, too. The *Wall Street Journal* makes a practice of this and other periodicals at least show what the previous day's bid price was, for the sake of comparison.

follow: if a stock looks very attractive to you, don't let the fact that it is unlisted deter you from buying. Many very interesting situations will present themselves in OTC securities so don't be prejudiced against them for that reason alone.

PART III

HOW TO JUDGE
THE STOCK MARKET
AND GAUGE WHERE
IT IS GOING

CHAPTER 7

The Market and How to Follow It

If nothing else is certain about stocks, one thing is: *the market will fluctuate.* To be up or to be down, that is *the question.* While the stock market is looked upon by many as a *thermometer* of business conditions, political climate, etc., I like to look upon it more as a barometer—as a *crystal ball.* The stock market is always trying to forecast what *will* happen, rather than reflect what has already occurred. That is why the axiom, "Buy stocks when things look at their worst" is so important. Because when things look their worst, the public is generally reflecting its pessimism by selling stocks on a wholesale basis. Smart investors are buying these greatly depressed stocks on the theory that, if things are at their worst, then they can only get better. In the stock market, if you wait until things actually *are* better, you'll be late. By that time, stocks will have risen in value by a goodly amount.

People are always amazed when a company announces higher earnings, a raised dividend or other good news—only to find the stock of that company go *down* in price after the announcement. Why? Because speculators had anticipated such good news, bought the stock before the announcement was made at low prices, and then, when the news finally broke, sold their stock at that time, forcing it down in price. Of course many times a stock will rise on good news (in fact, this is usually the case), but this does not refute this theory. It only proves that the good news had not been anticipated by the majority of investors and speculators.

The stock market in general is subject to the *same* "anticipation of news." The market is always trying to *forecast* events. And that is why I say the market is more a crystal ball than a thermometer. Now many times the crystal ball is real foggy—in fact, it can be as wrong as Madame Gadzooks, who tells you your future by reading the backs of tea leaves (or do they use tea bags now?). Sometimes people get real optimistic about the near future (and the market goes high), only to be wrong. For example, the 1956 stock market was rising and anticipating continued good business for some time to come, only to find business slump very rapidly in mid-1957 and 1958. Sometimes, the market will get worried about conditions, as it did in 1946–47, only to find that business was not bad when 1947–48–49 rolled around. The same thing happened with the 1962 market; no recession developed. Many, many times, however, the market is correct in its forecasts of things to come. The main thing is that you, as a potential buyer of stocks, should always *look ahead* and attempt to forecast, too. But you are probably asking how *you* are going to forecast complicated economic and political events and be just a little smarter than the next fellow. I think the following discussions will aid you in getting the jump. The facts are there—it's only a matter of knowing where to find them and then doing some interpretation.

WHERE TO GET THE FACTS

Many local newspapers will give you most of the facts you need to know in judging business and the stock market. But the "bible" in our business is *The Wall Street Journal*. This daily (5 days a week) publication will keep you current on economic statistics, reports by industries and individual companies, feature articles of interest, etc. There are countless other publications that are valuable and supplement the *Journal*, namely *Barron's* (weekly), *The Commercial and Financial Chronicle* (weekly—more economic theory and articles intended for bankers, brokers, etc.), *Business Week Magazine* (weekly—devoted to all aspects of business, including marketing, finance, labor, advertising, etc.), *Magazine of Wall Street* (strictly finance), *Forbes* (bi-weekly, exclusively devoted to the market and articles on stocks), *Financial World* and many others.

In addition, there are some government publications that will give you all the economic facts you can possibly digest, namely the Federal Reserve Board's monthly bulletin and two Department of Commerce publications—*Economic Indicators* (monthly business statistics in chart form) and the *Survey of Current Business*.

Furthermore, if you're willing to give up a few more dollars there are many investment "services" that will boil down these facts for you and make a policy of recommending individual issues as well as advice on the market in general. *Standard and Poor's* and *Moody's* are perhaps the best known of these services, but there are countless others such as *United Business Service, Value Line, Babson's*, etc.

Incidentally, let me point out one warning in following the investment recommendations of these services. Many times a widely subscribed service will put out a buy or sell recommendation on a particular stock. Now when such recommendations are mailed throughout the country and arrive at different locations on different days, there may not be any concentrated orders coming from this recommendation on just one day. Many such recommendations are mailed out, however, to arrive in the mail over the weekend. Hundreds of subscribers read their mail on Saturday or Sunday, call their broker and place an order for the opening on Monday morning and what happens? The stock is subject to a sudden spurt! Perhaps it closed at $30 on Friday, but orders to buy a few thousand shares are placed "at the market" on Monday and it opens at $33, or the stock has a concentrated rise during the whole day because of this recommendation. A person should beware of this, because chances are that, once this concentrated buying from the recommendation subsides (which may be only a day or so later) the stock may drop back near its Friday's close. In other words, be discreet with your order and don't become "one of a mob" which is rushing to buy the stock all at once. As example, a number of years ago a famed news commentator took up giving investment "tips" on his evening show (something which would be in violation of F.C.C. regulations today). Invariably these tips were followed by certain listeners and a rash of buy orders would accumulate the next morning and cause the given stock to rise suddenly and sharply. In the great majority of cases, these buyers would pay inflated prices and it generally took them quite some time to get even on their purchases. Some of us in the securities business used to say "Whatever Mr. _____ recommends on Sunday night, *don't buy, but instead sell short* on Monday morning." In practice this would have been one of the most consistent theories ever to exist in the stock market.

Actually there are countless economic factors for you to consider when reading the financial page of your newspaper. Like all statistics, these factors are only meaningful when compared with like figures for a previous period. First of all, let's take a look at some indicators which tell you how *business in general* is at the moment. Naturally, it takes interpretation (and a given amount of guesswork) to shape these factors into a projection of what kind of business lies ahead.

Gross national product (GNP) tells you the total goods and services produced in this country on an annual basis. Obviously the higher the GNP the better business in general is.

Employment figures are of course indicative of business. You notice I stress *employment* figures rather than *un*employment, mainly because the latter figure can be deceiving. For example, business may be booming and unemployment can actually be rising, if an exceptionally large group of 18–22 year old persons are suddenly added to the employable labor force. In other words, a bumper baby crop 18–20 years ago may now be added to the employable list after their schooling—and, unemployment figures might well indicate caution about business, whereas employment figures might remain high and be reassuring.

Disposable personal income tells you how much money people have to spend, which is of course basic to good business both currently and in the near future.

Index of industrial production gives you the amount of general business volume, shown as a percentage of the average which existed from 1957–1959 (given a base of 100). For example, an IIP of 150 means that business volume is 50% higher than the average of the base period.

Bank deposits—It's always nice to see bank deposits rising along with higher consumer spending. Were deposits to drop substantially it would be a sign for caution, because people can't draw down from savings forever. Savings provide future business.

Manufacturers' new orders, unfilled orders and inventories—The first two of these three factors are obvious in their importance. *New orders* received by manufacturers build up the amount of *unfilled orders* they have on the books; and the larger the unfilled orders the more assurance you have that business will be good in the time ahead. Not quite so obvious, but of the very utmost of importance, are *inventories*, which are of course the amount of goods already on the shelves of manufacturers.

Aside from the old story, "Salt," the more goods you have on your shelves the more cautious you are going to be about buying.*

Businessmen are willing to buy more than they require when they sense booming conditions, but the minute business starts to slip, they cut back on their buying of goods. And if they already have large supplies on hand, then they may delay buying altogether until their inventories get down to more manageable levels. *When inventories are rising from anything but depressed levels it is a sign for caution.* At least two of our country's recessions since the end of World War II were directly the result of inventory cutbacks—the cessation of buying because of having inventories too high already.

Consumer debt is another important indicator. People can only

---

* A customer entered a grocery store and asked, "Have you any salt?" "Salt?" replied the grocer, "Have I got salt? Take a look!" Behind him were shelves filled with salt. Then he took the customer to the back of the store and showed him more rows of shelves filled with salt. "Have I got salt?" he repeated again and took the customer by the hand to the basement, where he had a room full of salt. "Have I got salt!!" the grocer kept muttering.

The customer looked at him and said the obvious: "My, but you must sell a lot of salt every year!"

"Salt? Who sells salt?" cried the grocer. "Maybe three cases a year, I sell. But there's a salesman who comes here three times a year and, Wow-wow-wow-wow, can he sell salt!!!"

THIS IS DEFINITELY THE EXCEPTION TO OUR ECONOMIC REASONING ABOUT INVENTORIES.

owe so much and then they have to slow down their buying on credit. One of several contributing causes to the 1957–1958 recession was the large amount of debt piled up by consumers during the bulging 1955–1956 automobile sales. The public simply saturated themselves and had to hold off purchases of goods—especially those usually sold "on time"—till their debt payments declined. Consumer debt alone can be deceiving, however. Some effort should be made to relate it to personal income before reaching any conclusions about it being too high or too low.

Imports and exports naturally are important to the nation. While we encourage foreign trade and the building up of other nations, it is distressing to see an unfavorable balance of trade, wherein the U. S. is importing more than we are selling to others.

Business failures are of some significance, too, since a marked increase in failures denotes a credit caution signal.

The cost-of-living index indicates how much inflation we are having and is especially important when you have large labor contracts tied to this index.

SOME "MORE-SPECIALIZED" FACTORS TO WATCH FOR

Following are additional indicators, most of which have a double-meaning to forecasters and which should be watched:

Paperboard production—Certainly you should be interested in this statistic if you have an interest in paper stocks. In addition, however, this happens to be a very sensitive indicator of how business is trending. Why? Because everything that is produced has to be wrapped and shipped. And what is the most important material for this use? Paperboard, of course. Now remember that most companies report their earnings every three months. You have no way of knowing how a company's business is going in between these quarterly statements (unless the company issues a statement for the press in the interim). But the paperboard figures are shown weekly and they can tell you weeks or months in advance of a changing trend in business, which most certainly could affect the company you own and the stock market in general.

A similar indicator is *railroad carloadings*, which simply enumerate the number of railroad cars being loaded for shipment each week. If you own railroad stocks, here is the best indicator of how the rail business is going along. But these figures have added significance.

Everything produced must eventually be shipped and railroads handle most of the manufactured goods in the U.S. So when shipments decline, they show up *weekly* in the carloading figures. These carloadings are broken down for you by geographical location and by freight classification. Here again you can "be ahead" of those quarterly reports by following this important business indicator.

Electric power production is important for holders of utility stocks, but it can also give a check on over-all business conditions. After all, when business is good, more power is used and these weekly figures give a broad picture of activity.

Figures from two basic industries—*automobiles and building*— are very important. Aside from the huge sums of money paid out in wages to workers in these industries, think of the related industries which are so dependent on them. Auto-truck production has great effect on steel, glass, chemicals, rubber, aluminum and other metals, as well as on transportation. Building likewise involves steel, glass and aluminum and has considerable effect on cement, gypsum, asphalt, lumber and plywood, etc. Therefore, both new car-truck sales and building activity give you an insight into over-all business and especially into the major industries they involve. Auto-truck production figures are published weekly, while housing starts and other construction figures are more generally published on a monthly basis.

If you're following non-ferrous metal stocks (copper, zinc, lead, etc.), keep a close eye on *London metal prices*. Prices overseas eventually have an effect domestically. Incidentally, since non-ferrous metal prices fluctuate more than steel, aluminum, etc., they can give an indication of business activity. As copper prices rise, for example, it is usually due to increased demands—and these demands usually stem from higher production.

Steel production figures are released weekly by the American Iron and Steel Institute and of course give you early indication of what quarterly earnings of the steel companies will be.

Weekly *department store sales* not only tell how Macy's, Sears, etc. are doing, but also give a clue as to how the textiles and appliance makers should do.

Then, there are figures available of *life insurance sales, crude and refined oil production,* and countless other industries.

One not-so-noticeable statistic involves *wholesale price levels.* Food chains and soap manufacturers can be expected to *increase* their profits in years where wholesale prices are low.

Needless to say, an owner of stocks or a potential investor should follow the *earnings* and *dividends* of companies. Later on, we'll see exactly how to use these figures in determining what price a stock should be selling for in the market.

FEDERAL RESERVE POLICY

No discussion of business forecasting would be complete without mention of the Federal Reserve Board. The importance of this governmental body cannot be overemphasized.

The Federal Reserve regulates the amount of money which flows through our economic system. Because money is the root of all business activity, the "Fed" has great power. Briefly, the FRB has the following tools:

1. It sets the *discount rate*, which is the rate of interest that the banks have to pay in borrowing money from the Federal Reserve. If the Fed raises the discount rate from 5% to 5½%, it means banks have to pay more for some of the money they loan out. To compensate for this ½ of 1% increase, the banks will have to raise their interest charge by at least this amount. Theoretically, the higher interest charge should deter a certain amount of borrowing and thus the FRB has a method of restraint by raising the discount rate. In contrast, a lowering of the rate has the effect of lowering interest rates throughout the country, which should in turn invite more borrowing. This is not always the case, however. When people get cautious about borrowing, even abnormally low rates may not generate their enthusiasm. "You can lead a horse to water, but you can't make him drink."

Most economists agree that the discount rate is more powerful in restraining business than in stimulating it.

2. The FRB also sets the *reserve requirements* of banks. This has a direct effect on how much money the banks have available to loan out and naturally this has an important effect on the economy. The lower the reserve requirements, the more money the banks have "free" for lending, and vice versa. In addition, the FRB can affect banks' reserve positions through purchases and sales of government securities in the open market.*

3. The Fed has direct control over the use of credit in the stock market through the establishment of *margin requirements*. Margin is the amount of cash one has to put up in purchasing listed securities (you must put up all cash when buying unlisted stocks). When margin requirements are 70% a buyer must put up at least $7,000 in cash for the purchase of $10,000 in securities; the remaining $3,000 may be borrowed from the broker at an interest rate set by the local stock exchange. By raising margins the Fed requires more down payment and thus restricts speculation. Incidentally, changes in margins are *not retroactive*. If you were the buyer shown above with the $10,000 purchase and $7,000 in down payment and the FRB raised margins to 90%, you would not be affected. You could keep that $3,000 loan for as long as you like. As a matter of fact, you can replace a security held in a margin account with an equivalent dollar purchase (and stay under the "old rules") so long as the switch is accomplished the same day. Any new purchases, however, would come under the new regulations.

4. The FRB can utilize *credit restrictions* (i.e., force car or appliance buyers to put up a given down payment), but these have been used only under rare occasions such as war.

* No detailed discussion of this complicated mechanism is necessary, other than to know that the FRB decreases member bank reserve balances (restricts credit) when it sells government securities in the market, and vice versa.

The FRB has been criticized time and again for its policies. Tight money policies (higher discount rates, reserve requirements and margin requirements) are usually the brunt of attack by businessmen, because they tend to hamper business. That's why it is especially important to understand just what the FRB is trying to do. In short, it is trying to keep the economy on a steady rate of growth over the years and it wants to keep prices from skyrocketing. The FRB doesn't want a few years of boom and then a few years of recession and it doesn't want rampant inflation. The FRB knows the country's average growth rate and tries to keep it on an even keel. I like to contrast their attitude with an experience I'm sure all of you have had as a driver or passenger of an automobile traveling along a boulevard which has stop signals set for a certain rate of speed. Perhaps you've seen drivers who insist on going 60 miles an hour for two blocks, only to have to screech to a halt at the next signal, while you make all the signals without stopping by driving 30 miles per hour. What happens to the 60 m.p.h. driver? He wastes gas by rapid acceleration, wears down his tires and brakes by quick stops, and ends up with constant aggravation. This is just what the FRB is guarding against. It wants the economy to go 30 m.p.h. right along and get to the destination with greatest ease.

The trouble is, of course, that the FRB cannot regulate the economy like you can the gas pedal of your car. Restraint may well choke business and create lower activity than originally planned (this was the complaint of many during 1956–1957). But a temporary dip in business is always better than a sharp depression which might last for a long, long time.

CHAPTER 8

What's the Market Doing?

When people ask, "How's the market?" they want to know what the basic trend is. Many experts contend there's no such thing as a "general stock market." Instead, they feel there are separate markets for individual stocks and that an investor should be more concerned with what's going on in individual issues rather than the over-all list. While I, too, prefer this approach, one has to be conscious of a trend and that's what we're going to touch on here.

Most investors judge "the market" by what is happening in the Dow Jones Industrial Average. This average consists of an index of 30 stocks,* and measures their performance during the day. Actually, there are numerous disadvantages to this index. For one thing, it represents *only* 30 stocks and it doesn't seem fair to judge the whole market by just 30. Secondly, the 30 stocks are recognized blue chip issues and do not include any secondary stocks (since there are more secondary companies on the exchange than blue chips, the DJIA does not reflect the majority). Thirdly, the stocks in the average are not all equally weighted. In 1928 Dow Jones revised its average in such a way that any stock that splits has—after the split—less influence on the index than those which leave their price high. Because of this, in any given day a large

---

* The 30 include: Allied Chemical, Alcoa, American Can, A.T. & T., American Tobacco, Anaconda, Bethlehem Steel, Chrysler, duPont, Eastman Kodak, G.E., General Foods, G.M., Goodyear, International Harvester, International Nickel, Int. Paper, Johns-Manville, Owens-Illinois Glass, Procter & Gamble, Sears, Roebuck, Standard Oil of California, Standard of New Jersey, Swift, Texaco, Union Carbide, United Aircraft, U.S. Steel, Westinghouse Electric and Woolworth.

fluctuation in just one or two high-priced stocks like duPont or Union Carbide can distort the average considerably. Thus, while the DJIA has followed the over-all market trend *over the long run*, it is too often a very unreliable indicator of daily or weekly market action.

There are other averages one can follow. Perhaps the most inclusive are the Standard and Poor 425 Stock Index and the New York Stock Exchange Index which, because of their breadth, do not have certain of the Dow Jones Industrial disadvantages.

FACTORS TO CONSIDER IN JUDGING THE MARKET

There are countless factors to consider in judging what the market is doing. Following are some of the most important considerations:

1. *Do* follow some of the averages (Dow Jones Industrials, Railroads and Utilities and the S&P 425 or NYSE Stock Index), but remember that the most important consideration is the percentage change over one day or a long period of time. The newspaper headlines can be deceiving. *"Stocks Drop Six Points"* or *"Market Declines Total $3 Billion."* Remember that a seven point drop in the Dow Jones Industrial Average, which is currently around 900, is less than 1%. And that the total value of listed securities runs into hundreds of billions.
2. Look to see the ratio of *advances* to *declines* in the market on any particular day. If more stocks are advancing than declining then perhaps the market is really strong in spite of the fact that the averages showed a decline for the day.
3. Also useful in determining the breadth of the market in any given day is the number of individual stocks which made *new highs* versus the number that touched *new lows* for the year. Obviously a market with a preponderance of stocks reaching new highs cannot be termed weak, even if the averages do denote a decline.
4. What is the *volume of trading*? Like the preceding, this figure is shown every day in your local papers. The volume

of trading is just another way of saying "the number of shares that were bought and sold." The reason this is important is that *volume usually moves with a trend*. That is, if the market is advancing on *low* volume and declining on *heavy* volume, most probably *the basic trend* is *down*. By the same token, if the number of shares traded is consistently higher on days when stocks are strong then the over-all trend is probably up.

5. How many shares have been sold short? The so-called "short-interest" comes out once a month (gathered on the 15th and published a few days later) and shows how many shares of each stock are held "short." The larger the number of shares sold short the more pessimistic people are. Oddly enough, it is *not* a bad sign when the short interest is up. Why? Because the time to buy is usually when most investors *are* pessimistic, because that's when stock prices are low. And remember that a short seller must eventually buy back, so the more shares sold short the more potential buyers there are "lying in the weeds."

6. *How do yields on stocks compare with yields on bonds?* This "spread between the yields" is important because bonds and stocks are in competition for the dollar. For many years, stocks gave a higher return than bonds; this was natural, because there is more ordinary risk in stocks than in bonds. An investor would find the return on stocks anywhere from ½ of 1% to 2½% *higher than the yield on bonds*. As the 1958–1959 market boom progressed (stocks rose in value and bonds plunged downward) this situation changed to where a "minus spread between the yields" became standard procedure. By this I mean that bonds actually have provided a higher return than stocks (early 1969, 3¼% more return from bonds than stocks). The fear of inflation is primarily responsible for this "minus spread" since, as we have seen, bonds do not provide the desired hedge against inflation, whereas many common stocks do. From a historical standpoint, however, a minus

spread is a sign for caution and investors should watch these figures (shown weekly in *Barron's*, among others).

7. *What is "the public" doing?* One of the old adages of Wall Street is that "The public is always wrong." Who is "The Public"? Usually the smaller investor, who buys in smaller amounts—in odd lots. Therefore, we can gauge what he is doing by watching the summary of odd lot transactions, which shows how many shares in less than 100-share lots are bought, how many are sold and how many are sold short. Also from a historical standpoint, it is time for suspicion when odd lot buys greatly overshadow the odd lot sells. Conversely, think about buying when the odd lot figures show heavy selling on balance.

8. *How much speculation is there in the market?* This can be judged by the types of securities which are most actively traded. One guide is the Standard and Poor 20 Low-Priced Stock Index. Another is to scan the list of the most actively traded stocks on the exchange either daily or weekly. A predominance of speculative, low-priced, low quality stocks indicates that the market has "poor leadership," whereas heavy trading in the blue chips gives the market stature— good leadership. For the most part, low-priced stocks are not purchased by institutional investors, but instead by the public or by speculators. Large activity in lower-quality issues comes along only occasionally and it, too, presents a sign for heed.

   Another reliable indicator of speculation is the relationship of trading on the American Stock Exchange to that on the Big Board (NYSE). Let's face it, the ASE is hardly the haven for quality issues—at least as compared with the NYSE. Whenever the former (ASE) is experiencing volume much above 50% of what is trading on the NYSE, for an extended period, it constitutes a strong sign for caution.

9. *How many "secondary offerings" and "new issues" are coming to market?* Secondary offerings (large blocks of stock being offered at a given price at one time) and new

issues (shares of *privately*-held companies being offered to public investors for the first time) have one thing in common: they both take investors' dollars that might instead have ended up in stocks traded on the exchanges or over-the-counter. Too many of these "outside influences" must eventually place a drain on investors' resources and reduce the demand for other securities. Like other commodities, a very sharp increase in supply of securities without a corresponding increase in demand will lead to lower prices—and that is why you must be conscious of the secondaries and the new issues coming to market.

10. *How high is the market in relation to earning power?* We will see later how to judge an *individual stock's* merit on the basis of its earning power. The *market in general* should be judged the same way. Most statistical services show you how high the market is in relation to current earnings and in relation to projected profits—by figuring its "price-earnings ratio." This ratio is discussed fully in Chapter 20 but for now just remember that the lower the ratio the better, and a higher ratio is a sign of warning. Over the past ten years we have seen the market sell roughly between 14 and 20 times earnings with one year (1961) when the market sold well above 20 times earnings. Remember, however, that it is more important to determine how the market is selling in relation to *future earnings* (those of 6–12 months ahead) than of past or even present profits.

CHAPTER 9

The Bulls vs. the Bears

As you gathered from the last chapter, I believe it is important for you to know what is going on in the stock market. As you can see I encourage your attempting to analyze the market and I do so with a specific and important purpose. I am not simply trying to make a better newspaper reader out of you. Instead, the principal purpose of showing you what is going on in the stock market is to prepare you better to *forecast* what lies ahead. In other words, my preparing you is not just for your edification— it is for your possible enrichment in the stock market.

I say this because cycles of some kind are inevitable in the stock market, and I believe you should be prepared to spot these cycles *before they arrive.*

The stock market is a place where many thousands of people "vote" every day. In the market, of course, there are only two ways to vote: you vote that the market is going up, in which case you buy, or you vote it is going down—and you sell. Like political elections, a *trend* usually develops in favor of one party or another. If the trend is on the buy side, then the market goes up and we have what is called a "bull market." If, on the other hand, people are wholly pessimistic and are predominantly on the sell side we have stocks going down, which we label a "bear market."

Over the many years that the stock market has existed, we have witnessed many bull and bear cycles. Fortunately, the bull trends have dominated, as evidenced by the fact that the present market is close to its all-time high point. Also, a study of stock markets in the U. S. shows that bull markets normally last twice as long as the declining bear trends.

As a potential investor you certainly want to be aware of which trend you are in. Like a good fighter you want to roll with the punches and be a buyer in a bull market and be a seller if you spot a bear market coming along.

SPOTTING (AND DISTINGUISHING) BULL MARKETS

I said that you should recognize which trend you're in. This sounds silly; after all, if you're in a bull market stock prices are simply rising and in a bear market the reverse is true. Remember, however, how I keep emphasizing that you want to be *ahead of the crowd*. You want to prepare for the rain and take your coat and umbrella with you—not be suddenly drenched and soaked, with no rainclothes at all.

So now I am going to show you how to forecast—how to know that the clouds will be moving in, despite the prevailing clear skies. To start with, let's be aware of the characteristics of the final stages of a bull market. First of all, business is usually very good near the top of a market; this probably sounds paradoxical, but remember that the wise investors are looking ahead and they know that booming business cannot last forever; it is normally followed by a recession of some sort. Secondly, investors are enthusiastic and plum-full of confidence; everywhere you go you hear talk of the "new and golden era." Even the stock market "experts" are exuding confidence and are predicting higher markets ahead. In addition, the following factors generally exist:

1. The market has attracted wide public participation. The total number of stockholders in the country takes a sudden spurt. The odd lot figures mentioned in Chapter 8 show far more buyers than sellers.
2. Stock splits are commonplace; this is because stock prices have risen so high that there are just that many more high-priced issues (obvious split candidates).
3. Warnings mentioned in our last discussion appear: i.e., bonds are yielding way more than stocks, the market is selling very high in relation to current earnings, and there is a rash of offerings and new issues for the public to absorb.

(Watch out when the "hot" new issues suddenly turn cold and "sticky.")

4. Additional signs for caution show up:
    a) when rallies, which used to carry a long way, don't carry as far;
    b) when bond prices start to fall sharply, thereby offering much higher returns to investors (a lot of money is attracted away from inflated stocks into deflated bonds);
    c) the key stocks in the market begin to fade and sell off (the leadership of the market is weakened);
    d) volume of trading on the advances slows down considerably (the tide of enthusiasm is ebbing);
    e) the market does not react, as it used to, to good news (announcements which used to create excitement and cause stocks to rise, suddenly have no effect).

When you begin to spot these factors, then it is time to take heed and to get some cash. This is the time to switch from a heavily-invested position in common stocks to a conservative approach. And don't expect your actions to prove correct overnight. Don't expect the market to plunge the day after you have lightened your holdings. There is little chance of your selling at the top, so expect to see the stocks you have sold go higher in price. In other words, don't be greedy and expect the last ounce of profit and don't let a market which continues to roll on deceive you and "force" you to buy back hastily.

Naturally it is equally important that you be able to spot the end of a bear market, so that you know when to take a very aggressive position in the stock market. From a historical basis bear markets last anywhere from 1 to 4 or 5 years, although these over-all downward trends have been much shorter in duration over the last decade (usually lasting little more than one year). Exactly contrary to bull markets, the mood of a bear trend is morgue-like; everyone is in the dumps and interest in the stock market is apathetic. Oddly enough, a sharp decline in the blue chip issues is a sign that the end of the bear market is approaching (since investors hold on to these till the end). As this decline is nearing an end, an investor is able to find real bargains in the market: dividends are high and stocks sell very reasonably in relation to earning power. The market becomes resistant to bad news (announcements which used to cause stocks to sell off all of a sudden have little or no effect).

Once the market turns around and starts up, the volume increases, but gradually, and then you start witnessing more advances than declines, more new highs than new lows, etc. In short, the storm has passed and it is time to look for the clearest of skies.

Let me emphasize here that, despite what has been just presented, the stock market is not usually a feast-or-famine affair. There are stocks to buy in very bad markets, just as there are stocks to sell in a booming affair. I have presented this so you are aware of extreme danger signals, should they ever appear, and of exceedingly attractive opportunities which may present themselves sometime during your stock market life. "Everything is relative," and your success will come from having as much knowledge, information and insight as is possible. In essence, this is but one girder in the bridge to success. The other girders will fall into place as we go along.

PART IV

SOME FACTS OF LIFE
FOR STOCKHOLDERS

CHAPTER 10

Getting More Out
of the Financial Page

Chapters 8 and 9 have pointed out that there's plenty to be had from reading the financial pages. But there's still more! Now we'll take a look at the page that shows the daily performance of individual stocks.

DAILY PRICE MOVEMENTS ON COMMON STOCKS

Here are a few typical quotations from your daily paper.

Sls	Stock	High	Low	Close	N'Ch
266	GenMotors 4.30e	80	79½	80	+½
1520	Rohm & Haas 3bas	730½	724	726	—2

First of all, an explanation of the columns. Column 1, "Sls," means sales which took place in that stock on the particular day. These sales are in 100's; that is, you merely add two zeros to the figure under "Sls" to find out how many shares traded that day (in the case of General Motors above, 26,600 shares traded). The name of the stock follows—almost always abbreviated. Then comes the company's annual dividend rate, shown as 4.30e for GM, meaning GM pays $4.30 per share annually in dividends, including extras (which is what the "e" stands for). The "high" column signifies the highest price the stock reached during the day and naturally "low" signifies the lowest. "Close" indicates the very last sale which took place on the exchange that day. And

80

"N'Ch" means "net change," which is the change in market price of the stock between the previous day's close and this day's last sale price. In the GM example, the stock closed at 80 compared with yesterday's close of 79½ for a net gain of ½ point. Incidentally, stock prices are traded in fractions, with ⅛ of 1 point (12½¢) being the smallest fraction for most issues (on lower-priced stocks a dollar price is sometimes broken down to 1/16's and, in the case of "stock rights," they are often bought and sold in fractions as small as 1/64's).

Now let's take a look at this GM example again. What can we learn from it, over and above the simple facts just presented? First of all, watch the volume figures ("Sls") because, like the market in general, individual stocks many times show their *trend* by volume; that is, if GM consistently goes *up* on a large amount of "Sls" and shows consistently lower volume when it goes down in price, you might assume that the GM trend is currently *up*. In stock market jargon, such a pattern would "indicate a strong technical pattern" for GM stock. Secondly, notice in GM that the stock closed at its high for the day—hinting that enthusiasm for the stock was building up at the close, which in turn hints that the stock might open at higher prices on tomorrow's market.

There are a few stocks on the exchange that do not sell in *100* share round lots. Certain high-priced issues like Rohm & Haas (shown above) used to be so-called "10-share traders," which means that 10 shares constituted a round lot (1 to 9 shares constitute an odd lot). I say "used to be," as most of these very high-priced stocks have been split and their shares now trade in normal 100-share round lots. Rohm & Haas, for example, has been split and is a normal 100-share trading stock now. The only 10-share traders today are preferred stocks. In this case the dividend explanation usually includes the letters "as" which means "actual sales." In such circumstances, you do not add two zeros to the volume figures at the left; in our Rohm & Haas example, 1520 shares were the total traded during that day.

You might also have noticed the letter "b" after the "3" in Rohm & Haas. In this case, the "b" means the Company paid out *stock* dividends in addition to the $3.00 annual *cash* payout, but there are numerous other letters used to point out other information to the reader. By consulting some small print either at the beginning or at the end of the price list you can find out what the symbols mean.

ON PREFERRED STOCKS

Sls	Stock	High	Low	Close	N'Ch
10	NiagMhk pf 4.10as	64	64	64	—3
110	do pf 5.25as	82	82	82	+½
20	do pf 4.85as	75	75	75	

Our preceding discussion explains most of this. Just a few additions: the company's name is Niagara Mohawk; the "pf" stands for "preferred stock," and "do" means "ditto"—the same company as above.

Here we have three Niagara Mohawk preferred stocks. Perhaps you wonder why the big fluctuation of three points in the $4.10 preferred, especially since preferreds don't ordinarily fluctuate as much as commons. The answer: this preferred had not sold for quite some time—perhaps a month or longer—and the "—3" means the stock closed 3 points lower than *the last time it sold* (not the previous day, because it didn't trade then). You will often find large plus or minus signs on preferred issues and the time lag is usually the reason.

These prices on the three Niagara Mohawk preferred stocks serve as an ideal illustration of what has happened to preferred stocks in general in recent years as well as explaining how bonds and preferred stocks go up and down in price *with a change in money rates.*

Let's follow the history of these preferred issues to reveal this. In 1954 Niagara Mohawk needed some money and decided to sell some preferred stock to investors. The company determined that it would sell 210,000 shares at $100.00 per share. But what dividend would it pay on these shares? The decision was made by asking: "What are comparable preferred stocks paying?" After looking over numerous other such stocks, the company determined that it could sell all these shares if it offered a rate of return just over 4%—4.10% to be exact. Thus, a $4.10 dividend rate was set on the $100 stock to yield 4.10% yearly to its owners. The issue was sold on this basis. Incidentally, the company set a call price of 103¼ on this stock, which meant that the company could redeem all or part of the issue *at its discretion* at this price if it saw fit. *With such a call price, an investor knew he couldn't expect the stock to rise very far in price, no matter how long it was held.*

As years went on, money rates changed in the United States. Whereas in 1954 investors were attracted by yields of 4.10%, by 1957 people were not willing to pay $100 for an annual $4.10 in dividends. Instead they were willing to pay only about 79 for the $4.10 payout. The Niagara Mohawk $4.10 preferred had gradually declined in price where it, too, was selling at only 79.

Now Niagara Mohawk needed more money and decided once again to "float" a new preferred issue. It had only to look at its $4.10 preferred at 79 to know that a yield of around 5¼% ($4.10 divided by 79 gives you this yield of 5.25%) was "the going rate." So the company marketed 200,000 shares of a new $100 preferred with a $5.25 annual dividend rate, to yield this 5¼%. This time the company gave the buyers a little more upside potential by setting the call price at 107½.

Time marched on and once again money rates changed. Investors were getting lower returns on their money than in 1957 and were willing to pay more than $100 for Niagara Mohawk preferred with a $5.25 annual dividend rate. By the time 1958 rolled around, the $5.25 preferred had risen to 108 in the market price (pretty much a maximum price for the stock because of its 107½ call price) and the $4.10 preferred had come back to around 85. And once again Niagara Mohawk was looking for more capital and decided on issuing another preferred (the company had, over this history I'm referring to, sold considerable amounts of bonds and common stock, too). By looking at the $4.10 and $5.25 issues the company could see that a rate of around 4.85% was now attractive to investors,* so it set a $4.85

---

* The $5.25 preferred selling at 108 was yielding 4.86% ($5.25 ÷ $108 = 4.86%) and the $4.10 preferred was at a price which gave a 4.83% annual return ($4.10 ÷ 85 = 4.83%).

annual dividend rate on another $100 par issue. Call price this time was 106.

By 1969, money rates had changed again, this time rather drastically, and the example shown on page 82 shows them all providing an annual return, or yield, of around 6½ %. Further changes in yield will continue to affect these preferreds on the market. Niagara Mohawk's position as a company had not changed much over the years shown—it is still a strong utility company. Yet if investors get to a point where they are attracted only by a return of 7%, then we would find the $4.85 preferred selling around 70, the $5.25 selling at 75 and the $4.10 around the price of 58. If, instead, interest rates trend *lower*, the market prices of these preferreds—and other fixed income securities—will rise.

ON CONVERTIBLE PREFERRED STOCKS

While the majority of preferred stocks and bonds will fluctuate with money rates and do not provide a normal hedge against inflation, some such issues have a "kicker" in the form of a *conversion feature*. When a preferred or bond has this feature it gives the owner the right to convert it into *common stock at a given price* under certain conditions at *the owner's* option. For example, let's assume that back in 1960 you were considering the purchase of the Pacific Coast Company's $25 par value convertible preferred, which paid an annual dividend of $1.25 per share. Were this a straight preferred you could never expect more than the $1.25 dividend each year and you couldn't expect the stock to sell much over its call price, which in this case was $25 per share. It so happens, however, that this preferred was *convertible* share for share into Pacific Coast Company *common* any time until 1965. Thus, if the *common* were to rise to $50 per share, your $25 preferred would be worth $50, because you could take the preferred and exchange it into one share of common (worth $50) whenever you wanted, up to 1965. Thus, this conversion feature had given you a chance to grow with the common.

It so happens that the 1960 market price of Pacific Coast common was only $15—not $50—and thus the conversion feature was not of any *present* value. You certainly wouldn't turn in a $25 preferred for one share of common worth $15, so you had to hope the common would eventually move up in price past the price of the preferred. Because the common was at $15 and the conversion feature was of no present value, the preferred sold pretty much like any *non*convertible preferred (on the basis of its yield alone) and thus traded around $20.

In contrast, let's see what happens to a convertible preferred where the common advances in price and makes the preferred valuable. In 1966, as a result of a merger with Thatcher Glass Company, Rexall Drug and Chemical issued a preferred which carried a $2.00 annual dividend and which was to be convertible at the owner's option into one share of Rexall common stock. Needless to say, because the convertible preferred could be exchanged into one share of common at any time, the preferred should be expected to sell at least at the price of the common. Now let's see how both common and preferred showed in the newspaper in January of 1969:

Sls	Stock	High	Low	Close	N'Ch
286	Rexall .30b	45½	44½	45	+1
11	do pf 2	50½	50	50¼	+1

As you can see, the preferred sells for more than five points *more* than the common. This is because the former pays a healthy $2.00 per year to its owners in cash dividends, while the latter distributes a measly $0.30. Thus, investors are willing to pay a premium of over five points for the privilege of receiving the larger cash return. Of real importance here is the existence of the conversion feature. When the merger with Thatcher first took place, Rexall common was selling for around $35—and the preferred commanded a similar premium to that existing today and was trading slightly above $40. Now, of course, the common has increased in value (from $35 to $45) and the preferred has gone right along with it. Thus, *the preferred has proved valuable because of the conversion feature and can be expected to fluctuate up and down with the price of the common.*

ON CONVERTIBLE BONDS

Conversion features mean the same to bonds as to preferred stocks. It gives them an added potential. Let me show you two examples of convertible bonds.

1. *When the Conversion Feature is of No Present Value*

Example: Douglas Aircraft 4% convertible debentures,* 1977 maturity date; each $100 debenture convertible into 1.08 shares of common stock until 1977. This debenture was originally issued when Douglas *common stock* was selling around $85 per share. (All of this, of course, took place prior to Douglas' merger with McDonnell Aircraft). The debenture might have looked attractive at that time; after all, if Douglas common rose to 100 the bond would have been worth at least 108 (1.08 shares of common selling at $100) and the bond at that time would no doubt sell well above 108 because of its interest rate and the prospect that the common would rise further.

Unfortunately, Douglas common went the other way and declined to $35 per share in mid-1961. Was the conversion feature of this Douglas bond of any immediate value any more? Certainly not! To convert a $100 bond into 1.08 shares of common now selling at $35 would give only $37.80 worth of common (1.08 × $35 = $37.80).

Where was our $100 bond selling in 1961? Around *$80!* The bond never skidded down to $37.80 because investors were attracted to it almost as a straight (*non*-convertible) bond at $80. At $80 the $4.00 interest rate gave an annual return of 5% ($4.00 ÷ $80 = .05, or 5%) plus the fact that the bondholder knew that Douglas would have to pay back the original $100 at maturity (1977). Thus, the person who bought the bond at $80 in 1961 expected to realize a $20 gain by

---

* "Debentures" are bonds which have the general credit of the corporation behind them. No specific real estate, property or securities are pledged directly to debentures. Naturally these bonds rank above preferred stock in every way, but they are inferior to secured bonds.

1977—and this $20 plus the 5% yield attracted him.* For the conversion feature to be of any value Douglas common had to climb back to about $74 ($80 Bond price ÷ 1.08 = $74) —a long way from the then $35 market price. As it turned out, Douglas stock did stage a dramatic recovery. By the end of 1965 it was back to the $75–$80 level, which naturally brought recovery to the bond price, too.

2. *When the Conversion Feature is Presently of Value*

Example: R. H. Macy 5% convertible debenture, 1977 maturity date; each $100 debenture convertible into 12½ shares of common stock at $8.00 per share until maturity date. When this bond was first issued, Macy common stock was selling a little under $7.50 per share. Thus, the debenture gave the investor a 5% return, plus a long term call on the common at $8.00.

Since then, Macy common has risen from the approximate $7.50 figure to $37.50—up exactly five times since the 1957 issue date of the debentures. Obviously, the conversion feature of the bond has been of considerable value. Since each $100 bond can be exchanged into 12½ shares of common, the debenture can be expected to sell for 12½ times the price of the common. In this case, the common stock price of $37.50 makes the debenture worth over $468 (12½ × $37.50 = $468.75).

---

* In figuring bond yields it is important to figure both the current return of the bond *and* the increment in the bond's value to maturity (as a percentage rate of return). The combination of these two gives what is known as *yield to maturity*. In the case of this Douglas debenture, the $20 increment (the bond will be worth $100 at maturity compared to its present price of $80) amounts to a gain of almost 1½% a year over the 15 years remaining to the 1977 maturity. This 1½% plus the 5% current return gives a yield to maturity of almost 6½%. In this way you can compare the Douglas bonds with any others on a realistic basis. If, instead of selling below $100 (selling at a "discount" as we say), the bond sold over $100 (at a "premium") then you would have to subtract the premium to arrive at the yield to maturity. For example, a 5% bond due in one year which sells at 101 will have a yield to maturity of 4% (5% current return minus the 1% loss in capital = 4%).

A FEW RULES ABOUT CONVERTIBLE
PREFERRED STOCKS AND BONDS

There are a few generalizations which I think will be helpful to prospective buyers of "convertibles," as follows:

a) Do *not* buy a convertible issue unless you think the outlook for the company's common stock is especially good.

b) Try to figure what your maximum downside risk is before buying. Ask "What is the investment value of the bond or preferred as a 'straight' security—that is, what is the value of the security without the conversion feature?" This is your maximum risk, because even if the company's common stock market price declines substantially this is the lowest level that the bond or preferred should reach.

c) Most often when you buy a convertible bond or preferred where the conversion feature *is* already of value, the bond or preferred *will fluctuate directly with the price of the common.* In the case of the Macy convertible, if the common declines from 37½ to 30, the debenture will fall from 468 to 375 (12½ × $30 = $375).

d) In many cases where you find a convertible issue selling way above 100 you are better off buying the common stock directly. This is especially true if the common stock provides a higher rate of return than the bond at these advanced prices. For example, if a 4% bond is selling at 200 (giving a yearly return of 2%) and the common stock of the same company is yielding anything *above* 2%, you might as well buy the common directly.

e) Whereas your borrowing power on a corporate *bond* through your broker is limited to the existing margin requirements at that time (1969: 40% borrowing allowed on listed convertible bonds and 65% on listed non-convertible bonds), and whereas a broker cannot grant margin at all on *un*listed securities, *banks can lend large amounts* (generally between 50–75%) on such *un*listed securities. For example, assume you are considering the purchase of a 5% convertible bond of the XYZ Company. Let's say that each $100 bond gives you the right to convert the bond into 2 shares of common stock. XYZ stock is selling for $47. On a straight conversion basis the bond is worth 2 (the number of shares you get for each bond) × $47 (the price of each share on the market) or $94. The bond is certainly going to be worth more than this pure conversion value, however. The interest rate on the bond (5%) is probably higher than the yield on its common stock for one thing; but even if it isn't, the bond no doubt carries less risk than the common and, with the conversion feature giving you a long term call on the common, this minimized risk warrants your paying a premium.

Thus, the bond may be selling for 105, 110 or even more. Let's say we buy it for 108, which means that the common has to rise to 54 for us to be even (2 × 54 = 108). Let's also assume that the stock goes a lot further than 54—to 70! The bond will be worth 2 × 70, or 140, which is a 32 point profit on our $108 purchase, or an increase of almost 30%. But suppose we hadn't put up the full $108 purchase price. Suppose we had borrowed 70% of the $108 from the bank and invested only 30%, or $32 of our money. The 32 point profit on the bond is exactly the amount of our cash investment—and thus we actually doubled our money. Because of our borrowing, we turned a 30% gain into a 100% gain. By the same token, a 64 point rise in the bond would give us a 200% profit, a 96 point increase would mean a 300% advance, etc.

Naturally the reverse is true if the bond declines—a person will witness a larger percentage loss on his investment dollars because of the borrowing. Needless to say, borrowing of any kind involves risk and you should be very cautious about it, but you can see the dramatic possibilities which exist in borrowing on the right convertibles.

f) Convertible issues which provide more income than the common stock can be expected to sell at a premium over their conversion value (like the case of the Rexall preferred on page 85).

g) Most convertibles are "protected against dilution," in that the conversion feature changes along with the issuance of stock dividends, splits, etc. on the common stock. If XYZ convertible preferred, for example, is now convertible share for share into common and the common is split 3-for-1, the conversion privilege will change after the split. In this case, each preferred will become convertible into *3* shares of common, instead of 1. If you are considering the purchase of a convertible, make sure it *is* protected against dilution.

Also, *always find out if and when a conversion privilege expires or changes*. Not all convertibles give the owners the right to convert into common for the full life of the issue; and, in many cases, the original provisions of the convertible provide for a change in the conversion feature as time goes on.

h) Well-chosen convertibles can give you an excellent investment media. They can give you a high and stable return, a "senior" position above the common in the event things don't go too well for the company, and a chance to grow with the common stock over the years.*

---

* For more information on convertible securities, including a guide to "correct" pricing of them in the market, see Chapter 11 of *The Common Sense Way to Stock Market Profits,* published by The World Publishing Company in 1968, which was written by this author as a "follow-up" book to the first edition of *Stock Market Primer.*

CHAPTER 11

More About That Financial Page

STOCK SPLITS

Perhaps at some time you've opened to the financial section of your paper to see headlines like *"Minnesota Mining Splits 3-for-1."* Stock splits always make news. And they capture the imagination of investors and speculators alike. *Yet stock splits are merely the breaking up of a large pie into smaller pieces.* When a stock is split 3-for-1 the company gives you two new shares for each one you already own, giving you a total of three shares (including your original) for each one you started with. This would be sensational if the market price of the stock would remain the same after the new shares were mailed out to you. Unfortunately this is *not* the case! Once the new shares are mailed, the stock will sell for about ⅓ the price it was selling for before the mailing. In a way it's like a pack of gum. The pack of five pieces sells for five cents; open the pack and you have five separate pieces—each worth one penny. After you've opened the pack and *split* the gum into five separate pieces you have no more and no less than that with which you started.

Then why, you might ask, should people get excited and rush to buy a stock if they think a split is coming or after one has been announced? After all, aren't three shares of Minnesota Mining worth $60 each the same as one share at $180? Absolutely! Don't you still end up with "one pack of gum"?

The fact is there are many investors who won't buy a stock selling for as high as $180 per share. "How much money can I make," they ask, "by owning only 10 shares?" Yet they'll not think twice about buying 30 shares of the same stock selling for $60. That's just human nature. And, if more people are attracted to buying a stock at $60 than at $180, what does that mean? That the stock will *go up* in price after it is split and sells for $60. And this is the main reason investors are intrigued and attracted to newly split issues.

Actually there's another, and perhaps more basic, reason for being attracted to a company which has announced a split. That is because *a well-managed company will not split its stock unless it is optimistic about its future and can foresee the prospect of raising its dividend or showing higher earnings in the immediate future.* You can be sure when Minnesota Mining splits its stock that management is reasonably certain that business will be excellent in the current year. And chances are that the annual dividend rate will soon be raised and that it will exceed that of the previous year.

Management usually states that it wants to improve its stock's "marketability" by splitting it. It hopes that fluctuations will be less (even on a percentage basis) if a person wants to buy or sell the $60 stock than it would be at the $180 rate. This improved marketability is encouraging to investors and this, too, makes the split encouraging.

All of this brings us to one or two little warnings. First, be skeptical of $10–$20 stocks which announce splits. This smells of promotion, because there is really no reason to bring a stock down in price from these levels—they're low enough in price and there should be good marketability already. Secondly, never buy a stock only because it's being split; be sure you want to own that company and buy good values rather than splits alone.

Here's how splits show in your daily stock prices.

After stockholders approve the split proposed by the company's Board of Directors, a stock will be traded on the exchange two ways—"regular" (the stock at its old price) and "when-issued" (the new split price). It may show as follows:

Sls	Stock	Div	High	Low	Close	N'Ch
12	MinnMng&Mfg	1.60	183	179	180	+1½
45	do wi		61	59¾	60	+½

Trading will continue this way until the new stock is actually mailed out. The first day after the official mailing the stock will show with the word "New" after it, meaning that from here on out it will only be traded on the lower split price. The exchange allows the two-way trading as shown above as a convenience to buyers and sellers. Say, for example, you want to buy $6,000 worth of MMM stock. If there is no "wi" (when-issued) trading you have to buy 33 shares of the $180 stock; in this case, you have to pay the odd lot fee and you end up with 99 shares after the split and will then have to transact a one share buy order to round it out to 100. Both these disadvantages are overcome by buying 100 shares of the $60 stock. You pay no odd lot fee and you end up with the exact number of shares you want, without making another purchase. The term "when-issued" means you cannot take physical delivery of the certificate until the new stock is mailed out, but it's still your stock eventually and, if you turn around the next day and decide to sell it, you can do it (on the "wi" basis).

Splits do provide some extra speculative prospects, because margin regulations require that you put up only 25% of the money to buy "wi" stock (you can buy your $6,000 worth of MMM wi and only put up $1,500). Remember, though, that you have to put up the other 75% the day the stock trades "new." (After putting up the 75%, you can later convert the transaction to margin and thus withdraw in cash whatever amount existing market regulations allow).

MERGERS AND "ARBITRAGE"

Every so often two companies will announce they are merging, which is just the corporate way of getting married. For example, in March of 1958 Texaco and Seaboard Oil announced that the board of directors of both companies had agreed to a plan whereby the two companies would merge. In this case, they had agreed that each share of Seaboard would be exchanged into an equal share of Texaco (and that Texaco would be the surviving company). They announced that the stockholders of both companies would vote on the merger proposal and that the results of their voting would be ascertained at a special meeting on May 23rd. Here is the way the stocks of Texaco and Seaboard traded on the stock exchange between the time of the merger announcement and the day the merger became official:

| | Market Price on | | | |
	March 13	April 10	May 5	May 23
Seaboard Oil	58	60⅝	66¾	66
Texaco	61⅛	62⅜	67⅜	66
Difference in market price between the two	3⅛	1¾	⅝	—

Despite the fact the two companies' directors had agreed to the terms of the merger, you notice that there was a difference of 3⅛ points between the two stocks on March 13. Why shouldn't they sell at the exact same price? Simply because the merger was *not* official yet; many things could happen between March 13 and the May 23 date (maybe the directors would change their minds for a multiple of reasons or maybe the stockholders would not approve the plan or maybe the government's anti-trust forces would object to the merger). Thus, the market reflected this element of uncertainty, with Seaboard selling 3⅛ points less than Texaco.

As time went on, however, and it got closer to the approval date, the spread in price between the two narrowed: by April there was only a 1¾ point differential; in early May there was only ⅝ spread; and finally they sold at the same price after the approval. This is a typical illustration of a merger and respective market prices; in most cases, the spread will be far wider than the 3⅛ points (just 5% away from Texaco's $61 market price). Most often we will see a 10–15% disparity if the approval date is as much as a few months away and even a wider discount when there are additional elements of uncertainty involved.

Now let me show you a *guarantee* for making profits *if you believe the merger* is going to be approved. All you have to do is buy the Seaboard Oil in March at 58 and at the same time sell the same amount of Texaco stock *short* at 61, thereby giving yourself a 3 point gain (you eventually cover your short sale of Texaco by delivering your Seaboard stock—remember, the Seaboard actually becomes Texaco stock after the approval). The transaction would look something like this:

Sell 100 shares of Texaco short and receive appromiatcly	$6,100
Buy 100 shares of Seaboard and pay approximately	5,800
Your profit	$300

You have effected what is known as *arbitrage*, which is the buying and selling of similar securities for profit. Of course you have no guarantee of profit in the above, because the merger could be broken off and there you'd be, owning 100 shares of Seaboard Oil which you could no longer use to cover your Texaco short sale. Chances are that Seaboard would have fallen in price if the merger talks were terminated and you would stand to take a loss on your purchase. At the same time, Texaco would no doubt go up in price as short sellers would be rushing to cover—and thus you would lose on your short, too.

There are some types of arbitrage, however, which do *not* carry such risks and which actually do guarantee a profit, albeit small. Unfortunately, because of brokerage commissions, these profits are usually too small to warrant the public wasting its time on them. Brokers and members of the exchange, who do not have to pay commissions (they would only be paying to themselves), can make a nice living on arbitrage. One way to do this involves buying a convertible bond or preferred stock and selling the common of the same company short if it temporarily sells a little higher than the convertible issue. For example, let's assume the ABC company stock sells at 101 today and the company's convertible bond (which is exchangeable share for share into common) is selling at 100. A guaranteed profit will exist from buying the bond at 100, immediately selling the common short at 101 and then marching to the bank and exchanging the bond into the stock and delivering this stock to cover your short sale. In this case you make a one point profit with no risk whatsoever. The drawback is that you have to put up a lot of capital to do the buying and selling and thus the return on your money is small—perhaps only a profit of ½ of 1% on all your capital. But if you can get a guaranteed profit of ½ of 1% on your money 200 times a year, you end up with a 100% profit yearly and that isn't bad.

Not to carry this arbitrage confusion much further, but there is one thing to keep in mind here. Whenever a company has a convertible issue outstanding it *may* be subject to this arbitrage, which means that there may be constant short selling in its common stock. This constant selling may put temporary pressure on the stock and hamper its upward movement somewhat. If and when this convertible issue is called for redemption by the company, this short selling will cease and the stock will have an easier road.* Many of our country's very good growth stocks, however, do have convertible issues outstanding, so don't let that be a deterrent alone. As we'll see later, buy good value and the rest will take care of itself.

* Of course, the sudden conversion of bonds or preferred stock into a large amount of common results in the company having many more common shares outstanding. This tends to dilute earnings *per share*, which by itself should hamper the stock. Absence of the short selling—as described above —is usually a stronger factor than the dilution of earnings, however, and this is why the stock can be expected to do better after the conversion.

CHAPTER 12

About Those Dividends

IMPORTANT DATES TO KNOW

Ah, those lovely dividend checks! How important they are to so many millions of Americans. Despite their importance, however, there are a few things that are essential to know about dividends which are understood by only a small percentage of stockholders.

I'm referring mainly to the term "ex-dividend date" and its importance in determining just who is entitled to dividends.

There are four dates to consider when a company is paying a dividend to its owners, namely:

> Declaration Date
> Payment Date
> Record Date
> Ex-Dividend Date

The declaration and payment dates are simple: the former is merely the day the board of directors meets to consider paying a dividend; the latter is the date they set to *mail out the checks* for whatever amount of money is declared as a dividend.

Think of how many stocks change hands daily and you can imagine the problem of deciding who is entitled to which dividend. For this reason, the directors set a record date. They have to draw a line somewhere so they set a record date, which is the date you have to have your name *on the corporation's books* to be paid that particular dividend.

The trouble is that the corporation (or the transfer agent bank which generally handles dividend payments for the company) is not informed the very day a stock changes hands. As a matter of fact, a seller has *five business days* (excluding weekends and holidays) to deliver his stock certificate to his broker and a buyer doesn't have to pay for his purchase for the same five-day period. In other words, the company doesn't know for five days who sold and who bought its stock. Thus, if Friday is the established record date for a certain dividend, you have to buy it *five days* before—on the preceding Friday—to have your name on the company's books and be entitled to the payment. If you buy the stock *four* days before record date (in this case, on Monday) your name will *not* be on the books and thus you will miss the dividend. You can see, therefore, that there is a big difference between owning a stock four days before and five days before its record date. For this reason, the stock exchanges (and the OTC market) inform investors that they must buy a stock five days before record date to be entitled to a dividend and, if they buy it four days before, they are out of luck—they are not entitled to the dividend. To simplify this for investors (to save them from having to count back the days), the dividend declarations signify which day is *four (business) days before record date*—and they call this "*ex-dividend date*." "Ex-dividend" means "without dividend" and *anyone buying the stock on or after ex-dividend date* is *not* entitled to that payment. In other words, *as a prospective buyer, you have to buy before ex-dividend date to get that dividend.*

Obviously, the reverse is true if you already own the stock. If you sell before ex-dividend you miss the upcoming payment; if you sell on or after ex-dividend the dividend check is yours (even though you will receive the check a number of weeks after you have sold the stock).

Let's trace a theoretical 75-cent quarterly dividend by General Motors:

Declaration Date	Ex-Dividend Date	Record Date	Payment Date
April 10	April 19	April 23	May 30

If you already own GM you need to hold it *through* April 18th to be entitled to this May 30th payment. If you sell it on April

19th or after, the dividend is still yours. As a new buyer of GM, you must buy the stock *before* April 19th. The new owners on April 19 will not get the dividend. Now actually the buyer on April 20 is getting 75 cents less value than he would have gotten on the 19th. *For this reason, a stock should be expected to decline by the amount of the dividend on the ex-dividend date.* As a matter of fact, all open limit buy orders are automatically reduced on the specialist's book by the amount of the dividend each time a stock goes ex-dividend (in this case, the 75 cent dividend is equal to ¾ point, so all such orders on GM stock are lowered in limit price by ¾ point).

The stock exchanges designate that a stock has gone ex-dividend by putting the letters "xd" after the dividend figure in the daily quotations. General Motors, which in 1968 distributed a total of $4.30 including extras, would show "GenMtrs 4.30xd." If the stock closed at 80 the day *before* ex-dividend and closed the same price *on* ex-dividend date, the stock actually rose *in value* by the ¾ point dividend, so the paper will show the net change as +¾. In other words, the stock was expected to drop by that ¾ and because it didn't it was actually up ¾. If GM stock closed at 81— a one point gain over the previous day's close of 80—the net change would be "+1¾."

One general rule comes to mind here in answer to the obvious question: "Should I wait to buy a stock on its 'xd' date when it's lower in price, or buy it the day before and get the dividend?" *Given a static market,* I would always advise one to buy before "xd" (get yourself entitled to the dividend), because chances are the stock will come back up by the amount of the dividend not too long after "xd."* In the same vein, if you're going to sell a stock and it's the day before "xd" wait till the "xd" date or after because odds are that the stock will recover whatever amount it declined due to the "xd" and you will still be entitled to the dividend check when it comes a month or so later.

---

* Investors in extremely high tax brackets would be the exception here. They would prefer to buy the stock at the lower "xd" price rather than buy it before "xd" and have to pay a heavy tax on the dividend.

STOCK DIVIDENDS

Up to this time I have been discussing dividends paid out in the form of cash to stockholders. This is not the only type of payment made by corporations, however. Many firms either supplement cash distributions or substitute for cash with payments of additional stock; these stock payments are called *"stock dividends."*

Let's see the benefit of stock dividends both when they do supplement cash payments and when instead they are a substitute for cash. As a supplement stock dividends can be interesting. Suppose, for example, that Company A—whose stock sells for $100 per share and pays an annual *cash* dividend of $3.00 per share—declares an additional 10% stock dividend. This 10% distribution means that existing stockholders will get 1 share free from the company for every 10 shares owned. This sounds like a bonanza and would be except that, once the stock goes "ex" this distribution, it will drop in price by the amount of the stock dividend. Just as is the case with cash dividends, there is an "ex-dividend" date on stock dividends and all open buy limit orders on the specialist's book are reduced by the amount of the dividend. In the case of Company A its stock will drop by about 10% on the "ex" date—from $100 per share to about $91.* With this in mind you might then ask what is so valuable about a stock dividend. What's the difference whether you own 10 shares of a stock at $100 per share or 11 shares (1 extra share from the 10% stock dividend) of the same stock worth $91 apiece? Actually you are correct in your reasoning that there is no difference. Remember, however, that in this case Company A is also paying a $3.00 per share *cash* dividend and, *if no change is made in this payout, the stock dividend has the effect of increasing the stockholder's cash dividend income.* In our example, an owner of 10 shares of A stock was receiving $3.00 per share yearly in cash, for a total of $30.00 income. After the 10% distribution, ownership has increased to 11 shares—and these 11 shares with the same cash payout of $3.00 provide income from then on out of *$33.00* a

---

* 100 ÷ 1.10 (the 10% stock dividend) = $90.9, to be exact.

year. Therefore, the real advantage of the 10% stock dividend was that it increased the stockholder's cash dividends. If, instead of retaining the $3.00 cash rate after the distribution, the cash rate was reduced by 10% the stockholder would really have had no material benefit at all. *In the vast majority of cases companies do retain their present cash rate after a small stock dividend, and the increased income resulting is the main reason for viewing small stock dividends optimistically.* Incidentally, *large* stock dividends (50%, 100%, 200%, etc.) *are stock splits* and therefore fall under the discussion in Chapter 11.

After this conclusion you have probably gathered that *there is really no benefit to be had from stock dividends that are a substitute for cash.* If, in the example of A, the company is *not* paying out any *cash* dividends at all, what good is the 10% stock payout? In effect, the company is simply giving you more stock certificates, but these certificates in total are worth no more and no less than they were before the stock distribution. Many investors argue that the stock dividend without a cash rate gives the stockholder a tax advantage; that is, the stockholder is not forced into reporting cash income, on which he will have to pay income tax; then, if he wants cash income, he only has to sell off whatever stock dividends he gets and these sales will be taxable at the lower capital gain tax rates (Chapter 28) rather than at the high ordinary income tax rates. This tax benefit is valid. The trouble is that—*by selling the stock dividend—the investor has reduced his actual ownership in the company.*

Another argument for stock dividends without corresponding cash payouts is that, after the stock goes "ex" and is reduced in price by the amount of the distribution, it will go up in price back to where it was before. In theory, this should *not* be the case, because the company's earnings per share, book value per share, etc., are also reduced by the amount of the stock dividend. In practice, stocks often will recoup the stock dividend amount not too long after "ex." When this happens, we should really assume that the subsequent rise in price is truly not due to the stock dividend. Instead, it is due to the more important factors we will soon learn about, i.e., attractive industry and company, increasing net income, etc.

CHAPTER 13

Stock Rights

When a publicly-held company needs money it can resort to numerous channels. It can sell bonds, in which case it is *borrowing* money for a specified period of time. It can sell preferred stock, which gives it permanent capital (unlike bonds, there is no money to repay). Or the company may choose to sell more of its common stock.*

Assuming that it is decided to market more common stock, there are basically two ways this can be done:

1. through sale *to the public* of an agreed number of shares;
2. through the offering of stock to *existing stockholders*.

The first method may be the simplest, cheapest and speediest way to raise the money. The company looks at the present market price of its stock, sets the number of shares it will have to sell to get the needed money and then "hires" a group of brokers (called "underwriters") to sell those shares to the public at the existing market price. One of the difficulties of this plan is that it does *not* guarantee existing stockholders that they will be able to buy some of this additional stock if they choose. In other words, a stockholder's current ownership position is not protected: for example, if you currently own 10% of the XYZ Company and the company sells new stock—of which you buy none—you no longer own 10%. Assume the company has 100,000 shares outstanding, of which you own 10,000 (10%); if an additional 100,000 shares are sold and you buy none, you now own your 10,000 out of the

---

* Chapter 16 on leverage explains the pros and cons of issuing different securities.

102

new total of 200,000 shares, and thus your ownership has been decreased to 5% of the company.

For this reason, many companies prefer to offer new stock to *existing stockholders first* and always provide an incentive for the stockholders by giving them the right to buy the stock *at a reduced price*. But what happens if the stockholder has no more money to put into investments or simply chooses not to buy any more of the company's stock? Remember he has been given the option to buy the stock "wholesale" and this option to buy at a cheaper price than the prevailing market should be valuable to someone. It is! And the company allows its stockholders to sell this option if they want.

The option to buy stock at a price below the market is called a stock "right." Let's trace through an example of these rights, how they work and how to compute their value.

Assume the ABC Company has one million shares of common stock outstanding and its stock is selling for $50 per share on the market. The company has expansion plans and needs new money in the amount of about $4 million. It decides that it will offer new stock to existing owners at a discount of $10 per share from the present $50 price—or at $40 per share. At $40 per share the company will have to sell 100,000 shares to raise the $4 million. Since 100,000 shares constitutes one-tenth of the one million shares outstanding, you can see that the company plans to sell one new share (at $40) for each ten outstanding. In giving written evidence of this right to buy, the company *issues one "right" for each share outstanding and then explains that it will take 10 of these rights to buy one share at $40.*

Thus, if you own 100 shares of ABC Company stock, you will receive 100 rights from the company. Your 100 rights entitle you to buy 10 shares at $40 and, if this is what you want, you merely mail in your $400 to the company and wait for your new 10 share certificate.

If, however, you decide *not* to buy more stock you can sell your option to buy at $40 per share to somebody else. Because many people choose to sell their rights, the stock exchanges (or the over-the-counter market) set up trading in these rights just as they do in stocks. For the few weeks that the option is open to buy at $40, the letters "do rts" will appear under the name of the stock ("do" once again means "ditto" and "rts" means "rights"). For example, the financial page might show the following for ABC Company:

Sls	Stock Div	High	Low	Close	N'Ch
52	ABC Co 1	50	49	50	
150	do rts	1	⅞	1	

Notice that the rights have a value of $1.00 when the stock is $50. This is because it will take 10 rights to get the $10 discount (to buy one share at $40) and thus each right is worth $1.00. The formula for figuring how much rights will be worth is:

$$\frac{\text{Stock's Current Market Price} - \text{Subscription Price to Stockholders}}{\text{Number of Rights Needed to Buy One Share at Subscription Price}}$$

In the case of ABC, the formula would work like so:

$$\frac{\$50 - \$40}{10} = \frac{\$10}{10} = \$1 \text{ (the value of each right)}*$$

Naturally as the current market price of ABC stock goes up, the right to buy the stock at $40 has more value (and vice versa). If ABC common rises from $50 to $55, the rights will rise from $1.00 to $1.50 $\left(\frac{\$55 - \$40}{10} = \frac{\$15}{10} = \$1.50\right)$. Notice here the

---

* This is the formula for determining the value of rights *after* the stock has gone "ex-rights." Like regular dividends, you have to own a stock before it goes "ex" to be entitled to the rights being sent to stockholders. Also like regular dividends, you should expect a stock to decline on "ex-rights" day by the amount the right is worth, since the buyer on "ex-rights" day gets less in value than the person who bought the stock the day before.

Because there is the value of one right in each share before it goes "ex-rights," there is a different formula to use in computing how much each right is worth *before* the ex-rights date. Before this date, the formula is:

$$\frac{\text{Stock's current market price} - \text{Subscription price to stockholders}}{\text{No. of rights needed to Buy One Share at subscription price} + 1}$$

In our ABC example, the value of each right would be:

$$\frac{\$50 - \$40}{10 + 1} = \frac{\$10}{11} = .91 \text{ or 91 cents.}$$

speculative possibilities which can exist from the buying of rights. In this case, we're assuming the common goes up $5, which is a 10% rise on a $50 stock; yet the rights went up 50¢ each—a 50% increase on a $1.00 original price. By the same token, you can take a large percentage loss if you buy rights and have the stock decline very sharply during the rights period.

Now to some generalizations about rights which should be helpful to you in the future:

1. Under normal conditions, a stock will be somewhat depressed in price during a rights offering. This is because there are numerous stockholders who will decide to sell their option and, since the stock and the rights will fluctuate together during the offering period, any heavy sales of rights will not only force the rights lower in price, but will in turn also force the stock to go lower.

2. If you own stock in a company which is issuing rights, your decision whether to buy more stock at the option price or sell the rights should depend strictly on how you feel about the stock as an investment. Many people will argue: "How can I turn down the chance to buy the stock at $40 when it's selling at $50?" The answer is, if you decide to sell the rights instead of subscribing at $40, you will realize the $10 from the sale of your rights, so it's six-of-one, half-dozen of the other as to which you should do.

3. Remember you lose your proportional interest in a company by selling the rights. If you own 10% of a company and subscribe to the new stock you will still own 10%; if you sell your rights and do not add to your holding, you will own less than 10%. Since the average stockholder owns only a small fractional interest in his company, however, this is not of great consequence to him.

4. Any company issuing rights is adding to the number of common shares outstanding and thus it will have to increase profits to keep the net income *per share* at least equal to that of the previous year. In many cases the new money received from the offering by the company is for new production facilities, introduction of new products or other

elements which should increase the company's long range potential. Actual profits from these additions, however, will not usually show up for a year or more and thus you will often see earnings *per share* temporarily reduced.

5. Rights have a normal life of only a few weeks. Therefore, as a stockholder in a company such as ABC, be sure you either exercise the rights (buy the stock at the discount price) or sell the rights before their expiration date. If you don't, you have just thrown money away.

6. Rights do hold attractive speculative possibilities, but you have to consider #5 when you buy them with the prospect of making money on them. Since the rights are worth zero at their expiration, you have either to sell them before that date or be in a position to subscribe (by putting up $40 per share, in the case of ABC) before that date.

7. Since stocks are normally slightly lower in price during their rights offering period, this period can create attractive buying opportunities. Most often a stock will recover in price shortly after the expiration date of the rights.

SPECIAL SUBSCRIPTION ACCOUNTS

Oddly enough, one of the most intriguing speculative vehicles in the stock market is unknown to a vast majority of even the most sophisticated market followers. I'm referring to the "special subscription account," which provides large borrowing power for anyone buying stock rights. In generalization #6 above, I cautioned you to be prepared to either sell rights or subscribe to the stock at the option price before the expiration date. Assume you bought 1,000 rights of ABC at $1.00, hoping the stock would rise to $55 or thereabouts before the end of the offering period. Here it is two days before expiration and ABC common is still $50. You think ABC common is terrific value at $50 and you don't want to sell out at this level. So you decide to take those 1,000 rights, turn them in to the ABC Company and buy 100 shares at $40 per share. The only rub is that this takes $4,000—which you don't want to put up right now. What can you do? The answer: Instruct your broker to subscribe to the 100 shares at $40 under a "special subscription account."

This special account allows you to subscribe to the 100 shares by putting up only 25% of what the stock is selling for at this time. In the case of ABC, instead of putting up $4,000, you only have to put up 25% of the current $50 market price ($5,000 for 100 shares), or $1,250 in cash. You borrow the balance from your broker.

Actually, the regulations pertaining to special subscription accounts have changed significantly in recent years. At one time, a buyer could keep this 25% "down payment" indefinitely (and continue to borrow the remaining 75% without any time limitation for paying it back). Under these conditions, a person had exceptional speculative potentials due to this large borrowing power. Let's follow through on the ABC example under those conditions, simply because it will explain "leverage" (heavy borrowing) at its best. Remember, you put up $1,000 to buy 1,000 rights at $1.00 and you have given your broker $1,250 to subscribe to 100 shares. So, you have put up $2,250 in cash. Now if ABC moves up five points (or 10% on the stock's present $50 price), you will have made $500—or 22% on your $2,250 investment. Needless to say, if a person accomplished this type of experience five times a year he would more than double his money.

As mentioned, however, the regulations have changed on special subscription accounts. No longer can you keep your borrowing open for an indefinite period. Without going into complicated rules (which might be changed again), today's special subscription account buyer has to repay his "loan" in three stages and has to be *fully paid* within nine months of his purchase.

Thus, the special subscription account is now only suitable for those people who are looking for *short swings* (i.e., quick gains), and for those who have the money somewhere at hand to engage in the repayment. Only the very rich and the very secure can afford to borrow heavily (and repay rapidly) like this.

It must be obvious that it is especially treacherous when one buys low-grade, volatile equities this way. If you use conservative issues (like utility stocks) it is not much different from buying good real estate with a large short-term loan. But remember that you have to pay interest on any money you borrow; and do not lose sight of the possibility that you may be forced to put up funds faster than anticipated if the stock you have purchased declines substantially in price. In other words, like any kind of margin stock buying, do not consider it unless you can really afford it. As Harry Truman once said: "If you can't stand the heat, don't go in the kitchen."

There have been numerous times in the past (under the old regulations) when I recommended the purchase of stock rights and the possible use of special subscription accounts to appropriate people. At one time, utility stocks offered ideal prospects for this approach. One had to give important consideration, however, to the trend of interest rates in the U.S. at the time (Chapter 27 will discuss this fully). While the selection of reasonably priced utilities under rights once evolved into pretty much of a safe speculation vehicle, times changed—as interest rates soared and as utilities themselves became inflated relative to their growth prospects. At the time of this writing (mid-1969), however, the pendulum may well have swung far enough, so that they may prove to be decent candidates for such an approach again.

The important consideration to repeat is that which I pointed out in generalization #7—that you are generally buying a depressed stock when it is under rights. The stock is generally *artificially* depressed while under rights. There is nothing basically wrong with the company itself (other than that it is raising capital) —it is only the issuance of rights which has caused the stock to weaken. Naturally, you stand a good chance for profit when buying artificially depressed issues—and thus the reason for emphasis here.

CHAPTER 14

Warrants

"Make 1,000% on your money through warrants."

"A chance to make a fortune through warrants."

Perhaps you've seen advertisements like this in the financial pages of your newspaper or in finance magazines. These ads are not pure hokum—people have made fortunes by buying warrants and have done far better than 1,000% on their money through their purchase. As you can well imagine, these are very exceptional cases, but let's examine this explosive area and see what makes it tick.

In the previous chapter I explained how stockholders are sometimes given "rights" to buy more stock at a reduced price for a specified period of time. Warrants are just like rights. They, too, give their owners the privilege to buy stock at a set price. The difference is that warrants may be perpetual or have a life of *at least a few years* (remember, rights last only a few weeks) and the option price of a *warrant* is usually set *above the stock's market price at the time it is issued* (rights give you the option to buy stock at a discount).

Warrants are born differently than rights. Whereas the latter are born to raise money immediately for the issuing company, warrants are brought into the world as a "financing gimmick" and a method of possibly raising money for the company in the future. Warrants usually start out as a way of "sweetening up" a company's proposed new issue of either preferred stock or bonds.

Let's say that ABC company needs more money and decides to float a bond issue. Let's assume that, to sell an ABC bond today, the company would have to offer a 7% interest rate. This is a high rate for ABC to pay for its money, especially since the bond is going to have a 20 year life. If ABC were to throw in a "kicker," however, it could probably get away with offering a 6% bond, or even a 5½%.

The "kicker" in this case might be the use of a warrant. Each $1,000 6% ABC bond might carry with it one warrant which entitles the holder to buy 100 shares of ABC common stock any time over the next 10 years for $12.00 per share. The present market price of ABC common is $10.00 per share, but you can see that this warrant could become extremely valuable to its owner over the years if ABC Company does well and its stock rises above $12.00 per share. If this happens, the warrant owner can turn in his warrant and $1,200 (for 100 shares at $12.00 per share) to ABC and receive the 100 shares which has been set aside for him. If ABC common is now at $20.00 per share, his 100 shares is actually worth $2,000 in the open market and he can turn right around and sell the same 100 shares which cost him $1,200 for $2,000 and make himself an $800 profit. And remember he still has his $1,000 6% ABC bond.

Thus, by using warrants, the ABC Company accomplished two objectives: 1) it sold its bond issue successfully and with a lower interest cost; 2) it received an additional $1,200 for each $1,000 bond and this solved a future financing problem, because this money provided new cash which the company needed.

HOW TO EVALUATE WARRANTS

Shortly after the 6% ABC bond was sold, the bondholders were advised that they could detach the warrants from the bond if they desired. This gave them the choice to keep the bond and the warrant or sell either one separately. Then, instead of there being just one market for the bond *with* warrants, there commenced a market for the bonds themselves and the warrants by themselves.

In figuring how much the warrants should be worth, you should ask: "What is the worth of a piece of paper that entitles you to buy ABC common at $12 per share anytime in the next ten years, when the stock is now selling at $10?"

You might answer by saying that this piece of paper—this

warrant—isn't really worth anything. Why should you pay anything for this warrant to buy the stock at $12 per share when you can buy the stock itself right now for $2 less, for $10 per share. Right you are in your reasoning. But you've forgotten one thing. If you buy the stock right now you have to put up the $10 per share. But if you only have to pay, say, $2 for the warrant, you can get the option on five times as much ABC stock through the purchase of the warrants as opposed to buying the common stock outright.

For example, assume you have $1,000 to invest in ABC. You can buy 100 shares of the common at $10 per share. But if you buy the warrants at $2, you can buy 500 warrants, which in turn gives you the option to buy 500 shares of ABC at $12 per share over the next ten years. Assume that a few years from now ABC is selling at $20 per share. Had you bought the 100 shares outright at $10, your $1,000 investment would be worth $2,000. You would have doubled your money!

How did your 500 warrants come out? Assuming you sold your warrants instead of exercising the option—because you didn't want to put up any more money—here's how you would have ended up:

Each warrant would be worth a minimum of $8 ($20 current market price of ABC—$12 option price) and thus your 500 warrants would be worth at least $4,000—and you would have quadrupled your $1,000 original investment.

If ABC common had gone to $40 per share over this period, the comparison is even more startling. You would have quadrupled your money by buying the common outright ($10 stock advancing to $40). This is fine, but let's see how much the warrants would be worth now:

Market Price of the Common Stock	$40
Less Option Price of the Warrant	12
Minimum Worth of the Warrant	$28

Thus, the warrant you paid $2 for is now worth at least $28—your investment has appreciated at least 14 times.

You can see the possibilities that exist in warrants. You get a tremendous play for your money invested. For this reason, you will usually find warrants selling much higher than this ABC example. Instead of paying $2 for the ABC warrant you might find the market $4–$7, depending on how optimistic people are about the future of ABC company.

From a near term standpoint, once the warrants have established a base, you will often find the common stock and the warrant fluctuating by the same amount. In other words, once the ABC warrants are traded separately and the market is established at, say, $4 you will probably find the warrant going up one point to $5 if the common rises one point to $11. Of course a one point rise in a $4 warrant is a 25% advance while the one point increment in the $10 common is only 10%. By the same token, declines in the common would bring about much more severe declines in the warrants on a percentage basis.

Remember, too, that warrants never pay dividends—you must depend solely on the warrants going up in price to make your money. As I have shown, they can provide terrific gains for you, but they are highly speculative. If you find a stock you like very much—and find it has warrants outstanding—you should consider this medium for investing in the company. But do not buy warrants unless you are really enchanted over a stock's growth promise.

CHAPTER 15

Puts and Calls

The two preceding chapters have been devoted to forms of *options* to purchase stocks, namely:

1) *Rights*, which provide stockholders with the *temporary* option to buy more stock at prices lower than the existing market price; and
2) *Warrants*, which are originally issued as a financing "sweetener" and which serve as an option to buy stock at a set price for a longer period of time.

Both rights and warrants are issued by a company primarily for its own selfish purpose—to raise capital; the fact that these options are bought and sold after their issuance and that profits and losses result from their existence is incidental to their purpose. *As we have seen, rights and warrants are popular profit-making vehicles because they provide their owners with great leverage—with the opportunity to control a maximum amount of ownership for a minimum amount of invested capital.*

Another type of option—and one that provides even greater leverage than rights and warrants—exists in the form of *puts* and *calls*. In a book such as this, which intends to give you A to Z coverage and instruction in the stock market, some discussion of puts and calls is essential.

Let me point out at the beginning that these somewhat mysterious options (only a small segment of investors understand puts and calls) differ from rights and warrants in that the former are *not* issued by operating companies. These options are not corporate securities and of course have no place or effect on a com-

113

pany's capitalization, balance sheet, income statement, etc. Instead, puts and calls come into being through a small group of brokers and dealers who arrange for the buying and selling of these option contracts and who collect a fee for their work.

Now let's look at these unusual instruments and see what makes them tick. First of all, we'll answer the question: *What is a call?*

A *call* is a contract which gives its owner *the option to buy a specified number of shares of a stock* (usually 100 shares) *at a set price for a stated period of time* (anywhere from 30 days to 1 year). When you buy a call you are buying a privilege to purchase the stock any time during the agreed period at an agreed price. Naturally you don't have to exercise the option, you don't have to buy the stock; but if the stock rises appreciably any time within the contract period you can direct the maker (of the contract) to sell you the stock at the guaranteed lower price and make a nice profit.

A put is just the opposite of a call. A *put* is a contract which gives its owner the *option to sell a specified number of shares at a set price for a stated period of time*. In this case, you are purchasing the privilege to *sell* the stock anytime during the agreed period at the agreed price. You will of course profit if the stock declines substantially during the contract period, because you can buy the stock on the open market at the low price and direct the maker to purchase it from you at the guaranteed higher price.

You buy a call if you think a stock is going up in price and you buy a put when you think it is going down.

Basically, puts and calls are bought (instead of buying and selling the equivalent number of shares in the market place) because of the reason mentioned earlier—because of being able to control a lot of stock for a small amount of money. Assume, for example, that you wish to purchase ABC stock, which is presently selling for $50 a share. If you buy 100 shares, you will have to put up $5,000, or at least $4,000 if you are operating under 80% margin requirements. If ABC rises 12 points to $62, the resulting $1,200 gain amounts to a 24% profit on a $5,000 cash outlay, and a 30% gain if you margined your purchase and only put up $4,000. Assume that, instead of buying the stock itself, you purchase a 6-month call on 100 shares of ABC stock at $50 per share for a cost to you of $600. The $1,200 appreciation in this case is reduced to $600 (since the $600 outlay is gone—it has been paid to the put and call dealer) but this $600 gain amounts to a 100% increase on your cash outlay of $600.

The same thing goes for the purchase of puts. Suppose you believe XYZ stock is overpriced at $60 per share, where it is now selling. You decide you want to speculate that the stock will go down in price from these levels. To do this you have to sell XYZ short and, if you engage in a 100 share transaction, this will mean an outlay of $6,000 in cash, or $4,800 on 80% margin. To control the same number of shares through a put might cost you only $600, however, so you can imagine the prospect for greater return on invested capital from buying the put. For the sake of example, let's assume that your judgment proves correct and that XYZ does decline from $60 to $45 and that an approximate profit of $1,500 results. Here's how you will come out under the three possibilities mentioned:

a) Short sale of 100 shares at $60 with full cash outlay of $6,000: a $1,500 profit amounts to a 25% increase on invested capital (*$1,500 ÷ $6,000 = .25 or 25%*).

b) Short sale of 100 shares at $60 with 80% margin cash outlay of $4,800: a $1,500 profit amounts to a 31% enhancement (*$1,500 ÷ $4,800 = .31 or 31%*).

c) Purchase of a 6-months' put on 100 shares at $60 for a $600 cash outlay: the $1,500 profit is reduced to $900, since the $600 cash outlay is gone (it has been paid out to the put and call dealer); the net profit of $900 amounts to a 150% increase on invested capital (*$900 ÷ $600 = 1.50 or 150%*).

Thus, you can see how puts and calls offer money-making possibilities. In addition, I should point out that puts and calls have the advantage of *limited risk in dollars* for their owners. *The person buying either the call on ABC or the put on XYZ knows from the start that the very most that can be lost is the original $600 investment*, regardless of what happens to the respective stocks. Naturally you can't make this statement about the person buying or selling short on a regular basis. Of course, if the person loses the full $600 on the put or call, he is losing 100% of his invested capital and this is certainly terrible, so you can see that there are two sides to the coin. There are other disadvantages to put and call options and I'll cover these a little later. In the meantime, let's explore other motives for putting money into these contracts.

One such motive involves using puts and calls as a hedge when at the same time buying or selling stocks in the normal manner. Assume that you are interested in ABC stock at $50 per share. You feel that it will go higher in the next six months, but you want to protect yourself and limit your loss in case you are wrong. In this case, you might buy 100 shares of ABC on the market and, at the same time, purchase a 6-month put on ABC at $50 per share for, say, $600. Now you can relax some, knowing that —no matter how low ABC might go in price—you can always exercise your put and sell your stock to the put dealer at $50. Therefore, the most you can lose is the cost of your put, or $600 (plus commissions, taxes, etc.). Naturally if ABC goes above $50 you will let your option lapse and sell the stock itself in the open market. Obviously, whatever profit you make on the transaction will have to be reduced by the $600 cost of the put, so you can see that both your upside and downside potential have been tempered by this hedging. Certainly a hedge such as this is unsuitable for the vast majority of stocks; it would only make sense if you were buying the type of stock which might fluctuate widely either up or down. And the trouble here is that—on such volatile stocks—the cost of the put would probably be higher than the $600 example. Incidentally the reverse of this illustration can be accomplished by the investor who is selling short and wants to hedge with the use of a call option.

Another reason for buying puts and calls might be to protect a profit on a stock owned or on one sold short. Suppose you bought a stock some time ago and now have a sizable gain on it —to the point where you are worried about it declining sharply. Uncertain about the future, you can purchase a put on the stock. Then, if the stock continues to rise, you can eventually sell at a larger profit and disregard the option. If, instead, the stock plummets, you can fall back on your put and sell the stock to

the maker at the agreed price. By the same token, you can protect a profit on a short sale by the use of a call option.

A third motive for using options is to turn a short-term gain
into a long-term gain. Six months is the dividing line between a
short-term and the highly-advantageous long-term capital gain.
Sometimes a person has a short-term profit on a stock and is very
uncertain about the stock's immediate future; he wants to sell the
stock, but he also wants to avoid the excessive taxation of a short-
term gain. In other words, he wants to hold the stock for more
than six months, but he is afraid his profit will be reduced substantially by that time. He can solve this problem by buying a
put on the stock—one which will expire after the six-months
period since he originally bought the stock. If the issue holds its
gain beyond this six-month date, there is no need to exercise the
put; he can sell the stock in the open market. But if the stock
does fall sharply over this period, he can exercise his put and sell
the stock at the option price to the maker. By doing this, he has
preserved his profit, less the cost of option contract, and he has
accomplished this on the favorable long-term tax basis.

Now for some rambling facts which will familiarize you with
the ins and outs of puts and calls. To start with, your regular
stock broker will arrange to purchase option contracts for you.
Aside from the option price and Federal taxes, the buyer often
pays nothing or at most a small commission to the broker; if,
however, the option is exercised the broker will then charge what
would have been the New York Stock Exchange commission if
the option holder had either purchased or sold the equivalent
100 shares instead of buying the put or call on that 100 shares.
Then, if the option holder wants to move out of the security completely (sell the stock coming from the call option or buy the
stock coming from the put contract), there will be an additional
exchange commission. If any cash dividends are declared and a
stock goes ex-dividend during the life of the option, the exercise
price is reduced by the amount of the dividend; likewise, if a stock
goes ex-rights during the option period, the exercise price is reduced by this amount. If a stock dividend or split is declared, the
option holder will receive the additional or new shares when he

exercises the option. Puts and calls have no value for margin purpose, but any stock which an investor acquires through the exercise of an option can be margined according to regulation T (of the Securities and Exchange Commission rules). Special margin is allowed if a person exercises a call and sells the shares the very same day; in this case, the investor is required to deposit only 25% margin or $1,000, whichever is greater.

In addition, some interesting facts were uncovered by a thorough study of puts and calls by the S.E.C. in the year 1959. Here are some of the most pertinent of these findings, including my interpretations:

The majority of options written are for 6 months (6 months and 10 days is the usual actual length of the so-called 6-month option).

Option buyers paid an average of 14% of the value of the stock optioned for most 6-month calls. Excluding the very low-priced and very high-priced stocks, 6-month calls were priced at an average of 12% of their existing market price at the time.

The premium paid to buy 6-month options was about double the amount paid for *30-day* contracts (this means that the average fee for 30-day options was 6–7% of the stock's market price).

The premium paid to buy 6-month options was about 1½ times the amount paid for *90-day* contracts (the average fee for 90-day options was 8–10% of the particular stock's market value).

Calls are slightly more expensive to purchase than comparable puts.

Premiums charged on puts and calls depend not only on the market price of the stock involved, but also on the volatility of the stock. The stock which has a record of erratic price behavior in the market will cost more on an option than the relatively stable performer.

The S.E.C. completed a special survey of 6-month calls bought in June of 1959. Despite the fact that the stock market in general (as measured by the Standard & Poor 425 Stock Index) increased slightly over the 6 months from June of 1959 to January of 1960, the experience of call buyers was most disappointing. *Over-all, the public lost about 43% of its investment on these calls. Over half (54%) of the call money invested turned out to be completely worthless. Another 28% of the money wound up with losses amounting to an average loss of 60% of invested capital. Only 18% of the call money ended up with a profit—although this select group did reap a return of about 150% on investment.*

Before going into the disadvantages of puts and calls and some conclusions, I should point up two unusual contracts, namely "straddles" and "spreads." Both straddles and spreads are "double options" in that both a put and a call are written simultaneously on the stock involved. In the case of a straddle, the put and call options are written on the basis of the current market price of the stock; or, for a lower cost, an investor can buy a spread, in which the call will be a point or two above the stock's market price and the put will be a point or two below the market. These double options give their owners flexibility; they provide the opportunity to make money on both up and down swings in the market. Obviously, a person is extremely lucky if he makes a profit on both sides of a stock. Straddles and spreads are expensive to buy and a person has to count on wide price fluctuations in the stock to make them at all profitable.

SOME CRUCIAL WARNINGS

Time now for a magnifying glass look at puts and calls and some conclusions about them:

1. You receive no return on invested capital from dividends when you place money in puts and calls.
2. Puts and calls themselves have very limited marketability. While you can obtain marketability by exercising your option and then completing the transaction by either buying or selling the stock involved, you are at a distinct disadvantage if you want to sell the put and call option itself. There is no central market place and you are at a bargaining disadvantage in trying to sell it to put and call dealers.
3. You are limited by the time element of options. Good investments often take time—generally more time than 30 days, 90 days or even 6 months. Your idea might be completely right but you might be thwarted by the restriction of a short period of time in controlling stock through options.
4. The high cost of puts and calls places a burden on you

right from the start. You start out with a high break-even point when you purchase option contracts. For example, a 6-month call on ABC at $50 per share for $600 means that the stock has to advance to at least $57 ($600 option cost plus about $100 in commissions) for you just to break even.

My conclusion from all of the above is that *puts and calls should be used only on very rare occasions.* If you happen to come across a stock which greatly excites you, one in which you can visualize a very large advance in the market, then a call might be useful in your planning. Or you might consider the use of puts and calls for certain tax utility they possess (but this is complicated and takes professional tax advice, which of course cannot be covered here). Or, instead of buying options, *you can* take the other side and *sell them* through a put and call dealer (selling them is generally suitable only to very wealthy investors—and the procedure is too involved to discuss here).

If you do speculate in options I can throw in one bit of advice: *do not buy them with a time fixation in your mind.* Too many people purchase options with the fixation (either conscious or subconscious) that they will do nothing with them until the expiration date. Too often a person will see his price objectives on a stock reached before the option's expiration, only to procrastinate on exercising the option till the very end. Invariably the stock will retreat in the interim and the option holder will see that his profit has faded away. In other words, set some kind of price objective when you first purchase the option and do not let the expiration date of the option interfere with your investment judgment.

I wholeheartedly advise you against active participation in the put and call market. It is my contention that the percentages will "eat you up" in time. The statistics (you are working against a high break-even point and a time element) are against you from the start, so you will have to count on choosing unusually good stocks to make consistent profits in puts and calls over the years.

PART V

SECURITY ANALYSIS
MADE EASY

CHAPTER 16

Tools to Build Your Road to Success

One of the basic rules of investing is "Get the facts before you invest," or "Investigate before you invest." Fortunately—in stock market investing—the facts are available to you in research bulletins from brokerage firms, annual reports from individual companies, statistical services, etc. It's up to you to utilize these facts correctly and, if you do, your successes will be greater.

Part of these facts I mention involve basic fundamentals, such as understanding a little something about a company's financial position and earning power, etc. The basic aim of this book is to show you how to make money—big money—in the stock market. To understand what is yet to come I ask you to start by building the foundation for your success; after all, no builder starts with the roof.

THE BALANCE SHEET

Have you ever known a fellow who lives like he's earning $100,000 a year, but who doesn't have the price of a cup of coffee in the bank? Chances are he's up to his ears in debt and would be a very poor risk for you to lend twenty dollars, or even ten. Your good-heartedness in lending him anything might be termed a poor investment.

The same thing goes for certain companies which lack a strong financial position—they entail greater risk by you if you buy their stock. That's why it's important to know something about a company's financial status, all of which is available to you by a quick glance at its *balance sheet*. *The balance sheet tells you in detail a company's financial condition at one particular date.*

Perhaps the simplest way to familiarize you with this first tool is to compare it with the balance sheet of a typical American family. After all, we all have a balance sheet of our own. Following is just such a "Jones family" balance sheet:

JONES FAMILY BALANCE SHEET AS OF DECEMBER 31, 1960

Current Assets			Current Liabilities	
Cash		$ 500	Accounts Payable	$ 400
Savings Bonds		300	Balance due on Car	600
Common Stocks		1,200	Notes Payable	1,000
Total Current Assets		2,000	Total Current Liabilities	2,000
Other Investments		5,000	Mortgage on Home	12,000
Fixed Assets				
Automobile			TOTAL LIABILITIES	$14,000
Cost	$3,000		NET WORTH	15,000
Less Reserve for Depreciation	1,000			
		2,000		
Home		18,000		
Home Furnishings				
Cost	4,000			
Less Reserve for Depreciation	2,000			
		2,000		
Total Fixed Assets		$22,000	TOTAL LIABILITIES	
TOTAL ASSETS		$29,000	AND NET WORTH	$29,000

The left-hand column is titled "assets," which is just a fancy way of saying "these are the things we *own*." First of all, under assets, we have "*current* assets," which are simply those which are *easily converted into cash.*

Then we show "other investments" which could be anything, but in this case probably represents a small business thought to be worth $5,000.

Then we have "fixed assets," which are other tangible items we own but which are not as easily converted into cash as the current assets. Under fixed assets we have an automobile, home and home furnishings. Notice here that both the auto and the home furnishings have a "reserve for depreciation" which has reduced their carrying value on the balance sheet. Why? Because these items depreciate, or are worth less, as time wears them out. You know that the minute you drive a new car out of the show window it becomes a "used" car and is worth less on a resale than you paid for it. The same thing goes for furniture and other home furnishings. You might make the greatest buy of the century on a new sofa, but get it home and try to re-sell it and you'll know that it has already "depreciated."

Because of depreciation, you would only be deceiving yourself if you valued your car and furniture at their original retail price. To be fair—and to know truthfully what your assets are worth—you should subtract this depreciation from the original price of these items. In our Jones family balance sheet you can see that the $3,000 original cost of the auto has been reduced by $1,000 of depreciation giving it a more realistic net value of $2,000.

But, you might ask, how much depreciation should one account for? The correct way to figure this is to *estimate the life of the asset itself.* In the case of the car, for example, let's assume it has a useful life to you of five years, or 60 months. After that time, you figure it'll be ready for the junk heap. If you take the original cost of $3,000 and divide it by this 60-month "life" you'll come up with $50 a month depreciation to subtract from the $3,000 cost. At this rate, the car will be worth $2,950 after the first month,* $2,900 after the second and so on until, at the end of

---

* This is an example of "straight line" depreciation in which an even amount is deducted each month. Many companies use more realistic depreciation methods where higher depreciation is taken in the early stages of an asset's life. Such "accelerated" depreciation should really be used by individuals, too, because most assets see their re-sale value drop very sharply right after they are first purchased.

60 months, it will show on the balance sheet as having no value. Actually the car will have some small value at the end of this period and thus you can see that depreciation will seldom do an exact job, but at least it is realistic and gives you a good idea what you actually own as time goes on.

You will notice that I did *not* set up a reserve for depreciation for the Jones' home. This is because, in our day and age of rising real estate values, chances are 100 to 1 that the home has *appre-ciated*, not *de*preciated, in value over the years. To be correct in your figures, you should set up a reserve for appreciation by the amount you estimate the home to be worth.

Total all these things we own and we come up with our "total assets" of $29,000. Is this what we're really worth, though? No! We no doubt *owe* something to somebody and naturally we have to deduct this from what we *own* to find out what we're really worth. Now we come to the right hand side of this balance sheet, under the column titled "liabilities" (amounts *owed*). The first item shown is "current liabilities," which states the debts we have to pay *within one year* (here you have all your charge account bills and any other obligations you have to meet within the year).

Next we have to show our other debts—due over a longer period of time than one year. When the Jones family bought the $18,000 home shown under assets they borrowed $12,000 from their bank, which is to be paid off over the next 20 years. We have to show this *long term* debt and do so separately from the current liabilities. Now we've listed all the debts we owe and have totaled them together under "total liabilities" of $14,000.

At last we can tell what we are really worth, as follows:

Total value of what we *OWN* ("Total Assets")	$29,000
Less total amounts we *OWE* ("Total Liabilities")	14,000
Total amount we are worth, called "Net Worth"	$15,000

The balance sheet has served its purpose—to tell the world what our current financial position is and to determine what we'd be worth if we cashed in all our chips on the date this statement was compiled.

THE CORPORATION'S BALANCE SHEET

A company sets up its balance sheet just like an individual. Following is a typical corporate balance sheet (of the Ichabod Crane Company):

ICHABOD CRANE COMPANY BALANCE SHEET AS OF DECEMBER 31, 1960

Current Assets		Current Liabilities	
Cash	$2,000,000	Accounts Payable	$1,000,000
Marketable Securities	1,000,000	Notes Payable	1,000,000
Accounts Receivable	2,000,000	Accrued Wages, Taxes,	
Inventories	3,000,000	Expenses	2,000,000
Total Current Assets	8,000,000	Total Current Liabilities	4,000,000
Other Investments	2,000,000	Long Term Debt	4,000,000
Fixed Assets		Total Liabilities	8,000,000
Property, Plant and Equipment		Net Worth: Common Stock	
Cost	$10,000,000	(1,000,000	
Less Reserve for Depreciation	5,000,000	Shares)	$1,000,000
Total Fixed Assets	5,000,000	Capital Surplus	1,000,000
Prepaid Expenses, Deferred Charges Patents and Goodwill	} 1,000,000	Earned Surplus	6,000,000
		Total Net Worth	8,000,000
TOTAL ASSETS	$16,000,000	TOTAL LIABILITIES AND NET WORTH	$16,000,000

The "current assets" contain the very liquid items the company owns, but there are two items here which would not usually be found in the individual's balance sheet. A company in business has large sums owed to it by those who have bought its goods and these are shown as "accounts receivable." Then, of course, a company has a supply of its own products on its shelves waiting for sale (in this case, cranes) and these "inventories" are a part of the current assets. Naturally, in analyzing the current assets, we would prefer to see more of the cash items (cash, marketable securities, accounts receivable) than of inventories because the latter are less certain of being converted into cash.

There's no telling what you might find in a corporate balance sheet under "other investments." Most often you have to read some small print shown as "notes to the financial statement" to determine what these other investments include. Some very interesting facts can be learned from digging into these footnotes. For example, the Matson Navigation Company owned 500,000 shares of Honolulu Oil for years and always showed this holding under "other investments"—valued at Matson's original cost, which happened to be *50 cents per share*. Just in case you weren't aware of the real market value for Honolulu Oil (which was listed on the New York Stock Exchange) the footnote explained that this value as of the balance sheet date was *not 50 cents a share but closer to $50 per share*. Thus, instead of Matson's 500,000 shares being worth $250,000 as was shown, the holding was worth about $25 million. Quite a difference! There are many balance sheets like this (management is only being conservative by not writing up these hidden values) and the investor should be conscious of this "carry-all" category which can lead to profits for those who are alert. Incidentally, some large profits were made on Matson stock—the company partially liquidated in 1959 and stockholders realized how valuable Honolulu Oil stock was (its actual liquidation price was *$100.85* per share).

Next under the asset column of the corporation come the "fixed assets." Rather than show these fixed assets separately most companies lump them all into one category "property, plant and equipment." Like the Jones family's automobile and home furnishings, Ichabod is realistic and depreciates this carry-all asset and thus you see the "reserve for depreciation." Deducting this reserve from the original cost of the property, plant and equipment, you come up with a more realistic appraisal of the fixed assets.

The last asset items on Ichabod's balance sheet include what are termed "intangible assets." They include prepaid expenses, deferred charges, patents and goodwill, etc. I'd rather omit any detailed discussion of these assets. Just one word about "patents and goodwill." Despite the fact a company's patents may have large value and despite the fact that its name and reputation (goodwill) are also extremely valuable, it is conservative accounting practice to carry patents and goodwill on the balance sheet at the nominal figure of $1.00. This is because there is no satisfactory way of evaluating what they are worth. Beware when you find patents and goodwill carried for huge amounts on the balance sheet—management may well be deceiving you!*

Now we total all of the assets together—in this case they add up to $16,000,000. But, like our Jones family, Ichabod has some bills to pay, too.

First of all, we find "current liabilities"—those which have to be paid within one year. Here we have "accounts payable" (current bills we have to pay), "notes payable" (possibly to the bank), "accrued wages, taxes and expenses" (all of which are to be paid out in cash shortly), etc.

Just as the Jones family took back a mortgage on their home to be paid out over 20 years, Ichabod may have needed some money for a long period of time, too. This borrowed money is termed "long term debt" when it has *more* than one year to run.

Now we total the current liabilities and the long term debt and come up with "total liabilities" of $8,000,000. Finally we can gauge approximately what Ichabod is worth if it goes out of business tomorrow, as follows:

Total Assets	$16,000,000
Less Total Liabilities	8,000,000
Total Net Worth	$8,000,000

You can see that the total net worth of $8,000,000 is divided between "common stock," "capital surplus" and "earned surplus" on the balance sheet. It's not necessary in our discussion to distinguish between these terms. All three represent values to the common stockholder and the main thing to consider is the total of the three.

We're through now with the fundamentals of the balance sheet. The next step is to put these fundamentals to work and know how to judge whether a company is strong financially or not.

---

* An exception is when one company has recently purchased another, in which case it will possibly have paid for patents, goodwill, etc. and they will be written off (amortized) over the years.

CHAPTER 17

Some Simple Surgery on the Balance Sheet

Balance sheet analysis can become highly complicated. Ordinarily, however, there are only a few simple tests necessary to determine whether the stock of your dreams is sound financially or not.

Just like judging an individual's soundness, you want the answers to the following questions:

1. Can the company pay its bills?
2. What are they worth in the event they go out of business?
3. Have they gotten themselves too deeply in debt?

It may come as a surprise to you, but a very cursory glance at the balance sheet will answer these questions for you. Here's how.

1. *Can the Company pay its bills?*

You pay your bills out of your checking account, savings account or out of the money you have stored in the sugar bowl. You depend on your cash items. You do not depend on your auto, home, home furnishings, etc. to do this. In other words, you depend on your current assets (readily convertible into cash)—not your fixed assets—to pay your current liabilities (which have to be paid within one year).

Thus it's easy to see whether you can pay your bills by comparing your current assets with your current liabilities.

The same thing goes for a company. You can determine its ability to pay bills by comparing its current assets with its current liabilities. So that you can compare companies of all sizes you

129

simply divide current liabilities into current assets and arrive at what security analysts call the *"current ratio."* For example, Ichabod's balance sheet showed:

Current Assets of	$8,000,000
Current Liabilities of	4,000,000

By dividing current liabilities of $4,000,000 into current assets of $8,000,000 you obviously arrive at a current ratio of 2 to 1. In other words, there are twice as many current assets as current liabilities. The more assets the better and thus the higher the current ratio the better.

WHAT IS A "NORMAL" CURRENT RATIO?

Naturally a company is in bad shape if current assets are less than current liabilities. By the same token, a company with a current ratio of 1 to 1 (current assets the same as current liabilities) can't keep living from hand to mouth forever. *As a general rule we like to see a company have a current ratio of 2 to 1 or better. But the ratio will vary from industry to industry.* For example, your gas and electric company will no doubt have a current ratio of only a little over 1 to 1. It doesn't need any higher than this, because its revenues are steady and are all paid in cash monthly and it has no problem of carrying inventories on its shelves. In contrast, companies which have to build up inventories for seasonal sales will need a higher current ratio.

Two words of caution here! First, always look to see what portion of a company's current assets consist of immediate cash items. A company can have a high current ratio and have almost no cash in the till. A large portion of inventories is not as reliable because you can't be sure when and at what price these inventories will be sold and converted into cash.*

Second, don't buy a stock only because of a high current ratio. We'll see later just what to consider in buying and selling stocks, but remember that one of the disappointing stocks in the 1950–60

---

* To measure real liquidity, compare cash and marketable securities alone (omit accounts receivable and inventories) to current liabilities and get the company's "quick ratio." A quick ratio of 1 to 1 is very adequate.

decade—Texas Gulf Sulphur—had one of the highest current ratios—of about 11 to 1. Still, you should look at the current ratio for background because it's reassuring to know the company of your choice has the ability to pay its bills.

2. What are they worth in the event they go out of business?

You'll recall that we determined how to figure what an individual or a corporation is really worth. A balance sheet will usually set this out by the words "net worth." Then all the investor has to do is add to this any understatements of value (such as the Honolulu Oil–Matson situation discussed) and arrive at a true net worth.* Then divide this by the number of common shares outstanding and you get net worth, or "book value" as it is usually called, per share. This will usually be done for you by management in its annual report, but just in case it isn't, here's how Ichabod Crane book value would be figured:

Total net worth of $8 million ÷ one million shares = $8.00 per share.

In other words, this company would be worth $8.00 per share were it to liquidate tomorrow.

How important is it to know a company's liquidating value? I contend that it is important in only a small percentage of cases. After all, who cares what the liquidating value is of General Electric, International Business Machines, General Foods and a host of large companies *when they will never liquidate.*

Therefore, I insist that you *forget all about book value unless:*

1. There is a chance that the company might liquidate its business (this is a rare occurrence).
2. There is a chance that it might merge with another company in the future (in such a merger, book value would be given some weight in arriving at a merger price).

If you see little chance for either of these prospects, ignore book value in your appraisal of the stock. Incidentally, let me also point

---

* Preferred stock usually appears under Net Worth, but it should be deducted, since we are interested in what the *common* stockholders would get in liquidation.

out that the term "par value" has no significance whatsoever in the appraisal of a stock. The term appears on a balance sheet but it bears no relationship to book value, earnings, market price, etc. Simply ignore the words "par value."

3. *Have they gotten themselves too deeply in debt?*

Have you ever considered how much money to put up in cash to buy a home or another piece of property? If you can put up all cash—and not have to take a mortgage—you will have no monthly payments to make (except for taxes and insurance). Your worries will be small. You can even afford to lose your job and still know you'll have the roof over your head.

Assume, instead of paying all cash for this house, you have very little and you are forced to take a large mortgage from the bank. You borrow $25,000 and now you find you have payments to make of $150 or $200 per month. Now what happens if you lose your job and the income isn't rolling in? In short, you're in trouble.

The same principle exists when companies have to borrow to conduct their business. The more they borrow the more "monthly payments" they're going to have to make and the more risk they take. This is because the interest becomes a *fixed* charge which has to be paid through thick and thin.

I'm sure you remember the song "What a Difference a Day Makes." Following is a song you should get to know—let's call it "What a Difference a *Debt* Makes."

Assume you're looking to buy the business of the Hotentot Pot company. Last year Hotentot earned $20,000 before taxes, or $10,000 after taxes.* You and the present Hotentot owners agree on a selling price of $100,000 for the business and now it's yours.

You shell out $100,000 *in cash*. This year the business once again earns $10,000 after taxes and thus you are realizing a 10% return on your cash investment.

Then you think: "Why should I tie up all my cash in Hotentot? I can use some of that cash to buy some more businesses. And the interest rate from the bank is only 6%." So you arrange with your

---

* Actually the corporate income tax rate is only 22% on income under $25,000, but I have used 50% for the sake of simplicity.

banker to borrow $70,000 of the $100,000 purchase price—and to pay the bank 6% on the $70,000 or $4,200 per year interest. Now you only have $30,000 cash investment in Hotentot.

The next year Hotentot once again earns $20,000 before taxes. Of course, now you have an expense of $4,200 for interest and you have to deduct this from the $20,000. Here's how you'll come out:

Net Income before Interest and Taxes	$20,000
Less Interest Expense	4,200
Net before Taxes	$15,800
Less Income Taxes (50%)	7,900
Net Income	$7,900

Your net income shows at $7,900 instead of $10,000, but now you have only a $30,000 investment in the business. Thus, look what has happened to the return on your money:

Before: $10,000 Net Income ÷ $100,000 Investment = 10%
Now   : $ 7,900 Net Income ÷ $ 30,000 Investment = 26.3%

What a genius you are! Merely by borrowing the bulk of the purchase price you have increased your rate of return from 10% to 26.3%.

Next year Hotentot has a booming year. Net income before interest and taxes advances to $40,000. Let's see what this means to profits under both conditions (full $100,000 in cash and borrowing $70,000):

	All Cash Purchase	Borrowing $70,000
Net Income before Interest and Taxes	$40,000	$40,000
Less Interest Expense	None	4,200
Net Income before Taxes	$40,000	$35,800
Less Income Taxes (50%)	20,000	17,900
Net Income	$20,000	$17,900
Cash Investment Made	$100,000	$30,000
Return on Original Cash Investment	20%	59½%

Fantastic! You have tripled the return on your money by going into debt (by "leveraging" your investment as they say in investment circles). Of course, you know that there are two sides to this coin. So now we have to ask—what happens if Hotentot's business slides off? Assume net before interest and taxes declines to $4,000:

	All Cash Purchase	Borrowing $70,000
Net Income before Interest and Taxes	$ 4,000	$ 4.000
Less Interest Expense	None	4,200
Net Income before Taxes	$ 4,000	$ (200) Loss
Less Income Taxes (50%)	2,000	—
Net Income	$ 2,000	$ (200) Loss
Cash Investment Made	$100,000	$30,000
Return on Original Cash Investment	2%	Minus Return

The fixed interest charge of $4,200 looms big when business falls off and, because of this expense, you have a loss instead of a profit. The risk of borrowing has reared its ugly head.

I hope this discussion is helpful to you in deciding how much borrowing you should do if you buy a business, invest in real estate, etc. But back to stocks!

One of the things you should look for prior to buying a stock is the amount of borrowed money a company is using. Remembering that heavy borrowing entails risk and corresponding rewards, you ought to see what kind of leverage exists before buying.

Naturally we can't arbitrarily set a limit as to how many millions of dollars a company might borrow, because we will be looking at companies of all sizes. The debt figure means something only if we relate it to the amount of total capital the company has. A $5 million debt to a $100 million company is nothing, but to a $10 million company it constitutes half the capital. Here's the way to determine how heavily leveraged a company is:

1. Total all the invested capital in the business by combining these figures:
   a. All the *long term debt* shown on the balance sheet (this may include bank loans, notes, bonds, debentures);

   b. All the *preferred stock* (if any exists), also as it is shown on the balance sheet;

   c. All the *common stock money which is invested in the company.* Rather than use the common stock and surplus figures as they show on the balance sheet (we have just seen how this net worth, or book value, has little significance in appraising a stock's real value in the marketplace), it is more realistic to use *the market value of all the common stock outstanding.* In other words, *multiply the number of common shares outstanding by the stock's current market price.*

2. See what percentage of total invested capital (a + b + c) is represented by the securities which have fixed charges on the company—i.e., by long term debt (a) and preferred stock (b).

On Ichabod Crane's balance sheet you would figure leverage as follows:

1. Total all invested capital by combining:
   a. Long Term Debt, which in this case is .... $ 4,000,000
   b. Preferred Stock, which in this case is ....   None
   c. Common Stock
   Instead of using the $8,000,000 book value figure shown on the balance sheet, multiply the company's 1,000,000 outstanding common shares times the present market price on the stock (assume it to be $16 per share), for a total of ...   16,000,000

          Total Invested Capital $20,000,000

2. See what percentage of total invested capital ($20,000,000) is represented by long term debt and preferred stock ($4,000,000):
       $4,000,000 ÷ $20,000,000 = .20 or 20%

Thus, Ichabod has 20% of its capital in debt. Naturally the higher this figure the more risk the investor takes. Like the current ratio, the "proper" amount of borrowed capital will vary according to the industry and the individual company. Your gas and electric company once again can afford considerable borrowing because of its stability—and may well have two-thirds of its capital in debt and preferred stocks. This kind of leverage might be suicide for industrial companies. In fact, any time the leverage gets over 25% you have to be very conscious of the possible risks.

In a growing and profitable industry some amount of debt shows management aggressiveness. As in our earlier example, some borrowing can greatly enhance the return on your money. As a matter of fact, management may well leave itself open to criticism for not taking advantage of "cheap" borrowed money. After all, a company which consistently earns 10–20% on its invested capital may be foolish not to expand on 5% or 6% borrowed money.

I must mention, however, that there are some companies which are in the fortunate position of having ample cash to handle their business and take care of expansion. They may need no debt or preferred stocks. They have what we call a *"clean capitalization"— free of debt and preferred charges.* The stockholders of these companies can relax some, knowing that there are no fixed interest charges to cause extraordinary swings in their profits. Clean capitalization companies such as Otis Elevator, Gillette and Zenith Radio have given their owners both a feeling of security and some growth over the years.

From the standpoint of the investor, consider the leverage so that you know what risks the investment entails. It's just another "background" fact to know about a stock before making the plunge.

CONCLUSION

The current ratio—easily figured and usually computed for you by management in its report to stockholders—shows you a company's current financial position and tells you whether the money is there to pay the bills.

Leverage tells you whether the company is too heavily laden with debt and gives you a hint as to certain risks which may exist.

Book value has usage in only a few instances.

These are by no means the only yardsticks for balance sheet analysis, but if you understand the relative importance of these you have the background necessary to back up your decisions. I emphasize that they give *only background*, because, as we shall see very shortly, your decisions will stem from other considerations.

CHAPTER 18

Some More Road-Building Tools

We know now how to judge how solid a person or a company is by whether they can pay their bills, by determining whether they are too much in debt and by knowing how much they'd be worth if they were to go out of business tomorrow.

So far we've overlooked one all-important consideration: *How much money are they earning?*

As we'll see a little later it is the present and potential earning power which makes a stock a buy or a sell candidate. You can see that we would be remiss if we didn't know something about the accounting statement which tells the world about a company's earnings—the so-called "income statement" (also called the "statement of profit and loss" and/or the "statement of earnings").

The income statement tells *how much money has been earned over a given period of time.* Following is a sample income statement for the **Rum Dumb Rum Company:**

Despite the importance of the income statement its analysis is relatively simple. I'm sure most of the statement is self-explanatory to you. There are, however, a few pointers I'd like to pass on to you—all of which will prepare you for the ultimate: how to know what stocks to buy and when to buy them.

HOW EFFICIENT IS THE COMPANY?

You've no doubt had contact with inefficient, as well as efficient people. You wouldn't invest a plug nickel in the *in*efficient, I'm sure. Nor would you—or should you—be anxious to invest in inefficient companies.

RUM DUMB RUM CORPORATION
INCOME STATEMENT FOR THE YEAR ENDED DECEMBER 31, 1960

Net Sales		$100,000,000
Less:		
Cost of Goods Sold	$70,000,000	
Selling, General & Administrative Expenses	10,000,000	
Depreciation	5,000,000	85,000,000
Profit from Operations		$ 15,000,000
Less Interest Charges		1,000,000
Net Profit before Taxes		$ 14,000,000
Add Non-Recurring Income		4,000,000
Total Profit before Taxes		$ 18,000,000
Less Income Taxes		8,000,000
Net Profit		$ 10,000,000

Many investors have asked me: "How can I determine whether a company is efficient or not when I'm so far away from it and have no personal contacts?" The answer: by looking at its *"margin of profit."*

The margin of profit tells you how much gross profit the company is getting from each dollar of sales and is arrived at by relating the "profit from operations" on the income statement to "net sales." In the case of Rum Dumb, the margin of profit would be:

Profit from Operations ÷ Net Sales = Margin of Profit
$15,000,000 ÷ $100,000,000 = 15%

In other words, on every $1.00 sale, Rum Dumb makes 15%, or 15¢ (before interest, taxes, etc.).

Obviously a company which makes 15¢ on every $1.00 of sales must be far more efficient than one which makes only 10¢ on the same $1.00. Thus, *in the same industry*, you can compare the efficiency of any number of companies merely by comparing their margins of profit. You notice I have emphasized the comment that you must only compare companies *in the same industry* this way.

This is because each industry has its own profit structure and mode of doing business.

The food chain industry, for example, is a high volume business and the margin of profit on each $1.00 of sales is very low. You can't compare the margin of profit of Great Atlantic and Pacific— the world's largest food chain—with that of Caterpillar Tractor, for example. The latter sells high priced tractors, crawlers and other construction equipment and by necessity there is a larger profit in each dollar of sales than in the stable, high-turnover food business.

Assuming that you compare companies in the same line of business, we can conclude that *the higher the margin of profit the more effective is management in getting profit for the stockholders* and thus the better it is. Of course, the *trend* of margins is very important. It is very healthy to see them rising, so look for the trend in making decisions as to management's recent success.

BUYING "INEFFICIENCY"

Now that we've decided that it is better to buy the *most* efficient companies I have to turn around and say that *sometimes it can be very profitable to buy companies which have been plagued with inefficiency*. Of course it will be profitable only if there is some definite change of philosophy or a change in personnel which makes a sudden endeavor to improve efficiency and the margin of profit.

Take the case of Safeway Stores! The years 1949–1955 were spent building up sales for Safeway. But it is not volume of sales which pays off for stockholders—it is profits, and here is where Safeway had fallen down. Here's the company's record over this seven year span:

Despite the increase in sales, Safeway's profits per share had declined (the company had added to its common stock outstanding and this dilution forced earnings *per share* down over this period). As a result, Safeway common stock was a dull performer. Something was obviously wrong because the company was operating at a margin of profit *about half of what the average company in the industry was doing.*

	Sales (Billion)	Margin of Profit	Earnings Per Share
1949	$1.1	2.7%	$1.68
1950	1.2	3.2	1.61
1951	1.4	2.1	.75
1952	1.6	2.3	.67
1953	1.7	3.0	1.36
1954	1.8	2.8	1.16
1955	1.9	2.8	1.08

A change of management occurred in 1955 and it was the announced intention of this management to improve the efficiency —the margin of profit—of Safeway. This change of philosophy offered some real money-making opportunities to stock buyers. All you had to say was: "I believe that new management at Safeway will be able to reach industry averages of efficiency" (no more) and you could have bought the stock with assurance. After all, if Safeway doubled its margin of profit its earnings would at least double and the stock would be a good investment.

Here's what happened at Safeway in the ensuing four years:

	Sales (Billion)	Margin of Profit	Earnings per Share	Market Price of Safeway Stock
1955	$1.9	2.8	$1.08	19⅜–14
1956	2.0	4.1	2.04	23⅞–16⅞
1957	2.1	4.3	2.43	27½–20⅛
1958	2.2	4.4	2.60	41¾–24½
1959	2.3	4.5	2.82	42¼–34⅝

You can see the importance of efficiency here. Earnings went from $1.08 per share to $2.82 and the stock rose from a low of 14 to as high as 42¼. There are countless examples of constructive management changes which have achieved similar results. Beckman Instruments, Crown Cork and Seal, Greyhound, Sperry Rand, Hitco and (recently) Montgomery Ward are just a half dozen of hundreds of the successes made from "investing in inefficiency." Remember, however, that improving margins is not an easy task and do not assume that it will be accomplished overnight.

IS ANY PART OF NET PROFIT "UNUSUAL"?

Naturally you should be interested to know whether a company's reported profits will continue at the same levels in the future. You certainly want to know if one year's profits have been "bloated" by some non-recurring gain. Say, for example, a company sells a plant or some real estate in one year. They will have a gain to report and, since it may be many years before they sell off another large asset such as this (perhaps they never will), you should not be deceived by this gain.

Therefore, I caution you to look at a company's income statement to see if there are any large "non-recurring profits." Rum Dumb had just such an addition to its profits—in the amount of $4 million. You should deduct this $4 million (actually $3 million after 25% capital gain tax) from Rum Dumb's net profit to arrive at the company's "true" earnings for the year.

Usually management will do this for you: they will separate the non-recurring income from the normal income and tell you what the company actually earned on an operating basis. *If they do not do this, they are to be criticized.* To my way of thinking it's a sign of weakness if they don't have the fortitude to advertise the truth, rather than deceive the public. Look for this, too, in assessing management.

Likewise, a company may have some non-recurring *expenses* or *write-offs* which *reduce* normal profits. Write-offs will usually show separately on the income statement, but non-recurring expenses (such as the opening of new facilities, moving to a new plant, etc.) will usually be lumped together with normal expenses and not be separately shown. In either case, you can count on management to explain these non-recurring items and tell you how much they reduced profits. Naturally you'll want to allow for these items when you appraise the company's efficiency.

WHAT IS THE NET INCOME PER SHARE?

When you buy a stock on the market you pay for it on a *per share basis.* Whether you buy 10, 20 or 100 shares the important thing is what price you pay for each share. Thus, it makes sense that *you should know how much money the company is earning on a per share basis*.

Almost all companies report their earnings in both total dollars and *on a per share basis*. Just in case you're wondering how the latter is figured, it is done as follows:

Net income (after taxes and after preferred dividends, if any) ÷ Number of common shares outstanding.

In the case of Rum Dumb—which had 1,000,000 shares outstanding—net income per share would be:

Net income of $10 million ÷ one million shares = $10.00 per share.

Rum Dumb management would no doubt have deducted the non-recurring income for you and shown you that net income from operations would be $7 million after taxes, or $7.00 per share.

As we'll see later it is the relationship of a company's net income per share to its market price per share which tells us whether or not its stock should be bought.

WHAT IS THE "CASH FLOW" PER SHARE?

In Chapter 16 we discussed "Reserve for Depreciation" which is an accumulation of the periodic adjustments companies (or individuals) make in writing down their assets to realistic figures. There are various methods of computing depreciation: some companies use accelerated depreciation and write down their assets just as rapidly as possible, whereas others utilize the straight line method. A company that uses the *former* method is going to have *higher current depreciation expense and correspondingly lower reported earnings than the company using the latter*. For example, take companies A and B, both of which just completed new plants costing $50 million. Company A decides to depreciate this plant very fast and, in the first year, charges off depreciation expense of $5 million; company B uses a slower method and incurs a depreciation expense of only $3 million for the same year. Because of this accounting decision alone company A is deducting

$2 million more than B from its sales and, for this reason alone, A will have to report lower net income than B. It is obvious that A is not really any less profitable than B and therefore it should be obvious that an investor has to be conscious of depreciation expense in an income statement.

In order to compare companies like A and B more fairly, analysts use what is known as *"cash flow"—which is the total of net income after taxes plus depreciation*. As is the case of net income, it is important to compute this figure on a *per share basis*. In the case of Rum Dumb, cash flow per share would be:

Net Profit (after deducting non-recurring income)	$7,000,000
Add Depreciation	5,000,000
Total Cash Flow	$12,000,000

Per Share ($12 million ÷ 1 million shares) = $12.00 per share

In the same industry, it is often very important to compare companies on the basis of *cash flow per share*. In extreme cases like that of A and B, cash flow per share can be the most realistic measure of comparison.

CONCLUSION

The investor can easily learn what he needs to know from a company's income statement. You now know how to judge a company's efficiency and how—in rare cases—you can profit from spotting inefficiency (accompanied, of course, by a change in management or a change in philosophy). You also know how to uncover some hidden items and how to arrive at the all-important net income and cash flow per share. All of these will be valuable tools for you to use in your future investing.

PART VI

HOW TO BUY
THE RIGHT STOCKS
AT THE RIGHT PRICES

CHAPTER 19

What to Buy

Studies have shown how workers are happier when they have soothing background music while they work. Not only are they happier, they also get more work done and this increased productivity leads to higher wages for themselves and higher profits for their employers.

In a way, the last few chapters have provided you with the "background music" for investing in the stock market. Your "productivity" should improve by knowing the few important facts I've emphasized.

But background music isn't enough. If a worker hasn't been properly instructed in how to assemble the product he's working on, the music will do him little good; in fact, it might just put him to sleep.

The same thing goes for your investing. We've turned on the background music—now let's see how to assemble the product and know *what to buy* in the market.

Knowing *what to buy* involves using a very simple and very logical procedure. Actually it's just like buying a house. When you shop for a house you're most interested in the location of your abode. Regardless of how beautiful the house may be you're not going to buy it if it's located next to the city dump. The most logical approach to house-hunting is to determine *where* you want to live and then find the house you want for the right price in this approximate location.

Buying stocks involves the same approach. The first thing to do is to find the best location for your money. In this case the best location is the *best industry*.

MY INDUSTRY APPROACH THEORY

Most of the mistakes made by investors stem from not giving ample weight to the industry in which a company is engaged. People get excited about certain companies for a variety of reasons, but in so many cases they could save themselves a lot of time, bother and money by sitting down and putting a magnifying glass on the industry involved. After all, even the very best company in a poor industry will, generally, be only a mediocre investment. And a mediocre company in a poor industry will be a very poor investment.

Therefore, follow my industry approach theory. It involves only one basic rule:

"Before you invest a penny, be satisfied that the industry is attractive."

The industry approach theory is not a new one. All security analysts are trained this way. My theory involves asking only a few questions about the industry you are considering. Here they are:

1. *Is the industry growing?*

This is so obvious I'm almost ashamed to list it. But the person considering putting his dollars into International Buggywhip in the early 1900's—just when the automobile was getting into mass production—knew to ask this, too. His answer would certainly have been: "No, this industry is not growing—it has reached maturity and will eventually be replaced by the advent of the automobile." Yet I'm sure there were many people who lost "Buggywhip" money at that time. They failed to isolate themselves and specifically ask whether the industry was in its early stages of growth or whether it had reached maturity. You might ask the same question today about steel (aluminum, plastics, glass, all aiming at markets which now belong to steel), oil (atomic energy will replace certain uses), rayon (newer synthetic fibers are making sharp inroads into rayon usage), etc. Don't *you* forget to ask this first important question about the industry you are investigating.

2. *How important are labor costs?*

It is said that there is nothing certain in life but death and taxes. Add "and higher labor costs" to this and you have a broader truism. As you know, labor unions have gained great strength in recent years. The job of union leaders is to improve working conditions and wages for their members. This they have done in the past and I'm certain that they will continue to reap such benefits for their members in the future. Companies with high labor charges have to depend on either:

a) Corresponding increased productivity from their workers, or
b) Increased selling prices of their products,

or—they will see their profits squeezed in the future. Naturally there is no guarantee that they will be able to accomplish either of these remedies over the years. Therefore it is important for you to recognize the importance of labor costs in the industry you are considering.

3. *What is the pricing structure of the industry?*

Certain industries compete solely on the basis of the selling price of their products and are always having "price wars" among themselves. Other industries are not subject to these wars—they have disciplined themselves (naturally, I am only attracted by firm-price-policy groups which do *not* resort to collusion or price-fixing), realizing that price wars are injurious to everyone involved.

I always think of asphalt, plumbing fixtures and plywood (among others) when I think of industries which are often engaged in price wars. The record will show that most companies in these industries have lacked the consistent year-by-year increases in profits that you find in certain other industries.

In contrast, I always think of the time Bristol-Myers brought Bufferin to the market. Here was a product which was intended to penetrate the aspirin market. Your first thought might be that Bufferin would be brought out at a price either under aspirin or at the same level. If it were sold *under* aspirin's price, then the aspirin producers might be forced to cut their prices and down would go profits for all the companies involved.

Instead, Bufferin was brought out to sell *much higher* in price than aspirin. Bufferin, of course, was a success. It did penetrate the aspirin market and it became a profitable item for Bristol-Myers. And what happened to the aspirin producers? They subsequently *raised* the price of their branded aspirin and are probably making as much money—or more—on this product than they did before the advent of Bufferin.

Proprietary drugmakers (proprietary drugs are those which can be purchased *without* prescription) have found that price is *not* the important thing in marketing their products. If the public thinks Bufferin or Pepto Bismol or XYZ formula will accomplish the job in mind, the public will pay the price. For example, right now test your own "knowledge" of prices of non-prescription drugs which you might buy to relieve yourself of some discomfort. Think of products like cold pills, laxatives, pain relievers, cough medicines, etc. Then see if you can pinpoint the selling prices of these products. Chances are that you won't be too accurate. Of even greater importance, however, ask yourself whether an extra dime or twenty cents added to these product prices would cause you to switch to something else. If the products are any good at all, you'll stick with them *despite the slight increase in price*. Of course, this type of loyalty is of great benefit to the manufacturers.

The earnings record of companies such as Bristol-Myers, Norwich, Plough, Sterling, all bear this out: every one of these four has shown steadily rising profits *in every year* since as far back as 1953.

Other industries which have at least a fairly well "disciplined" price structure include cosmetics, soft drinks, tobacco, automobiles, dress patterns and selective "service" areas.

4. *How easily can new competition come on to the scene?*

A famous American industrialist made an extremely sage and interesting statement some years ago. The statement: *it is easier to make a million dollars than to make ten thousand.* The comment was shocking to many people, but actually it made a great deal of sense. Why? Simply because there are relatively few people in the world who have the capital, the know-how and/or the fortitude to engage in million dollar deals, whereas the world is full of individuals who are trying to make ten thousand. How very true this is. And how valuable this lesson can be to investors— so valuable that I insist you keep it in mind at all times when you consider an industry for investment.

Naturally you don't want to invest in an industry in which new competition can easily set up business and cut into your market. Don't invest in what I call "garage" industries—ones in which persons can set up similar operations to yours in their garage. Invest in industries which require some real know-how, or heavy capital requirements or control of important resources, etc. In short, invest in industries where new competition is going to be scarce.

A few years ago, there was a wild flurry for boat stocks in the market. As sure as night follows day, I was convinced that this flurry would end in partial disaster for most investors. The reason: small boats can be made locally for competitive prices by small operators and it was obvious that most glamour boat companies would soon fall by the wayside—which, in fact, they did.

5. *Is the industry cyclical? (Does it fluctuate up and down with the business cycle?)*

I mentioned earlier that the Federal Reserve Board and other monetary authorities are endeavoring to keep business on an even keel—growing gradually upwards. Despite this, some fluctuations are of course inevitable. We are bound to have our ups and downs in business over the years.

Certain industries are very sensitive to changes in business conditions. When business in general is good, they thrive. When business turns bad, they show rather drastic declines. I will discuss later how money can be made from buying and selling so-called cyclical stocks (those which *are* so sensitive to the general economy). I personally don't recommend the average investor buying cyclicals. Buying cyclical stocks requires great flexibility, which most investors lack. From a mathematical standpoint it doesn't make sense, either. *Buying cyclical stocks entails making two decisions instead of one* (when you buy a steadily growing industry—not a cyclical one—you generally have only to decide what to buy and you hope the strong growth trend can allow you to forget about having to sell). The average investor has a hard enough time making the one decision, much less the two.

Therefore, in determining whether an industry is *for you*, take a good look at the industry's past record and see whether it has been subject to ups and downs. If it has, then you need only ask one question:

Has anything in the industry changed to eliminate this fluctuation?

If not, then you should beware!

6. *What is the over-all outlook for the industry?*

This is merely a summation of what we have just discussed and many other factors which have to do with the future. Here is where you have to let your imagination run wild in deciding what the future has in store. Here is where I recommend my "vacuum approach" in reaching a conclusion. Put yourself in a vacuum! Tear down all those emotional ideas you have with some negative thinking. In other words, become completely objective about the plus and minus factors and decide what the over-all outlook is for the industry you are considering. Later on—in Chapter 26—I will do some of this vacuum thinking for you.

CONCLUSION

By now you should be able to make a decision about the industry involved. If your feeling is negative, then go no further. Look elsewhere for your success. You simply can't stress the importance of this industry approach enough.

CHAPTER 20

What to Buy—Part Two

MY COMPANY APPROACH

Assuming you've decided that a certain industry is attractive for investment, the next step is to rate *the company* you are considering. I have compiled a few questions you should ask of every company you consider for investment. Don't neglect to ask:

1. *How good is management?*

Obviously management of a company is all-important. A company is no better than the people who make the major decisions and form the backbone for its progress. There are countless examples of what a difference good and bad management can make in an organization.

Perhaps the classic example is that of Montgomery Ward and Sears, Roebuck. In 1947, sales of Montgomery Ward were $1.1 billion and those of Sears amounted to $1.9 billion. Both companies had been battling for the consumers' business and both had achieved considerable success. Following the war, however, the two companies differed enormously in their attitudes about the future:

Montgomery Ward was pessimistic about the future of the U.S. Management felt a depression was right around the corner. Now was the time to conserve cash and reduce operations so that overhead and expenses were at a minimum.

Sears felt that the pot of gold was right around the corner. Americans had had their buying of almost all items curtailed during the war and there was a pent-up demand for good merchandise. Now was the

152

time to modernize existing stores, build new ones, go into suburban shopping centers.

The results are startling. Here's what happened to Sears and Montgomery Ward from 1947 to 1967:

	Sales		Per	
	1947	1967	Share Earnings	
	(billions)		1947	1967
Sears, Roebuck	$1.9	$7.3	$0.75	$2.51
Montgomery Ward	1.1	1.9	4.43	1.31

And here's how the stockholders of these two companies fared over the same period:

	MARKET PRICE OF STOCK Mean Price		Percent Increase Over	Dividends Per Share		Percent Increase Over
	1947	1967	20 Years	1947	1967	20 Years
Sears	5⅞	52½	793%	$0.29	$1.20	314%
MW	28½	26	decrease	1.50	1.00	decrease

What a difference—and it was all due to a difference in management philosophy and know-how. There are countless other illustrations of companies engaged in identical fields, where performance of sales, earnings, dividends, etc. are as different as day and night. In the vast majority of cases, the difference between success and failure is attributable to management and management alone.

Perhaps you're wondering how you can judge management from your living room chair. Well, there are many ways of doing this. First of all, your broker can help you most. His research people call on various companies throughout the year and they give you a first-hand "feel" about management through the research reports they publish. Secondly, I always recommend that a person read the annual report of a company he is analyzing. You can get your own "feel" on management this way. You can read their ideas and their planning. There are many other management guideposts, some of which will be discussed in a moment. Among them are: stress on research, ability to bring out new products, efficiency of marketing and distribution of products, trend of profit margins, trend of sales and profits, etc.

2. *How good is the company's research?*

As you know, research is the backbone for the future. Top companies all possess strong research teams and put a strong emphasis on this. Here are a few hints in analyzing a company's research:

a) Is the company spending a higher or lower *percentage of sales* on research and development than other companies in the same industry?

b) How many new products has the company developed successfully in the past few years?

c) What percentage of last year's sales came from products recently introduced?

Don't think research is important only to glamourous industries like electronics, chemicals, etc. It's equally important in even the most conservative food company. What has made the Carnation Company out-perform its competitors? Strong research and new product development, for one thing.

The future lies with those who prepare for it. The efficient research companies will continue to outstrip their competitors, so give this element strong consideration when you are considering a company for investment.

3. *Is the company diversified?*

As you know, it's dangerous to have all your eggs in one basket. Likewise, it's dangerous to own companies which have only one product. Someone comes up with a better mousetrap and you're out of business.

I always think of a company in which my firm had a substantial interest for many years—Clorox Chemical. Here was a well-managed business—a product which had become a household word. Yet for the lifetime of Clorox Chemical it lived under a "one-product black cloud." Suppose someone developed a capsule which, when dropped into a gallon of water, made a bleach like Clorox. The latter's extensive bottling facilities would have become relatively obsolete. Here was a risk which Clorox stockholders faced every day of their lives—whether they knew it or not. Like most one-product companies, Clorox eventually merged with another company (in this case, Procter and Gamble) and stockholders finally could breathe easily with good diversification. (Later, P&G was forced to divest itself of Clorox and thus the latter became an independent entity again.)

Most companies have sought diversification in recent years. But some have *over*-diversified, and have entered a variety of industries on a helter-skelter basis. It's a difficult job indeed for management to become familiar with the ins and outs of all these businesses and be able to make correct decisions for all. The experience of such over-diversified companies in the stock market has indeed left much to be desired.

To my way of thinking, proper diversification should fit a pattern: it should be done in related businesses. American Home Products is a good example. This fine company diversified from drugs into foods and related household products. This makes sense, because drugs and foods go to similar markets, take similar merchandising, distribution, production, etc. Success is not so difficult to achieve when diversification is in a related field.

4. What new products does the company have?

It's really unnecessary for me to tell you to watch for new products which might suddenly increase a company's sales and profits sharply. Yet I would be remiss if I didn't at least list this as a factor to consider.

Some new products are easy to observe. Remember the boom that Kent cigarettes provided for Lorillard? All of a sudden, everyone you knew had switched to Kent and Lorillard stock was an obvious candidate for some near-term profits. The same thing goes for the Polaroid Land Camera and the automatic pinspotters produced by American Machine and Foundry and Brunswick.

Other new products are not quite so obvious, but can be equally important. A friend of mine put me on to one (imaginative friends can be helpful to you, too). This friend called me one day and asked me about Otis Elevator. Otis stock a dozen years ago was recognized as a pretty good income stock, but one which had no growth potential. I asked my friend why he was considering Otis. He told me that an Otis salesman had just explained how the changeover from manual to automatic elevators in his building would save him loads of money and a lot of aggravation over the years. We bought the stock on the basis of this "new product" and it certainly was profitable for him, particularly over the 1955–1961 "conversion" period.

5. *What kind of patent protection or specific know-how "protects" the company from outside competition?*

This is just as apparent as our #4, but has to be mentioned. Remember how duPont had the synthetic fiber market to itself for so many years, till other companies developed their own processes. Minnesota Mining's Scotch Tape patent protected it for many years. Kimberly Clark's "pop-up" Kleenex patent allowed it to get a hold on the tissue market. Owens-Corning was one of the few companies in the country which had the know-how in production and fabrication of fiber glass. Polaroid would have plenty of competition were it not for its patent position. Xerox' office copying literally destroyed those which had only wet-process machines.

These are but a few examples, but they point out how you have to consider patent protection, know-how, etc. in analyzing a company's strength.

6. *How well does the company control its costs?*

As we saw in the discussion of profit margins, some companies operate far more efficiently than their competitors. It goes without saying that an investor will fare much better with an efficient company than with one which is a bit sloppy in its control over costs of doing business. Some companies simply have better manufacturing plants, some have better labor, some boast more efficient distribution of their products and some know how to control their inventories better. Naturally these should be prime considerations in analyzing an individual company and I urge you to consider them. In addition, there is one important factor which has much to do with the answer to the original question and that is: *How dependent is the company upon others for raw materials, etc.?*

Confucius might well have said:

Housewife who depends on neighbor for sugar three times a week will eventually drink *un*sweetened coffee.

I think it's safe to say that a person will be happier if he doesn't have to go through life depending on other people for everything. The same thing goes for being in business. The less dependent you are on others the better off you are.

Thus, in looking at prospective investments, give more consideration to self-sufficient companies than to those who must depend on everyone else for their existence. These self-sufficient ("fully integrated") companies have the following advantages:

a) they have control over their resources;

b) they are not as liable to shortages (e.g., Chrysler: after some very lean years, they finally came up with a model car in 1959 that was slated to sell pretty big. What happened was that their glass supplier got involved in a drastic strike. Result: Chrysler had another bad year).

c) From the standpoint of reported profits, certain companies with their own resources can choose which resources to use at what time and thereby "fix" their reported profits. Example: Georgia-Pacific. Georgia-Pacific now has huge timber holdings. When plywood prices are low they can cut low-cost timber and thus show good profits even though their final selling price of plywood is way below last year's levels. Obviously, other forest product companies with low-cost timber have the same potentials.

d) If you believe inflation is here to stay, natural resource companies (such as those owning timber) should see their reserves worth more and more over a long period of time.

e) Companies which have to buy from others have to pay their suppliers a profit—a profit which would be their own if they did the work themselves.

Naturally, there are notable exceptions to this reasoning. A company such as Bristol-Myers, for example, does not want its capital or management efforts tied up in the production of containers for its products. For one thing, it prefers the flexibility of being able to switch to whatever container it desires, rather than be tied to its own manufacturing output. In other words, management concentrates on producing the right products and putting the most efficient merchandising behind these. The small profit paid to someone else for the right container is insignificant in relation to the central goal.

7. *What is the company's past record and future outlook?*

In many cases, a company's past record will give a good clue as to its future outlook. Therefore, just as in analyzing the over-all outlook for a specific *industry*, you should start out by looking at a company's past record and ask: "What, if anything, makes this company's outlook any different today from what it has been over the past three or five or ten years?"

If the answer is, "Nothing is any different," then it should be relatively simple to project the future. Most often, however, it is not that simple. Things are seldom static in this world of ours. Thus, you have to consider all the previously mentioned factors and arrive at a conclusion as to whether the company's rate of growth will be faster or slower than its recent past.

CONCLUSION

Now we have satisfied ourselves that the *industry* we are considering is attractive and that the *company* within this industry is for us. Does this guarantee us a successful investment? No. Because our timing may be wrong in buying the stock.

Our next step, therefore, is to determine when a stock should be bought and when it is overpriced and should be sold.

CHAPTER 21

What Tools to Use

Earlier I discussed some yardsticks to use in analyzing the stock market in general. I hope you will use these yardsticks, but I feel it is even more important for you to learn when individual stocks are too high or too low. I emphasize this because there are many times when individual stocks will rise sharply even while the general stock market is declining—and just as many times when individual stocks will fall while the market in general is rising.

You're probably aware that there are a multitude of yardsticks and ratios which can be used in analyzing stocks. Actually I don't think it necessary that you bother yourself with most of these.

We've already discussed balance sheet analysis and decided that the various yardsticks given can be used to bolster your confidence in a company or to warn you of certain dangers. We concluded, however, that it is very seldom that the balance sheet should be the determining factor in deciding whether a stock is a buy or at what price.

It's one thing to conclude that a company is sound and attractive for investment over the years. It is another to conclude that the stock is ripe for buying now or ripe to be sold. Actually there are only two yardsticks for you to consider in arriving at this conclusion, namely *yield* and *market price in relation to earnings*. Let's consider these separately.

YIELD

"Yield" is just another way of saying "annual rate of return on your investment." This is figured by *dividing the yearly dividend rate of a stock by its present market price.* Thus, a stock paying $4.00 per year in dividends and selling at $100 gives an annual rate of return (yield) of 4% ($4.00 ÷ $100 = .04 or 4%).

This is just like figuring the return you get when you put money in the bank in your savings account. If you put up $100 and keep it there a year, the bank will pay you $4.00 interest, for a yield of 4% on your money.*

Many people give great weight to yield in figuring whether a stock should be bought or not. This is fine if current return is your investment objective. If you are living on the dividends from your stocks and if you have to depend on these dividends for your everyday living or for necessary "luxuries" then yield should be your consideration in buying stocks.

Oddly enough, most investors today don't really need the dividends right now. Most investors are looking to the future. They are more interested in building up capital for their retirement and in building up *future* income, rather than being concerned with yield now.

If growth of capital is your objective, *do not give consideration to yield.* If you have invested your money in a growing company, it is better that they do *not* pay out high dividends now. Here's why:

1. If dividends are paid to you, you will have to pay income tax on them.
2. You will probably spend the dividends and not "let them ride" and compound for you.
3. If you don't spend them, you will certainly not be able to reinvest the dividends at the same high rate that the company could invest them for you. Most growth companies earn 10–20% (and some considerably higher) return on their invested capital. I ask you—where could you invest your money and achieve such a high rate of return? Most probably the dividends would be placed in a savings account paying 4–5%.

* Actually you will get slightly more than 4% if the interest is computed more than once a year.

Thus, if it's growth you want and you're looking to the future, forget about dividends and yield now. Most important, consider annual growth of your capital as the major part of your "annual return" equation.

I should point out that yield can be important in a declining stock market. It can provide a "floor" for your stock and limit your downside risk. Take a stock paying a $1.00 annual dividend and selling for $16 on the market, for a yield of over 6% ($1.00 ÷ $16.00 = .0625 or 6¼%). If that $1.00 dividend is safe, what is the lowest you figure that stock can go? If it declines to $10, the $1.00 dividend gives a 10% yield and this is awfully high. Perhaps the lowest the stock would go is 12½ or so, because the yield there would be 8%—and this is high, too. In other words, because of the $1.00 dividend, you can feel sure your stock will not go below 12½. If there is no dividend on the stock, you cannot say this. Who knows, maybe the stock will go to 10 or 8. Thus, yield should be a consideration if you cannot afford much risk in your investments.

The above illustration does point up, however, how yield *can* provide some *temporary* appreciation in stocks. The example of the stock which declines to 12½ (with a secure $1.00 dividend) is a case in point: the very high yield of 8% attracts considerable interest from investors and, before long, this "bargain" stimulates buying and the stock recovers—perhaps back to the 16 level or higher. The rise from 12½ to 16 (a gain of almost 30%) is due to yield and yield alone. The trouble is, of course, that this rise will probably constitute the major part of the stock's appreciation potential, *unless the company's earnings are growing.* Incidentally, the 8% example is an extreme one in today's (1969) stock market, where existing yields are very low. Instead, an illustration of a stock going from a 5–6% secure yield to about 4% is more realistic. Still, the theory is the same, and the important thing to remember is that—unless some real earnings growth potential exists—the appreciation will be limited.

As you see, I contend that *the best defense is a good offense.* Buy a stock that you think is a good value and that you feel confident will go up in price. If you're right and the stock goes from

$16 to $20, $25 or $30 then you shouldn't have to worry about it going down to 12½ or even 16 or 18 anymore.

It is difficult, of course, to have your cake and eat it, too. High yielding stocks generally lack any growth potential. As a matter of fact, they *generally indicate weakness*. Many times I have had clients call me and ask about a given stock "which looks attractive because it's paying X% yield." Nine times out of 10 there is good reason for the stock to be selling so low on the market that it provides a very high yield. It is usually the case of:

a) the fact that the outlook for the industry or the company is very poor and investors have no reason to buy the stock; or

b) the dividend is *not* adequately covered by the company's earnings—to the point where the present dividend rate is *not safe*.

A number of years ago a client called me and asked about Waldorf System common stock (listed on the New York exchange). My client was interested because Waldorf stock was selling at 16½ and paying a $1.00 annual dividend, for a yield of over 6%. I took a look at this company and found that it was in the restaurant business, which at that time was not a popular industry with security analysts and/or stock buyers. I went over Waldorf's record of earnings for the last five years, which showed as follows:

1955	$1.01 Per Share
1956	.90 Per Share
1957	.98 Per Share
1958	.91 Per Share
1959	1.08 Per Share

The company had exhibited little growth over this period; unless there were some new developments in the Waldorf scene, you couldn't get excited over this stock for growth. The stock's major attraction was its $1.00 dividend which, as my client pointed out, gave a yield of over 6%. But was the $1.00 dividend secure? Definitely not! First of all, Waldorf was paying out $1.00 in dividends out of a bare $1.08 in profits. In other words, there was a tiny 8¢ extra coverage of the $1.00 payout rate. Only a minor decline in Waldorf's business would put earnings *below* the $1.00 dividend and the dividend would no doubt have to be reduced.

Furthermore, a check of Waldorf's earnings for the first few months of 1960 indicated that profits were running below the 1959 levels. Now it was doubtful whether there was *any* coverage at all of the $1.00 rate.

With the appraisal of Waldorf's business and the discovery that the dividend was not well-protected, I advised my client against investing in Waldorf stock. It was only a few months later that Waldorf was forced to reduce its quarterly dividend from 25¢ to 15¢; now the $1.00 rate had suddenly become only $.60. That 6% yield had faded to only 3.6%—and this was not especially attractive. It wasn't long before Waldorf stock reflected this and fell to a price of 11½.

Remember then that there is usually a good reason for a stock offering an exceptionally high yield—and it is a real mistake to reach for high yields. Experience has proven this. Here's one motto which sums it all up:

If growth of capital is your goal, concentrate on *outcome*, not income.

WHAT YARDSTICK SHOULD YOU USE?

If you were to buy a business or a piece of real estate, what would determine the price you would be willing to pay? The answer: *the present and potential earning power* of the business or property.

Common stocks should be bought the same way. You should buy them according to their present earning power and according to what you believe they should earn in the future.

To achieve this, you should emphasize one ratio and one ratio alone—the price-earnings ratio (or price-earnings multiple, as it is most often called). This is not a new yardstick—it has been the backbone of security analysis for years. But the applications of this multiple have changed considerably over the years.

My application of this yardstick is somewhat different. It is one which will help you decide when a stock is good value and when it is overpriced in the market.

First of all, let's see exactly what the price-earnings multiple is. It is simply the relationship between a *stock's market price and its earnings per share*. It is arrived at by *dividing a company's earnings per share into the market price of its stock*. For example, suppose Co. A earned $1.00 per share last year and Co. A stock is selling for $10 per share. The price-earnings multiple is 10:

$10 Market Price ÷ $1 Earnings per Share = 10

Let's suppose that Co. A had earned $2.00 per share instead of $1.00. What would the price-earnings multiple (let's call it P/E multiple from now on) be?

$10 Market Price ÷ $2.00 Earnings per Share = 5

Naturally you'd rather buy Co. A stock at $10 with *$2.00* earnings (P/E of 5) than with *$1.00* earnings (P/E of 10). Thus you can see that *the lower the P/E multiple the more value you are getting*.

Another way of looking at this is to say that the P/E multiple tells you how many years you will have to wait to recoup your investment *if earnings remain the same in the future*. In Co. A's case, if it continues to earn $1.00 per share each year it will have earned your $10 market price back in 10 years (remember, 10 was the P/E multiple or, as we say in our business, "the stock is selling at 10 times earnings"). If Co. A earns $2.00 per share every year you will only have to wait five years to have your $10 market price earned for you.

Naturally the quicker your investment is earned back for you the better—which is just another way of saying that the *lower* the P/E the better.

If companies earned the same amount of money every year it would be easy to decide which stocks were the best buys: all you would have to do would be to compute the P/E multiple and buy the one which had the lowest figure. The trouble is, of course, that companies do *not* earn the same amount of money year after year. There will always be some fluctuation, either up or down. Thus, *you can't buy stocks on the basis of P/E multiple alone*.

Instead, *the price you pay for a stock should depend on what you expect the company's profits to be in the future*. Let me show

the vast difference between four theoretical companies, all of which
are now earning the same $1.00 per share—but which are going
to grow very differently over the next ten years. The first of these
is a *supreme growth company*, with an expected 30% annual compounded growth rate over the next ten years; the second is a
normal growth company, with a 10% annual growth rate; then
come *stable company* (no change in earnings expected at all) and
the *stagnant company*, which is going downhill.

Here's how these four will change in this ten-year period:

Year	Supreme Growth (30%)	Normal Growth (10%)	Stable (no change)	Stagnant (declining)
Base Year	$1.00	$1.00	$1.00	$1.00
1st	1.30	1.10	1.00	.95
2nd	1.69	1.21	1.00	.91
3rd	2.20	1.33	1.00	.87
4th	2.86	1.46	1.00	.83
5th	3.72	1.60	1.00	.80
6th	4.83	1.76	1.00	.76
7th	6.28	1.94	1.00	.73
8th	8.16	2.13	1.00	.70
9th	10.61	2.34	1.00	.67
10th	13.79	2.57	1.00	.64
Total Earnings For The Ten Years	$55.44	$17.44	$10.00	$7.86

What an amazing difference between these four companies.
Supreme earned a total of $55.44 over the ten years, which is
more than three times what *normal* earned ($17.44), about 5½
times what *stable* earned ($10.00) and over seven times what
stagnant reported ($7.86).

In addition, take a look at the difference in earnings per share
in the tenth year. Supreme is earning $13.79 per share in this year,
which is over five times *normal's* $2.57, almost fourteen times
stable's $1.00 and over 21 times *stagnant's* $.64.

It is obvious that you should be willing to pay a far higher market price for the *supreme growth company* than the others; by the same token, you should pay more for the *normal growth company* than the other two; and that you shouldn't be interested in buying either of the latter two, *if growth is your objective.* As a matter of fact, you could have paid $50 or even $100 per share for the *supreme growth* stock in the first year and only $10 for the *stable company* (5 or 10 times as much for *supreme* as for *stable*) and still had a far better investment from the growing company. So it is obvious that *you should be willing to pay a premium in the marketplace for growing companies.*

But just how much? How does one know whether he should pay 15, 20, 40, 80 or 100 times earnings for a growing company?

The answer lies in my *compounding growth theory.*

A COMPOUNDING GROWTH THEORY

Whereas guesswork is always going to have a lot to do with the stock market, it is amazing how stock prices *eventually* revolve around their basic values. Said another way, both the general market and the evaluation of individual securities seem to adjust (in time) to what kind of growth is in store. In short, low P/E multiples evolve when growth rates are falling and high P/E's result from an acceleration of profits.

For example, at the time of *Primer*'s first edition, I computed the growth in profits in the United States over the fifteen years which followed World War II—and then became more specific and did the same for the companies constituting the Standard & Poor 425 Stock Industrial Index. I found that the figures coincided at about 4% (growth) per year. Then I looked at the stock market itself over the previous decade and found that its average multiple of earnings was around 14½ times. Thus, investors had been willing to pay around this multiple for an average of 4% growth.

A few years later, I re-computed—this time using the 1951–1965 span. Here I found that earnings were going up approximately 6% per annum and that the market had adjusted to this acceleration and had averaged around 16 times earnings over the period. And now, in 1969, we can take all types of periods and see that further increases bring higher evaluations. A 7% growth rate, for example, seems to allow a P/E average of 17½ times.

Let's see whether there is any common thread running through all this. To make it simple, let's substitute an individual company for the whole market and see what five years of growth at various rates do when we start with a base year's profits of $1.00 per share —and then apply the kind of average multiples described above both to the base year's earnings and to those five years hence. Here is the way 4%, 6% and 7% growth companies would look:

| Annual | | | Market Price Paid For | |
Growth	Base Year	Fifth Year	Base Year	Fifth Year
4%	$1.00	$1.22	$14.50	$11.88
6%	1.00	1.34	16.00	11.90
7%	1.00	1.40	17.50	12.50

The interesting statistic here is contained in the last column on the right, where all the figures coincide around $12. Thus, whereas the price of $14.50 was paid for $1.00 earnings for the 4% growth company in the base year, that $14.50 amounts to a price of $11.88 for the $1.22 earnings in the fifth year ($14.50 ÷ $1.22 = $11.88). The same thing goes for the 6% and 7% companies. *The purchase price today amounts to approximately 12 times earnings at the end of the 5th year.*

According to this formula, let's see what market price an investor should pay for a company growing at a 10% compounded rate. Here's the way a 10% growth company's record will look over five years:

Earnings per Share

Now	$1.00
1st Year	1.10
2nd Year	1.21
3rd Year	1.33
4th Year	1.46
5th Year	1.60

Earnings per share will be $1.60 in five years. The investor should be willing to pay now a market price equal to about 12 times this $1.60 figure, or $19.20 per share (12 × $1.60 = $19.20). Thus, whereas we paid $14.50 for the 4% growth company, we should pay around $19 for this 10% growth stock.

Now let's look back at our *supreme growth company*—with a 30% rate:

Earnings per Share

Now	$1.00
1st Year	1.30
2nd Year	1.69
3rd Year	2.20
4th Year	2.86
5th Year	3.72

Multiply 12 times the $3.72 earnings (12 × $3.72 = $44.64) and we find that we should be willing to pay almost $45 for this stock, compared with $19 for the 10% company and $14.50 for the 4% stock.

Setting this up mathematically, here is what we should be willing to pay for stocks according to their projected rate of growth over a five year period:

The Company's Expected Annual Rate of Growth in Earnings per Share Over the Next Five Years	This is the Price-Earnings Multiple You Should Be Willing to Pay
5%	15.4
10	19.2
15	24.0
20	29.7
25	36.6
30	44.5
35	53.7
40	64.3
45	76.7
50	91.0

All of this assumes you can project a company's earnings over a five year period—*which is indeed difficult to do*. Because of this, I insist that certain changes be made to this pure mathematical formula.

First of all, I vigorously warn you not to assume companies will grow at such high rates as 25–50% a year indefinitely. After all, *the areas which promise such growth invite competition* and this competition will no doubt cause a reduction in the growth rate of almost all individual companies in the field.

Secondly, many companies which are growing at a 25–50% rate are smaller companies which don't have to show a very large increase in their business *at the beginning* to achieve such large percentage increases. For example, a company with $20 million in sales need add only $10 million the next year to show a 50% increase and perhaps just one or two new products will add this $10 million. As the company becomes larger, however, it naturally takes larger increases in volume to continue this growth rate: once this same company reaches $100 million sales it has to add a whopping $50 million the next year to keep up the 50% growth rate and this may necessitate bringing out more new products than it is capable of doing.

Thirdly, the industries which are showing the fastest growth rates are generally the ones which are in some phase of technological advancement and they are dependent on new discoveries to realize their growth. The industries which are advancing at slower rates may be depending mainly on population increases or gradually changing habits of consumers—and these are more dependable than technological breakthroughs. The spending on health and beauty aids is an illustration of a more dependable growth pattern and that is why you can project with more assurance the growth rate of Bristol-Myers, Johnson & Johnson, etc. than that of many small electronic companies which are now *apparently* in this 25–50% growth class.

For these reasons, I insist the pure mathematical table on page 168 be changed. (A new table is presented to you in Chapter 23.) The P/E multiples for companies projecting unusually rapid growth should be lowered. Each case has to be considered on its own merits, of course, but you have to be pretty positive of your growth projections to pay more than even 20 or 30 times earnings for a stock.

But there's another reason why you cannot rely on a mathematical table alone. The reason is that investors, being human, may appraise two companies with identical growth patterns in entirely different ways. Take Company A and Company B, both earning $1.00 per share and both expecting to grow 5% a year. You may find Co. A stock at $15 per share, while Co. B stock is selling at $30. The reason for this discrepancy may be due to Co. B simply having more glamour in the eyes of the public.

My method for making maximum gains in the stock market combines both mathematical and emotional elements. Before I give you this method, however, let's explore the emotional aspects of buying stocks a little further.

CHAPTER 22

Sex Appeal in Stocks

The past few chapters have taught us how to judge what to buy and what price to pay. It's simply a matter of

1. choosing the right industry,
2. selecting a good company in this industry,
3. paying a price which is reasonable in relation to the company's growth trend.

All of this assumes that investors are completely objective in buying and selling stocks. Nothing could be further from the truth! Human beings live by their emotions and it's tough suddenly to shut them off when investing.

Have you ever seen a movie and "fallen in love" for 90 minutes with the glamourous, curvaceous beauty—the leading lady (or if you're a female, with that strapping, handsome leading man)? Psychiatrists tell us it's not abnormal to do this, but I ask you: "Did you, during the whole 90-minute movie, even once consider whether your love of the moment could cook, raise a family or provide any of the countless characteristics necessary for a life of more than 90 minutes?"

Stock buyers fall in love with stocks, too. The love lasts more than 90 minutes—sometimes it lasts for a lifetime. But the analogy doesn't stop there. Just as you'd gladly pay $3.50 to see Raquel Welch in the movies, you might feel cheated paying 85 cents to see Hilda Duffledinker exhibit her wares. Because of *glamour*, investors are willing to pay a premium for some stocks while others remain in the "85 cents" category.

Because of emotional influences, stock prices often get out of

171

line with their growth rate. Why, for example, does Minnesota Mining and Manufacturing sell at around 35 times earnings (which, according to the pure mathematical table, means the company should be growing at a 25% rate) when MMM's growth rate over the 1962–1967 five years averaged only 11%? There are many recognized blue chips like MMM which sell at higher P/E ratios than their recent growth rate would dictate. Take a representative list like the following and see how they are selling at premium prices:

Stock	Annual Compounded Growth Rate Over Five Years 1962–1967	P/E Ratio They Should Sell at Based On Growth Over These Five Years On a Pure Mathematical Basis	Approximate P/E Ratio at Which They Were Selling in 1967
Corning Glass	12%	22	48
Eastman Kodak	20%	30	32
Honeywell Corp.	9%	18	32
International Business Machines	15%	24	43
Minnesota Mining and Mfg.	11%	20	35
Owens-Corning Fiberglas	Flat	?	34
Scott Paper	3%	13	20

All of these stocks were selling at higher prices than their actual growth rate dictates. The reasons for this are:

1. Their names alone indicate strength in the minds of investors.
2. They are recognized leaders in their respective fields—all of which are glamourous.
3. They have shown growth over a long period of time, and they have shown the ability to make money "through thick and thin." Likewise, in most cases heavy depreciation charges are causing earnings to be understated (but certainly not so understated as to narrow the gap between the "mathematical P/E" and the present P/E significantly).

4. They are well-managed enterprises.
5. Their outlook is for continued success in the future.
6. They are on approved investment lists of banks, insurance companies, pension funds, and other large institutional investors. They are consistently purchased by these investors for their long-term benefits and this constant demand keeps their market prices higher than "normal."

Because of these six points, investors feel more confident owning these stocks than other not-so-well-known companies. Buying them is like buying a home with an underground bomb shelter. These stocks provide—*in the minds of their owners*—a *shelter*: a shelter against attack from outside competition, from recessions, depressions, and from all sorts of catastrophes. Buying these stocks has always proved profitable, so why not keep riding a winning horse!

Chances are that these stocks will continue to sell at premium prices in the future, although, if growth rates do not improve, some of the premiums will no doubt narrow. You can sum this up by saying that all these stocks sell at high multiples because they have profit-sex appeal. In the minds of the public and in the minds of institutional investors, they all have glamour.

There are, of course, many *non*-blue chip stocks which also sell way out of proportion to their growth in earnings over the last 3–5 years. In these cases, the premiums paid by investors emanate, not from a sense of stability such as is the case for the blue chip issues shown on page 172, but from an expectation that future growth will be faster than recently shown. This projection of accelerated growth may or may not be a figment in the imagination of the investor. Only time will tell this. In the meantime, such stocks are selling way above what one might expect because of the glamour status which has been built up. Needless to say, overpriced stocks such as these carry substantial risks; if projections fail to materialize, these stocks, which generally lack any consistent institutional buying, can "fall out of bed" sharply. The sellers' exit can get mighty crowded.

At any rate, you can see the importance of judging what kind of glamour status a stock might take on. The human mind can do strange and interesting things; it can place rockets *and* stocks into orbit.

Look, for instance, at the common stocks of Automatic Canteen (the vending machine company now known as Canteen Corp.) and Merchants Fast Motor Lines (a trucking company operating almost exclusively in the state of Texas) as they appeared early in 1961. I choose these two because, five years before their per share earnings were almost identical. Here's how they grew from that 1956 year through 1960:

	Automatic Canteen	Merchants Fast Motor Lines
1956	$ .67	$ .61
1957	.72	.64
1958	.76	.80
1959	.91	1.18
1960	.73	1.40

Perhaps you'll be amazed to learn that—despite Merchants having grown more consistently and twice as fast—Automatic was selling in early 1961 for three times the market price as Merchants. At $45 per share Automatic commanded a P/E multiple of about 60; while Merchants ($15 per share) sold at little more than 10 times earnings. The reason, of course, is accounted for mainly by sex appeal. Automatic's vending machine business had captured the imagination of the public (whose judgment incidentally is most often wrong), while the trucking business had no such glamour and hence the very wide disparity in price between the two stocks. This happens to be a very extreme example—a case where one stock was simply *over*-glamorized and the other *under*-glamorized. As a matter of fact, Automatic subsequently dropped in half from 1961 to 1965, while Merchants increased some in value. Extreme as these two illustrations may seem, I could cite scores and scores more—and provide many more exciting re-evaluation-upward situations than Merchants'. What the Automatic vs. Merchants comparison shows, of course, is what glamour, or lack of same, can do to a stock.

Thus, it must be obvious now that one has to assess a *stock's potential glamour appeal as well as its expected growth rate* in determining what P/E multiple it should (or might) command in the market. By combining what we have learned in the last two chapters, we are now ready to lay out a guide in black and white for selecting the all-important "proper P/E."

CHAPTER 23

My Compounding Growth Guide

From the very beginning of the stock market, investors have been seeking a guide which will tell them when a stock should *definitely* be bought and when it is too high and should definitely be sold. Unfortunately there will never be such a *guaranteed* system! If there were, the stock market would almost cease to exist, because those stocks which showed as buy candidates by the infallible system would be bought by everyone and sold by no one—and then no market would be needed. By the same token, those stocks which were signaled as sell candidates would find few buyers, thereby creating the same confusion.

Despite this pessimistic attitude, I have developed a guide which I believe will be extremely helpful to you in making these heretofore difficult buy and sell decisions. I call this my Compounding Growth Guide.

My Compounding Growth Guide combines the elements I described in the last few chapters. Your judgment is, of course, needed. You have to decide the approximate rate of growth expected for the company in mind over the next 3–5 years and you have to decide whether the company's glamour-appeal is *super*, *above-average* or only *average*. Once you have decided this, then all you have to do is consult my guide and see what P/E multiple the stock might reasonably be expected to sell for.

Let me emphasize again that this is *only* a *guide*. It is not a formula for guaranteed profits. The market is too fickle for such a thing as that. The guide makes no representation that a stock which looks too high will not go a lot further up in price. Even if you're dead right in your assessment of a glamour status and annual growth rate, you can be wrong. Look at Studebaker stock in 1959. No line of reasoning would have prompted a sensible investor to buy that stock anywhere along the line on its rise from 10 to 29¼. And yet that's where the stock went. (Of course, it reversed itself sharply and dropped back to 8 within the next year.) The same thing can be said of innumerable situations.

The Guide naturally cannot be all-inclusive. It is based on growth in earnings and on market psychology, but an investor has to be flexible with it. The guide helps you to conclude what market price appears warranted for a stock, but you must remember that the market for stocks fluctuates substantially at times—sometimes to the extremes of either great optimism or great pessimism. In other words, the Guide provides the market prices that investors should be willing to pay for the various growth rates *as an average*. As I pointed out in Chapter 9 (The Bulls vs. The Bears) investors in some years will pay only very low multiples for stocks, whereas in other years they will pay very high P/E's for the same stocks. Naturally one has to roll with the punches and attempt to judge the market's over-all tone.

The main thing about my guide is that *it forces you into organized thinking and into judgment based on value*. As I will repeat again and again in this book, buying *value* is the best guarantee for success in the stock market and thus I believe that my guide, properly used, can be very helpful to you.

Now let's look at the guide—and then we'll see some examples of its usefulness.

While there are bound to be additional elements which have to be considered in arriving at the "proper P/E," I want to add one specific factor to the Guide—namely, *institutional support*. We saw how a stock which is widely held by pension funds, insurance companies, investment trusts, etc., and is on the approved purchase lists of most banks commands a much higher P/E than might be expected. Assuming that the institutional stock's general outlook has not changed materially from its historical pattern, it will no doubt continue to command some kind of premium in the market. For this reason we should adjust our guide for such institutional support and add an approximate 3–5 P/E for the widely held stock as opposed to that which has no institutional following.

MY COMPOUNDING GROWTH GUIDE

	This is the Price-Earnings Multiple You Should Pay if it is		
The Company's Expected Annual Rate of Growth in Earnings Per Share Over the Next Five Years	Super Glamour Company	Above Average Glamour Company	Average Glamour Company
5%	18–20	15–18	10–15
10	20–25	18–20	16–18
15	25–30	20–25	19–20
20	30–35	25–30	20–25
25	35–40	30–35	25–30
30	40–45	35–40	30–35
35	45–50	40–45	35–40
40	50–55	45–50	40–45
45	55–60	50–55	45–50
50	60–65	55–60	50–55

NOTE: You can assume that any company which has prospects for success or for increased earnings has at least average glamour. The company which is going downhill is the one which is below average glamour. Naturally, no column has been constructed for below average glamour companies because, if you believe a company falls in this category, you should not buy it for growth.

You are probably wondering how you can find out what kind of institutional support a stock has. I recommend you use either the widely distributed *Data Digest*, which is sent free-of-charge by most brokerage firms to customers who want it, or the *Standard & Poor Stock Guide*, which is usually also available through your broker. These publications show how many (out of a total of more than 2,100) financial institutions hold each stock. As a general rule, anything over 50 indicates good following, but you have to relate this figure and the number of shares actually owned by these institutions to the amount of stock outstanding in order to conclude how substantial the support is. For example, it stands to reason that American Telephone—which has almost 550 million shares outstanding—should be owned by many, many institutions (it is owned by 1,050), whereas a company like Addressograph-Multigraph—which has a comparatively low 8 million shares outstanding—commands excellent support through being owned by some 110 institutions. As a matter of fact, the *January 1969 Data Digest* shows that 1.2 million of the 8 million Addressograph shares—or 15% of the capitalization—rests in such hands. A 15% figure, incidentally, connotes strong ownership. (In contrast, A.T. & T. has only about 3% of its shares in such institutional coffers.)

HOW TO USE THE COMPOUNDING GROWTH GUIDE

The Guide is really simple to use. It involves your following a short and logical procedure, as follows:

1. Look at the past record of the company you are considering and approximate what its rate of growth in earnings per share has been over the past 3–5 years. Incidentally, I have shown you how to arrive at a company's annual compound growth rate on Appendix pages 339–342. I suggest you familiarize yourself with these pages at this time. Naturally you will want to check the growth rate over the most recent year or two, to see whether the trend is increasing or tapering off.
2. Determine whether there is any reason for the company's basic trend to change.
3. Consider any new elements in the company's outlook (new products, larger production facilities, added competition in its field, etc.).
4. Decide whether these new elements will increase or decrease the company's previous rate of growth.
5. Arrive at a reasonable growth rate for the next 3–5 years (naturally barring any drastic recessions in the economy).
6. Decide which glamour category the company deserves.
7. Consult the compounding growth guide and see, according to its expected growth rate and glamour status, what P/E multiple is suitable for the stock.
8. Determine what kind of institutional support the stock has. If it is widely held by institutions, add a 3–5 higher P/E.
9. See what P/E multiple the stock is now selling for.

10. Conclude whether the stock should be bought or not. If the present P/E is lower than the guide indicates it should be, the stock is undervalued and should be bought. If, on the other hand, the stock is selling at a higher P/E than the Guide indicates, the stock is overvalued and should not be purchased.

Now let's see how effective the Guide can be and go through some examples of its use.

I. A. Let's look at General Foods stock, as it appeared in 1960—and then in a number of years thereafter. In 1960, the Company's most recent five years looked like this:

Year	Earnings Per Share
1959	$2.48
1958	2.21
1957	1.99
1956	1.81
1955	1.66
1954	1.33

Following the steps outlined, here is the way General Foods should have been analyzed in 1960.

1. General Foods has shown a 13% annual compounded growth rate since 1954. Appendix pages 339–342 show you how to compute a company's annual compounded growth rate. In this case, it is figured as follows:

   a) General Foods has shown an increase in earnings per share of 86% over this five year period ($2.48 — $1.33 = $1.15; the $1.15 increase ÷ the $1.33 base year figure = 86%).

   b) On Appendix page 341, glance down column A of the table till you come to 85% (the nearest figure to the 86%).

   c) Look to your right and go to column D—the "5 year period" column (we are using General Food's 5 year record from 1954–1959).

  d) Conclude that an 85% growth over 5 years amounts to a 13% annual compounded growth rate.

2. There is no reason for any change in the company's basic trend (population is still increasing, consumers are eating better and spending more on convenience foods, etc.).

3. Just as in the past, the company will introduce new products, and General Foods' established lines (Postum, Post Cereals, Jell-O, Maxwell House Coffee, Baker's Chocolate, Calumet Baking Powder, Minute Rice and Tapioca, Birds Eye Frozen Foods, etc.) will provide consistently growing volume.

4. The rate of growth may decrease slightly as it is reasonable to assume that other food companies will enter the "convenience" market. Also, GF's heavy dependence on coffee makes it somewhat vulnerable to commodity fluctuations; and competition is building up in this area.

5. A 10% rate of growth seems reasonable for the Company.

6. GF should probably command a glamour status of Above Average. While foods in general do not generally create great excitement in the minds of investors, GF's stress on convenience products, its well-regarded management and its consistent record over the years warrant it receiving something of a premium. Result: a stature somewhere above the Above Average, but not as high as Super Glamour.

7. The Compounding Growth Guide shows that the high P/E for Above Average Glamour is 20 and the low for Super Glamour is the same 20 for a 10% growth company. Thus, use 20 as a P/E starting point.

8. GF stock had fairly decent institutional support, with over 300 institutions owning about 8% of its stock. This should lead to a higher multiple—by about a 3–5 increment. Thus, GF stock "deserves" to sell at about 23–25 times earnings.

9. GF stock was selling around $50 per share. In 1959, the Company earned $2.48 per share; therefore, the stock was selling for just over 20 times earnings ($50 ÷ $2.48 = 20.2).

10. GF is selling at 20 times earnings, whereas our conclusion in #8 was that it should sell at 23–25 times. With the stock selling below what we deem it should, it qualified as an undervalued situation and thus the conclusion that it should be purchased.

RESULT: Over the next year and a half, GF stock rose steadily. It went to 25 times 1961 results of $2.90 per share, or up to around $75. Then it proceeded to go way beyond these figures— up to the 30–35 times multiple range.

B. Now look at GF stock as it appeared in the five years following 1960:

Without going through all the details as shown above, the record of General Foods through this period is indicative both of how value rules out in the long run and how our Guide can be useful in both the purchase and sale of stocks. In 1962, the median price of GF was $78; in 1963–65, the median was $84, $86 and $84, respectively. In other words, each time the stock rose past 25 times earnings it ran into selling pressure. As a matter of fact, the stock's median P/E for the years 1962–65 was as follows: 24.5; 25.2; 24.9; and 23.3.

C. And here is how GF stock looked in 1965:

Once again shortening the procedure used in "A," we should start with the company's growth for the latest five-year period. GF showed profits of $2.69 per share in 1960 and $3.73 in 1965. This amounted to a 39% advance or, according to our Appendix, a 7% growth rate. This diminution in growth had relegated the stock to no more than Above Average status; a look at our Guide indicates that 7% growth for such a company is only worth a P/E of about 18 times. Adding the aforementioned institutional support of 3–5 gives a P/E range of only 21–23 times. Multiplying this by the $3.73 earned for 1965 gives a price of only $82 (22 × $3.73 = $82). Conclusion: That the stock deserved no more than this price, unless there were new developments to alter the future outlook.

RESULT: GF stock ran into considerable selling pressure through the 1965–68 period. As a matter of fact, the latest five-year period (1963–68) showed a further slowdown in growth—to about a 5½% level. The stock's median P/E has slipped accordingly, to about 18 times.

II. A. An analysis of Hewlett-Packard Co. common stock in mid-1961. First of all, here is Hewlett-Packard's record from 1956 to 1960:

Year	Earnings Per Share
1960	$.43
1959	.40
1958	.26
1957	.27
1956	.20

Now to our procedure in evaluating Hewlett with the use of our Guide.

1. Hewlett's earnings per share had grown 115% over this four-year span ($.43 — $.20 = $.23; $.23 ÷ $.20 = 1.15 or 115%). The four-year column C for a 115% growth (on Appendix page 341) shows a figure of 21%. Thus, Hewlett-Packard has grown at a 21% compounded annual rate over this period.
2. The company's basic trend should not change. Demand for electronic measuring instruments should continue to increase, and Hewlett's reputation for quality is almost unchallenged.
3. The company will continue to bring out new products. In addition, Hewlett is interested in making acquisitions, any of which will no doubt increase its earnings per share.
4. Balancing these elements against the realization that, as a company gets larger it is more difficult to sustain very high growth rates, one might conclude that H-P's rate over the next 3–5 years will approximate the past.
5. A growth rate of 20–25% seems attainable.
6. The company certainly deserves a Super Glamour rating.

7. A 20–25% Super Glamour company is entitled to a P/E of 30–40.

8. Hewlett was at that time gaining institutional support—something which was fostered by a recent listing on the NYSE. This support, from a low base, might add an extra 5 to the multiple. Thus, the stock should command a 35–45 P/E.

9. At the then-current price of $48, H-P stock was selling at an astronomical 110 times earnings ($48 ÷ $0.43 earnings = 110).

10. It should be obvious that the public had inflated H-P stock. Despite the conviction that the company represented a solid and exciting vehicle in a rapidly growing field, the present price was simply "too rich."

RESULT: Certainly we did not need any guide to tell us that the stock was overpriced at that time and that it should be sold. Perhaps the thinking process described, however, would have taken the dangerous emotion out of any decision-making and would have set an investor straight relative to the real values which existed.

A truly better proof of our Guide as it pertains to H-P comes from an appraisal of its use in years subsequent to 1961. Just to trace the facts, H-P stock dropped from the $48 level to around $32 in a short six-month span. Quite interestingly, a full five years later than 1961, the stock was selling at $38. By that time, the Company's earnings had risen to $1.12 per share—for a 21% annual growth rate (over the five years). The then-$38 market price amounted to 34 times the $1.12 profits. Finally the stock had hit real buying levels, according to our Guide (which concluded that it deserved 35–45 times earnings). And from there the stock proved to be a good value, as it has risen to around $80 today (1969).

III. Here is an analysis of one of my favorite growth companies over the years, Bristol-Myers, using a year as base which was a top for the general market for a few years to follow, namely 1961:

| | Earnings |
Year	Per Share
1960	$1.03
1959	.85
1958	.73
1957	.68

1. Bristol-Myers earnings grew from $0.68 in 1957 to $1.03 in 1960; this increase of $0.35 amounted to a 51% increase over this three-year period ($0.35 ÷ $0.68 = .51 or 51%). Appendix Page 341 shows that a 50% growth over three years (Column B) amounts to a 14½% annual compounded rate.

2. There is no reason for any change in the company's basic trend.

3. A flow of new products plus continued strong demand for existing lines plus steadily rising product prices augur well for the outlook.

4. Conclude that these elements will at least retain—and possibly enhance—the growth rate.

5. A 15% rate of increase is a reasonable expectation over the next 3–5 years.

6. Management image of this company is supreme; thus, Super Glamour.

7. A Super Glamour company with a 15% growth rate deserves 25–30 times P/E.

8. The stock is widely held by institutions; some 193 own almost 11% of the number of common shares outstanding. And the rate of accumulation is expanding. Adding a 5 P/E to the 25–30 gives a 30–35 "deserved" multiple.

9. Bristol-Myers stock is selling for $35 per share. In 1960 the Company earned $1.03 per share. Dividing this $1.03 into the $35 market price gives a multiple of 34, right in line with our conclusion of 30–35 times above. Therefore, the stock can still be purchased, with the expectation that appreciation percentages will about parallel the Company's earnings growth from here on out.

RESULT: Four years later, the Company's net income had risen from the $1.03 figure to $2.65 per share. This increase of 157% over the five years was actually slightly above a 20% compounded gain. Over this period, BMY stock rose from the $35 figure of 1961 to $95, a rise of 171%. The P/E based on 1965 earnings was 35.8, a slim premium over the 30–35 times range which our Guide would have indicated a full five years prior. As indicated, purchase of Bristol-Myers stock did work out well—and it did about parallel the Company's profit growth.

IV. Let's see whether our approach would have helped in the buying or, all-important, holding of one of the nation's great growth companies, Xerox. Let us assume we were considering the stock sometime *after* the introduction of the 914 office copier—in mid-1963. In this case, it would only be deceptive to go way back in the company's history and establish a growth rate; obviously, the 914 had brought a new pattern. In 1962, the first year of sizable deliveries of the 914, Xerox earned $0.72 per share. By 1963, the quarterly results were giving the indication that profits would rise to the $1.10–1.20 range, up almost 60% over the previous year. Thus:

1. Xerox was apparently growing at a fantastic rate; many analytical projections pointed to a 50–60% compound growth rate over the next 3–5 years.
2. The above projections were not difficult to substantiate because of the rental nature of Xerox's business.
3. New elements would obviously come into the Xerox scene (i.e., extensions of the 914, new products based on xerography, etc.).
4. Certainly it would be difficult to anticipate a greater average rate of growth than 50–60% compounded, as competition would no doubt build up.
5. Keeping our fingers crossed, we conclude that a figure of about 50% is obtainable, at least over the short term.
6. No question about glamour status for this company: Super.
7. 50% growth with Super Glamour allows multiples in the 60–65 range.
8. Avidly sought by institutions, some premium over growth

rate is apparently deserved, perhaps to a 65–70 range. (Do not have figures for 1963, but in March of 1966, 223 institutions owned over 16% of the Xerox outstanding common shares.)

9. Xerox stock at $60 per share was selling at 50–55 times the $1.10–1.20 per share earnings forecast for the current (1963) year.

10. Despite the apparently astronomical multiple, Xerox stock was still well within buying range and actually cheaper than our Guide would indicate it deserved at the moment.

RESULT: Xerox stock was, of course, a profitable performer over the next few years. In the following year (1964), profits rose from the $1.13 reported for 1963 to $1.88—an advance of over 66%. The stock proceeded to sell as high as almost $132 during the year; high as this looks, the resulting multiple of 70 times was still in the ball park of our 65–70 P/E conclusion in #8 above. The year 1965 saw Xerox earnings rising to $2.78 per share, up 48% over the previous year; during this year the stock jumped to the $200 range—but once again the multiple was around 70 times.

Obviously, there is considerable guesswork involved in the assessment of a company such as Xerox. The risks of being wrong about growth rates are large, but—if achieved—our Guide would have kept you on the Xerox track and allowed you to buy it along the line or retain it if you owned it—even though your emotions or the apparent high multiple might have frightened you into deferring purchase or selling it out.

Time now for some additional, and very pertinent, comments about the use of our Compounding Growth Guide.

First of all, as the examples indicate, be sure to key in to your thinking the kind of earnings expected for the *coming* year. Last year may well be an indication of the future, but it is really ancient history as far as the stock market is concerned. Thus, be sure to relate the present P/E to the immediate future—not to the past.

Secondly, an investor has to reassess his stocks against this Guide (or any other) as time goes on. In other words, time flies by and conditions change; and the successful investor stays current and continues to anticipate the future. He alters his earnings estimates continuously—and of course he reassesses market prices and their potentials according to the new figures. Most important, you have to check continuously to determine whether your appraisal of growth rates is on the beam, or whether instead the company's pattern is changing.

Thirdly, you can see from the examples that our Guide is valuable mainly in evaluating *growth companies*. The next chapter will show the Guide's usefulness in four specific money-making ways in the stock market, but there are many areas which defy analysis by our Guide. Non-growth situations, for example, will generally sell on a basis of either yield or asset value (since there is no definable growth rate). In addition, typical cyclical stocks are really difficult to evaluate through a Guide such as this; and certain industries (i.e., the oils) have a heavy bias towards some deeply entrenched historical basis and do not generally sell at prices which relate directly to annual growth rates.

Lastly, I want you to realize that there is method in my madness of choosing very high P/E stocks as examples in this chapter. I did so because the premium multiple equities are most often the most difficult for people to buy (their fear that the premium might disappear inhibits them). Stocks which are cheap on earnings (i.e., 10–15 times earnings) do not pose the "psychological block" problem as do those in the 25–50 P/E range. Obviously, it would have been simpler for me to show a raft of examples pinpointing the wisdom of purchasing stocks at 12 times earnings (as a matter of fact, we will see some great examples similar to this in the next chapter). By understanding the right procedure in buying growth companies, which are unfortunately not usually found at dirt-cheap multiples, and by understanding how money can be made in high P/E stocks, too, I believe I have given you a well-rounded and sophisticated approach.

Needless to say, this whole approach involves some judgment on your part. But then, what successful endeavor does not! Furthermore, I want to make it clear once again that the stock market is not as precise as all of the above might make it out to be. I have felt it essential, however, to prove the point that the key to long-range success is in *paying the right price for the right growth rate—*

and this is what my Guide helps you to do. Over the long term, your largest stock market profits should come from owning companies which *are* growing, and the Compounding Growth Guide should be very valuable to you in assessing these growth companies correctly.

PART VII

HOW TO MAKE MONEY
IN THE STOCK MARKET

CHAPTER 24

Five Roads to Big Profits

Our Compounding Growth Guide helps us decide when a stock is too low or too high. The Guide is flexible—it considers a company's growth rate and how public psychology and institutional support might affect its price. The Guide allows you to analyze companies of differing qualities and quantities.

When correctly used, the Guide will help you to buy good values and to sell those stocks which have run up beyond their values. The Guide revolves around value and, in the stock market, value will eventually prevail.

I believe that there are five major ways to make money in the stock market. Our Growth Guide will be useful in all but one of these approaches. Let's consider these five roads to big profits separately.

ROAD NUMBER ONE: CYCLICAL STOCKS

Buying "cyclical" stocks when they're at the bottom of their cycle. Certain industries go through definite cycles over the years. They have a year or two of very good business and then they go into the doldrums for a few years. Most cyclical industries ride along with the cycle of business in general: when the economy is rolling along at high speed they prosper famously, but when the country's business starts slipping they face sharp cutbacks. Automobiles, heavy machinery, copper, steel and railroads are some of the foremost industries which follow the economy in this way.

Other industries have cycles of their own—not necessarily right in line with business in general. Building (which can be expected to get a boost when *lower* business activity forces the Federal Reserve to grant easier money and lower interest rates), farm equipment and insurance (fire and casualty) are a few cyclical industries which fluctuate in their own way.

All of the above lack a strong enough growth trend for their products to overcome this sensitivity to ups and downs. In all of the above you can be pretty certain that, when business is booming, it will not be too long before things are slipping once again. Automobiles are a perfect example! Autos are "durable goods" —they can be made to last a long time if necessary by their owners. When you run out of food you have no choice but to buy more, but when your car runs down you can make it workable by a motor overhaul, a new set of tires, etc. Thus, people are not compelled to buy new cars. They do so in vast quantities when times are good, but the minute business and/or employment sloughs off, people defer new purchases. You can see from this that new car sales may enjoy one, two or even three good years in a row, but it is almost inevitable that the booming sales will be followed by a decided dip, at least temporarily. Thus, auto sales are extremely sensitive to the changes in the business cycle and auto stocks must be classified as "cyclical."

This gloomy picture does *not* mean that people cannot make money in auto stocks or other cyclical stocks. They can. Stock prices will generally follow these cycles: in the case of steel, for example, when steel production is falling, steel stock prices will generally go lower and lower and lower. Then it's only a matter of guessing how low steel production will go and *buying* a steel stock sometime *before* production improves drastically (remember, the stock market is always looking ahead and, if you wait for production to rebound sharply, steel stocks will already have had a good part of their rise). For example, you can be sure that steel production will not remain at 50–60% of capacity for long. Barring a sharp general business recession, the country needs more steel than that and thus the rate will have to be increased before too long.

The trouble with cyclical stocks is that you *do* have to plan to sell them for maximum profits. Just as the steel stocks were a buy when production was at very low levels, they should be sold when the operating rate is very high. After all, what more can you expect when the industry has attained an operating level of 95–100% of capacity—certainly not 150%.

Our Growth Guide will *not* help you in buying and selling cyclical stocks (the growth rates are so erratic that they cannot be depended on). You have to approach cyclical stocks by acting directly opposite to the way business is. You assume that the public is not smart enough to be buying when things are bad (they are probably selling their stocks in a state of panic) and then you have to fight your own emotions and *sell them when things look their very best.*

All of this takes flexibility and the strength of your convictions. It is not easy to buy stocks when the news is bleak; and it is even more difficult to sell them when everything looks rosy. This is one reason why cyclical stocks are not ideally suited for the average investor. The other reason is that a person will do better to buy a company with a stronger inherent growth trend—where he doesn't have to worry about selling and where he feels confident that his gains over the years can be *big* (not the smaller profits—after taxes—which generally come from the buying and selling of cyclical stocks).

Incidentally, there are two chapters in *The Common Sense Way to Stock Market Profits* which I honestly believe are unique in their approach to cyclical stocks. For those who are intrigued with their use, Chapter 19 on "How and When to Sell Cyclical Stocks" is a "must," as is Chapter 7, which deals with the uncovering of "cyclical-growth" stocks.

ROAD NUMBER TWO: MANAGEMENT "PLAYS"

Buying companies which have new, more aggressive, more efficient management.

Many companies are held back by poor management. Give them some new blood and the profit picture can change tremendously. Safeway Stores (see Chapter 18) was a good illustration of this, although not nearly so dynamic as some of the profits which were made in companies such as International Telephone, Crown Cork and Seal, Raytheon, Joy Mfg., Norton Simon Inc. and countless others over the past few years.

Beckman is a good example. Here was (and still is) a strong research company with many glamorous products. Management made the mistake of getting so interested in its research that it neglected the backbone of success—profits. Earnings in 1956 were $1.36 per share; by 1957 they had slipped to $.16 per share and by the end of that year the company was operating at a loss. Beckman stock had followed this trend: from a high of 47¾ in 1957 the stock had sunk to a low of 18⅛. Time had come for a change of managerial philosophy and Beckman's board of directors set about to do just that. Some personnel changes were made and a complete housecleaning was accomplished. While these changes were being made, Beckman was still in the red and ended up the 1958 year with a loss of $.70 per share. By the end of this year, however, the company started "turning the corner" and profitable operations were foreseen again. In 1959 Beckman earned $1.30 per share and in 1960 net income was a fat $2.25. By that time, Beckman common stock had soared to over $100 —a wonderful five times higher than its low of just two years before.

Our Growth Guide is helpful in knowing what price to pay for these "new management" companies. *In these cases, however, the past record is no indication of what might lie ahead and thus it's a matter of picking a normal earning power for the company and projecting a growth rate ahead for it in determining what price to pay.*

Let's look at the aforementioned International Telephone and Telegraph in 1960. Here was an old established company which embarked on a management change (Mr. Harold S. Geneen, who did such a good job at Raytheon, joined I.T. & T. in 1959). I.T. & T.'s earnings over the previous five years from 1955–1959 averaged $0.83 per share, with $0.92 being the average for the last two (1958–1959). The company had announced that it expected sales to double by 1965 and, since Mr. Geneen's forte has always been for the improvement of profit margins, you could have assumed a 20% annual growth rate over this period. I.T. & T. would be a Super Glamour company but for the risk of its large overseas operations. Thus, we might have concluded that it deserved an Above-Average rating. Consult our Guide and you can see that a 20% Above-Average growth company should sell at 25–30 times earnings. Multiply this 25–30 P/E times last year's $0.90 earnings and you come up with a price of $22–27, compared with a market price at that time of about $18. It is obvious that this "management-change" stock looked very reasonably priced at that time, according to the Guide. Interestingly enough, it was only a year later that I.T. & T. stock was selling in the $25–30 price range, right in line with our Guide projection.

ROAD NUMBER THREE: RECOGNIZED STOCKS

Buying a company which is correctly priced according to both glamour and growth rate and holding it for continued gains over the years.

On pages 184–6, we discussed the stock of Bristol-Myers and concluded that Bristol stock was selling just about where it should considering its glamour status and expected growth rate. In such a case, we concluded, the stock should be bought for consistent gains—about in line with the company's earnings progress over the years. There are many stocks like Bristol-Myers—stocks which are already selling at high P/E multiples, correctly evaluating their glamour status and growth rate. So long as they continue to increase their earnings and retain their glamour, investors will make money owning them.

Take the case of duPont (E.I. duPont deNemours, to be exact) stock. Back in 1946, duPont was recognized as a blue chip growth issue. The stock had a median price of $50 during 1946; it earned $2.36 per share that year and thus had a median P/E of 21 ($50 ÷ $2.36 = 21.2). As of 1960 duPont was selling for $195; the company earned $8.92 per share in 1959, so the P/E was 21.8 ($195 ÷ $8.92 = 21.8). Here's what has happened to earnings of the duPont company and to the market's evaluation of duPont stock over this 14 year period:

The stock market gave the same over-all rating to duPont in 1960 as it did in 1946—a P/E multiple of around 21. Because of this, the growth in duPont stock *came mainly from the growth*

Year	Earnings Per Share	Median Market Price	P/E Multiple
1946	$2.36	$50	21.2
1959	8.92	195	21.8
% Increase from 1946 to 1959	277%	290%	

in earnings: these earnings grew 277% and duPont stock grew 290% over this 14-year span. *Whenever you pay a very high multiple for a stock you can assume that your stock will increase about in line with its increase in earnings over the years.* Thus, when you buy a duPont or a Bristol-Myers or any of a host of stocks which are selling about in line with their growth and glamour ratings on our Guide, be satisfied with gradual but consistent gains as time goes by.

ROAD NUMBER FOUR: GLAMOUR PLAYS

Buying companies where you can foresee an improvement in their glamour status.

In Chapter 22 we discussed the importance of sex appeal in stocks. If you can foresee an improvement in a company's glamour status you can make big money without any appreciable growth in earnings at all. Many times an industry will lack appeal to investors for years on end. Then, all of a sudden, investors will fall in love with the industry's growth prospects and go on a buying spree which will hike stock prices of the whole group. Stocks may double or triple in a short time despite the fact that actual growth prospects of the group may not be much better than before.

Consider the stocks of B. F. Goodrich Company in 1946 and Crown Zellerbach in 1950.

At the end of World War II the rubber stocks had little following. Investors were concerned over the fluctuation of natural rubber prices in the world market and over the industry's dependence on new car sales for growth. Because of this, rubber stocks were "cheap": Goodrich for one was selling around $11.00 with earnings of $2.95 per share, for a P/E of less than 4. A person with foresight could easily have become enthusiastic over the industry because: a) synthetic rubber plants built during the war had lessened the dependence on natural rubber; b) a large re-placement demand for tires would build up as more autos were on the road.

Thirteen years after 1946, Goodrich's earnings had grown only 42% (from $2.95 to $4.18) yet Goodrich stock had climbed from the $11.00 figure to a price of $90.00—an increase of over eight times. *Despite very limited growth in earnings, Goodrich stock had advanced greatly because its glamour status had improved.* (This improved glamour status, which was aided by a rather general re-appraisal of stocks in the market, brought about a higher P/E and it was this—not earnings growth—which accounted for the stock's appreciation.)

The case of Crown Zellerbach is similar. In 1950, paper stocks were not regarded as growth vehicles. Crown Zellerbach earned $2.73 per share in 1950 and sold around $13.00—at less than five times earnings. Nine years later, Crown's earnings were at the same level of 1950—$2.76 to be exact—and yet Crown Zellerbach stock was now selling at $55.00. *Despite the lack of earnings growth the stock had more than quadrupled.* Obviously this appreciation was due to an increase in the company's glamour status, as net income had failed to advance.

While on the subject of glamour status alone, let's turn to what turned out to be a fad area of the late-1950's—the vending machine stocks. With the introduction of an automatic bill-changing device in 1959, investors suddenly fell in love with this industry and two companies in particular, Automatic Canteen and Universal Match (both of which are known by different names today), became star performers through 1959–1960.

Early in 1959 Universal Match stock was selling as low as $12, or at about 10 times the year's expected earnings of $1.20 per share. The company had shown a growth rate of about 13% over the 1955–1958 period. According to our Guide a 10–15% growth company should sell as follows:

	Super Glamour	Above-Average Glamour	Average Glamour
10%	20–25	18–20	16–18
15%	25–30	20–25	19–20

It is obvious that the market felt Universal Match (at 10 times earnings) had only *below*-average glamour. As an investor in 1959 you only had to say to yourself: "Universal is an industry which should have at least above-average glamour and possibly super glamour—because of its potentials."

On the basis of this alone, you would have bought Universal. After all, an above-average glamour multiple of 18–25 (times the $1.20 earnings) makes the stock worth $22–30 and a super glamour multiple of 20–30 makes it worth 24–36 *without any increase in the growth rate at all.*

Thus, our Guide would have given you the "go ahead" signal to buy even if you took the most conservative approach and figured no increase in the growth rate. Then, had you allowed for an increase in the growth rate, too, you could have looked for spectacular results from the stock.

As it turned out, Universal ran into some severe operating problems in 1961—and actually earnings declined sharply. Before that, however, the stock had experienced the kind of gain shown above as possible. Actually, I have used Universal as an example for a reason—to illustrate how stocks will advance or decline based on what people *think* may occur. The lasting results, however, will come about from what *does* happen—and our Guide must assume performance of some degree from the company involved.

This leads us to the ultimate—

ROAD NUMBER FIVE: THE ULTIMATE, GROWTH *AND* GLAMOUR

Buying companies where you can foresee an improvement in both their growth rate and glamour status.

Here's the way to make really *big* money in the stock market. Find a company or an industry where you can visualize both a stepped-up growth rate over the next few years *and* a re-evaluation of the glamour status (upwards, of course). This double-barrelled effect will lead to explosive profits for you.

Let's look at one stock which captured my imagination a number of years ago, namely American Photocopy Equipment.

Back in 1957, the stock of American Photocopy was sold to the public for the first time (it had been a privately-held stock until then). The company's record of earnings from 1954–1956 and the company's 1957 earnings were as follows:

Year	Earnings Per Share
1957	$.26
1956	.23
1955	.17
1954	.13

Apeco's earnings over the 1954–57 period had increased at an average rate of about 25% per year (a 100% increase over a 3-year span equals a 26% compounded rate—Appendix page 341). Going through the procedure shown in the last chapter, it should have been apparent that the company's growth rate would at least continue at this 25% figure. This reasoning was based on the development of a good product and hard-driving marketing. In addition, the reasoning was based on the fact that each photocopy machine sold "built-in" an ever-increasing demand for photocopy *paper*—and this replacement demand was an extremely profitable item for Apeco.

Apeco stock was brought to market at a price—adjusted for stock splits which have taken place since then—of $1.50 per share. While a very limited supply of Apeco stock was available at this $1.50 price, I found there was a considerable supply of stock available around $2.50 per share, which was about 9 times the 26 cents per share earnings Apeco had achieved in 1957.

Now let's see what our Compounding Growth Guide shows you should pay for a 25–30% growth outfit like American Photocopy looked to be at that moment:

	Super Glamour Company	Above-Average Glamour Company	Average Glamour Company
25% Rate warrants	35–40 times earnings	30–35 times	25–30 times
30% Rate warrants	40–45 times earnings	35–40 times	30–35 times

The Guide would have shown you how very cheap Apeco stock was at only 9 times earnings. Even if the stock had only Average glamour, it should have sold at 25–35 times earnings; and, as a super glamour company, the stock might sell at 35–45 times earnings, or at between $9 and $12 per share at that time (35 times 26 cents = $9 and 45 times 26 cents = $11.70), compared with the then-existing price of $2.50.

The results of Apeco stock were of course startling. The double-barrelled effect of *increasing earnings and a higher glamour status* (as reflected by a rising P/E) brought the following results:

Year	Earnings Per Share	Median Market Price of Stock	Median P/E
1957	$.26	$3	12
1958	.30	5½	18
1959	.47	12	25
1960	.57	21	36

At the close of 1961, Apeco stock was selling around $38 per share, which amounted to over 57 times the 66 cents earned for the year which ended in November. This very high multiple came about through the expectation by the public of even faster growth in 1962. Actually, the combination of a multiple which greatly exceeded the range indicated by our Guide plus my fears about the advent of dry-process (Xerox-type) copiers caused me to alter my opinion on Apeco. By April of the following year, all of my people had sold their shares in this company, most with gains of 10–20 times their original investment.

Aside from the fact that our Growth Guide would have prompted us to buy Apeco stock in 1957 *and in every year thereafter (through 1960)*, there are other lessons to be learned from this great success story. First of all, you can see that the re-evaluation, or upward revision, of the P/E did not occur overnight. As a matter of fact, it took a full three years for the P/E to get to the 35–45 level which the Guide indicates it could have commanded right from the start. Therefore, the investor had to exhibit patience to realize the maximum gains on this fine stock.

Secondly, you can't expect every year to show the same rate of growth in earnings. For example, Apeco's 1958 earnings of 30 cents per share were up only 15% over the 26 cents earned in 1957; but 1958 was a recession year in the United States and a 15% increase under these conditions was remarkable (when business returned to normal in 1959, the company experienced a 57% increase in profit).

Thirdly, the fact that Apeco had doubled or tripled or quadrupled in price over the two years from 1957 to 1959 did *not* mean that it had reached its maximum potential. Too often investors are scared away from buying a stock merely because "it already has tripled in the last . . . years." Despite a quadrupling in price to $6 per share in the latter part of 1958 Apeco was still a great buy. This is a perfect example of how you should appraise a stock on the basis of its merits, not on the basis of where it has been in price.

The private airplane industry affords another illustration of an improvement in growth rate and glamour status. In 1955 the private airplane stocks in general—and Cessna Aircraft in particular—could be purchased at about six times their earnings. The group had little glamour appeal! Over the next few years, the net income of these manufacturers increased (Cessna outperformed the group) and suddenly investors took notice and began paying higher and higher P/E multiples for the stocks. Look what happened, for example, to Cessna:

CESSNA AIRCRAFT

	Earnings Per Share	P/E Median Multiple	Price Range of Cessna Common Stock
1955	$1.12	5.7	8¼– 4⅝
1956	1.66	6.0	13¼– 6¾
1957	1.53	6.3	13¼– 5⅞
1958	1.87	6.3	16⅜– 7⅛
1959	2.47	9.9	34⅝–14⅝

Because of an improvement in growth rate and glamour status, Cessna provided gratifying results for its owners. Over this five-year period Cessna common stock went from a $6.00 average price in 1955 to as high as 34⅝ in 1959, and up to $40 in 1960 (not shown above).

Zenith Radio is another case in point—one which brought some worthwhile profits for my clients. Despite this company's top management, quality product, efficient distribution system, strong financial position and some interesting "kickers" from pay-TV and the advent of color TV, I found that Zenith stock in 1958 was selling at only 9 times its previous year's earnings. I strongly recommended Zenith stock, which was then at only (adjusted for subsequent splits) $4.50 per share. In 1958, despite a recession in the U. S., Zenith reported record profits of $0.68 per share and investors were attracted by this amazing performance. The year 1959 again saw new highs in earnings and the stock was spectacular. Here's what happened to Zenith in a period of less than two years:

	Earnings Per Share	Median P/E Multiple	Price Range of Zenith Stock
1958	$0.68	11.2	11⅝–3⅜
1959	0.94	17.4	22⅞–9⅞

The combined effect of increasing earnings and a higher P/E multiple had shown Zenith stockholders a fast quintupling in market price. But that was not the end of this success story. The next year (1960) Zenith had a minor dip in earnings, but 1961 was on the uptrend again and in this year the stock was a dynamic performer again, as shown:

	Earnings Per Share	Median P/E Multiple	Price Range of Zenith Stock
1960	$0.85	21.5	21⅝–14⅞
1961	1.00	28.9	41⅜–16⅛

In a period of just 3½ years (from May of 1958 to November of 1961) my Zenith owners had seen their stock rise from $4.50 to $40 per share. This increase of almost 10 times their original investment was brought about by a combination of advancing earnings and a higher P/E multiple. Of additional interest is the fact that the person who bought Zenith stock through most of 1958 really was taking very little risk. He had the assurance that he was buying the stock at a very reasonable price in relation to earning power; he knew that, so long as Zenith's profits merely held around their existing level, the stock would not fall very far in price. This, of course, is in direct contrast with the person who buys a stock selling at 40 or 50 times earnings; in this case, one certainly cannot expect much upward revision of the P/E; and, if earnings fail to advance or if profits begin to trend downward, there will be a lot of "air" in the stock (having small earnings to begin with, the stock could retreat a long way before it becomes reasonable on a P/E basis).

Not all of these rags-to-riches stories emanate from multiples of less than 10 times earnings. Take the case of Simplicity Pattern, a company which had all the industry and company characteristics emphasized in Chapters 19 and 20. Earnings per share from 1960 to 1963 had compounded at a 20% annual rate and the outlook for the future was apparently bright enough so as to consider this as a future trend objective. Referring to our Guide (Page 178), you can see that a mere Above Average Glamour dictates a 25–30 P/E. Allowing *no* upward evaluation for institutional support, the stock's P/E of around 17 times—as related to our Guide—indicated its attractiveness. Since that time (1963), Simplicity's profits have about tripled—at an *annual* rate of about 25%. And Simplicity stock has gone from a median price of $12 in 1963 to around $75 today.

So you can see the potentials of road number five—of having a double-barrelled profit-making effect working for you.

In all of these examples, our Growth Guide would have shown the value which existed in these stocks and would have given us a definite "buy" signal. Apeco, Cessna, Zenith and Simplicity Pattern were obviously not correctly valued relative to their growth rates or glamour status at the beginning. The important thing is that the Guide would have given us the confidence to buy them *right along their upward trend.*

CONCLUSION

The Growth Guide gives you a tool to use in four of these five roads to big profits. It should be valuable to you in assessing future profitable ventures in the stock market; of course, imagination on your part is going to play a big role in selecting the star performers of tomorrow. The next two chapters will give you some food for thought and some ammunition to use in making such selections.

CHAPTER 25

Spotting Growth Companies

So-called "growth stocks" have been in fashion for many years now. They have done far more than just provide a hedge against inflation for their owners—they have built up small and large fortunes for their owners. The success of growth stocks has actually changed the theory behind investing in the stock market.

Years ago investors were advised to buy stocks for their yield —for the high dividends they paid to their holders. The stock market represented a medium for achieving a higher current return than was available through various other investments. Buy stocks that yield 6%, 7% or more! After all, a 6% return compounded (that is, with the dividends added to the investment each year) will double your capital in just 12 years.

Suddenly in the early 1950's many investors woke up to the realization that it was better to buy a growing company with a very low yield than to buy a non-growth company with a high yield. One very startling fact became apparent:

That stocks of growing companies not only gained more in market price over the years, but that *they actually provided more dividends for their owners over the long run.*

Remember our comparison of supreme and normal growth companies with stable and stagnant companies. To save you looking back, I'm repeating the table of earnings growth of the supreme (30% growth rate) company with the stable (no growth). For the sake of this discussion, though, let's see what might have happened to *dividends* of these two companies over the ten year period. We'll assume that the supreme outfit pays out one quarter

206

(25%) of its earnings to its stockholders in the form of dividends, while the stable company pays out three-quarters (75%).

| Year | Supreme Growth Company | | Stable Company | |
	Earnings Per Share	Dividends Per Share	Earnings Per Share	Dividends Per Share
Base Year	$1.00	$.25	$1.00	$.75
1st	1.30	.33	1.00	.75
2nd	1.69	.42	1.00	.75
3rd	2.20	.55	1.00	.75
4th	2.86	.72	1.00	.75
5th	3.72	.93	1.00	.75
6th	4.83	1.21	1.00	.75
7th	6.28	1.57	1.00	.75
8th	8.16	2.04	1.00	.75
9th	10.61	2.66	1.00	.75
10th	13.79	3.45	1.00	.75
Total Dividends Received over 10-Year Period		$13.88		$7.50

Supreme's growth allowed it to increase its dividend consistently over these years. By only the fifth year, this growth had brought the dividend rate to a level surpassing Stable (93 cents for Supreme vs. 75 cents for Stable). And see how Supreme stockholders received $13.88 in dividends over the 10-year span compared to Stable's $7.50. Of even greater importance is the annual dividend rate of Supreme at the 10th year: the $3.45 dividend is more than 4½ times that of Stable's $0.75.

Supreme stockholders have indeed benefited. And chances are that they will continue to in the future. After all, Supreme in the 10th year looked like this:

Earnings Per Share	$13.79
Dividends Paid Out	3.45
Money Left to Be Re-invested in the Business	$10.34

By comparison Stable is still earning $1.00, paying out $.75 and still has a measly $.25 per share to re-invest in the business.

While this theoretical example may seem extreme to you, I could cite countless cases to verify the point. To illustrate, let me show you how a $5,000 investment in 1958 in stable Consolidated Edison and Wrigley Company compares ten years later with normal-growth Sterling Drug, above-average growth Bristol-Myers and with supreme-growth Xerox.

A $5,000 Investment In 1958 Would Have Bought	Which Would Have Paid You the Following Dividends in 1958	Here's What Your $5,000 Investment Would Be Worth Now	Your Yearly Income in 1968 Would Be
185 Con. Edison at $27	$249.75	$ 6,100	$ 333.00
60 Wrigley Co. at $84	270.00	6,900	330.00
500 Sterling Drug at $10	170.00	19,000	350.00
900 Bristol-Myers at $5.50	162.00	61,200	1,080.00
1250 Xerox at $4.00	50.00	323,750	2,000.00

Despite the fact that both Con Ed and Wrigley paid (by far) the highest dividends in 1958, the growth of the other companies brought a *higher yearly rate* in 1968. It is obvious how much more successful Sterling, Bristol-Myers and Xerox were market-wise. The $5,000 investment in Xerox, for example, is worth some $316,000 more than Con Ed and Wrigley; at the latter two's current dividend rate it would take almost 1,000 years to amass this amount. While Xerox is hardly a standard case, the experience of Bristol-Myers is also startling. And even conservative-growth Sterling finds itself with market appreciation of around triple the two stable companies—and with more dividend return than either of them at the end of the tenth year.

History has proven over and over how profitable it is to buy growth companies. As I've pointed out before, investors are willing to pay great premiums for growth stocks.

Corporate management has reacted accordingly. Most companies take great pains to point out to stockholders, security analysts and the general public why their company qualifies as a growth company—hoping the label will stick and the company's stock will be better received (and qualify for a higher P/E) in the market. For this reason, many people are confused as to which companies actually should be considered as true growth vehicles.

Professional investors have found that there are certain fundamental elements which enable one company to outperform others, with the result that the stock of this one company greatly outperforms the general market.

So that you can distinguish a growth company on your own, here's a checklist to follow:

1. Growth companies have top management, which shows up as follows:
   a. They will have a record of better-than-average increases in sales and earnings over the years;
   b. They will have a record of introducing new products over the years and these products will develop larger markets and good profits.
2. Growth companies will spend a greater portion of their sales dollar on research and development than their competitors.
3. Growth companies will earn a high return on their invested capital.
4. They will plow back a good part of their earnings into expansion (new plant and equipment, etc.). This means that dividends paid out to stockholders may be very small at the beginning.
5. They will have some great advantage over competition because of either patent position, manufacturing know-how, low cost natural resources, strategic geographical location, etc.

Whenever you find these characteristics in a company you will probably have to pay a premium for it in the market place. *Your timing in buying a growth stock is not quite so important as with non-growth companies: the inherent trend of the growth company will usually bail you out even though your timing has been wrong.*

Let me warn you, however, that growth stocks are not resistant to declines. As a matter of fact, when public psychology changes and the public becomes pessimistic, growth stocks may well decline faster than the averages and so you, as an owner, can have some uncomfortable months. Just be sure that the company's growth is sufficient to give you profits *in the future*. Once again let me stress the value of our Growth Guide. It should give you reassurance in the event an original purchase was temporarily ill-timed. Value will win out in the long run and the Guide allows you to make a value judgment for each stock.

PART VIII

LOOKING AHEAD:
A FORWARD VIEW
TOWARD FUTURE
SUCCESS IN STOCKS

CHAPTER 26

Food for Thought

We have already determined that the logical approach to investing is to believe in *the industry* in which a company is engaged. Thus, I thought you would be interested to know the basic characteristics of the major industries in our country. Look at the pros and cons as they appear today. Keep in mind that there may be some "sleeper" industries—ones which are not highly regarded today but which may turn out to be the super glamour babies of tomorrow.

Following is a summary of the industries. I have tried to be objective in giving you both sides of the coin. I've also tried to plant some seeds along the way. Let your imagination bring them to blossom. Naturally I've had to be brief and put everything in capsule form—anything more detailed could fill a few volumes.

Follow this procedure:

1. Read over the pros and cons of the industry.
2. Argue these points and conclude just how much the pros outweigh the cons, or vice versa.
3. Decide what glamour status you would objectively assign to the industry and what kind of growth you might expect *in the future.*
4. Look at the approximate P/E multiple the industry sells for in the market (which I have shown after the pros and cons).
5. Conclude that the market is under-evaluating or over-evaluating the group (or evaluating it about the way you would). Of course, you should be especially attracted to any industry group which is selling on a lower P/E multiple than you think it should.

6. Start investigating individual companies within the groups you like.

Here we go! !

PRO	CON
AEROSPACE	

PRO	CON
Companies also heavily engaged in more glamourous electronic and other technological projects.	Remote possibility of world disarmament or reduced tensions in cold war.
Less chance of contract cancellations than in prior years (i.e., no duplicate programs awarded to more than one producer).	Heavy dependence on government spending.
	Possibilities of contract cancellations.
Govt. incentive contracts can mean greater profitability.	Profits subject to renegotiation by government.
Long range potentials for helicopters.	Massive R&D expenditures required to exist.
	Heavy labor factor.

Average P/E Multiple: 8–15

AIRLINES

PRO	CON
Tremendous growth in revenue since World War II.	Regulated by the Civil Aeronautics Board (CAB).
Low saturation point (still very low percentage of adult population use the airlines).	CAB pressure to keep rates low.
	CAB has allowed more and more competition along routes.
Jets allow greater utilization of equipment (can fly more miles with less planes).	Companies need huge capital to pay for new equipment.
	Companies carry large debt.
Air freight in its infancy.	Operating earnings have been erratic.
Increasing leisure time.	
Faster and larger planes coming up.	Larger planes may hinder earnings progress at the beginning (heavy introductory costs; temporary excess capacity).

Average P/E Multiple: 12–16

ALUMINUM

PRO	CON
Light weight, durable metal, easy to fabricate.	Sensitive to level of industrial and construction activity.

PRO   CON

ALUMINUM (*cont.*)

Making inroads into many new uses.

Tremendous potential demands exist from aluminum engine blocks, aluminum cans, etc.

Doubling of demand expected over next decade.

Major companies are aggressive marketers.

Industry temporarily plagued by oversupply.

Recent trend of profit margins down.

Government no longer buying for stockpile.

Earnings of major companies disappointing over 1955–68 period.

Metal subject to price-cutting on occasion.

Government looks upon metals as inflation "scapegoat."

Average P/E Multiple: 13–16

AUTOMOBILES

More two-car families.

Cars have become a "status" symbol in the U. S. (New car is a sign of success).

Possibility of reducing the frequency of style changes (like certain European cars), which would lower costs of production.

Burgeoning "family formation" population (ages 18–25 increasing rapidly).

Expanded highway system.

Fairly "blind" price item (gives manufacturers firm price structure).

Autos are durable goods—they will last a long time if owners choose to delay new purchase.

Sales very sensitive to consumers' personal income, personal debt, savings, etc.

Style changes expensive for producers.

Hard to gauge which manufacturer's style will be popular.

Foreign car competition.

Average P/E Multiple: 9–13

AUTOMOTIVE PARTS

Those companies selling to replacement market benefit from increasing number of vehicles on the road.

Suppliers to Big Four forced to operate on low profit margins, are subject to fluctuations in new car sales. Always the risk that Big

PRO	CON

AUTOMOTIVE PARTS (*cont.*)

| | Four may manufacture parts for themselves. |
| | Possibility that new developments might outmode certain parts. |

Average P/E Multiple: 10–15

BANKS

Services being expanded.	Competition from savings and loan associations.
New holding companies provide diversification prospects.	Loan volume depends on business conditions.
Mergers reducing overhead expenses.	Labor costs a sizable percentage of expenses.
Most have shown consistent growth over the years.	Most employees earn less than in a comparable job in another industry.
Higher money rates are beneficial.	
Mechanization of work is increasing.	
Use of capital notes amounts to favorable financing method.	

Average P/E Multiple: 12–16

BROADCASTING

Growing use of TV advertising.	Limit of radio and TV outlets for each company set by FCC.
Home entertainment the most convenient; should grow in usage.	Have to operate within FCC requirements—which can mean non-income guidelines in part.
Opportunity to automate radio broadcasting; following "master plan" for all stations leads to maximum efficiency.	Advertising bound to be affected by general economy.
	CATV might infringe on markets. Pay-TV could change whole structure (this could turn out to be strong positive factor).

Average P/E Multiple: 15–20

PRO	CON

BUILDING

Represents an important segment of economy and thus government tries to avoid drastic declines.	Easily postponed by consumer if he chooses.
Family-formation age groups should create increased demands.	Been subject to ups and downs over the years (no steady growth).
Public construction should increase.	Labor rates are expanding sharply.
New Housing Act calls for accelerated construction over next decade.	Most materials lack uniqueness; this leads to excessive price competition.
Much potential in modernization of older buildings.	
Modular construction will lower costs and open up new outlets.	

There are countless distinct segments of the building industry (asphalt, cement, gypsum, plywood, paint, plumbing, etc.). Each requires a separate study.

Average P/E Multiple: 15–22

CHEMICALS

Production has grown almost twice as fast as the general economy.	Ample capacity in most lines.
	Subject to price competition.
Strong research continues to bring out new products and uses.	Companies have high fixed overhead expenses.
Plastics making inroads into countless markets.	European competition building up.
Takes considerable capital and know-how to operate—which excludes small competition.	Somewhat sensitive to business cycle.
Many companies develop proprietary products for consumers.	

Like the building field, there are many distinct areas, which have to be taken separately.

Average P/E Multiple: 13–20

PRO	CON

CONTAINERS

Attractive packaging an excellent sales medium.	Aluminum foil and plastic film provide new competition.
Trend to supermarkets makes good packaging essential.	Possibility that customers might manufacture own materials.
	Possess few proprietary products.
	Ample production capacity exists.

Average P/E Multiple: 12–16

COPPER

Most of the world supplies are controlled by a small group.	Demands very sensitive to economic conditions.
Most companies boast very strong finances.	Aluminum making inroads.
	Prices fluctuate widely.
Widely used in some attractive industries (i.e., electronics).	Persistent labor troubles and foreign government interference.
	Rising labor costs necessitate rising copper prices and the latter makes competing products more attractive.
	No control over prices because of sensitivity to world metal conditions.

Average P/E Multiple: 9–11

COSMETICS

Expanding middle-income population.	Heavy advertising programs necessary.
No severe price competition.	Promotional expenses large.
Increasingly vanity-conscious population (both men and women).	Some products have seasonal patterns.
High return on invested capital.	Consumer buying patterns can be fickle.
Usage commencing at earlier ages.	

Average P/E Multiple: 18–25

| PRO | CON |

DISTILLING

PRO	CON
"Drinking age" population expanding. Tax-free bonding period now extended; aged whisky no longer dumped on market.	Beer pretty much a non-differentiated product. Little increase in per capita consumption over past 10 years. Industry has excess production capacity. Nationally advertised brands meeting severe competition from private label merchandise. Many institutional investors will simply not own liquor stocks.

Average P/E Multiple: Beer: 20–25   Liquor: 14–18

DRUGS (ETHICAL)

PRO	CON
Huge volume can be generated from new products. Breakthroughs in heart disease, cancer, common colds, etc., yet to come. Broadened medical insurance leads to increased use of drugs. Expanding old-age group will use more and more drug remedies. Expanding markets overseas. Labor costs insignificant. Not affected by fluctuations in general economy.	Heavy research expenses are necessary for company survival (products have rapid obsolescence). Competition is severe and price cuts are common. Subject to occasional government investigations and criticism of high profit margins. Threat from greater use of generic drugs. Medicare could lead to more governmental intervention.

Average P/E Multiple: 20–30

DRUGS (PROPRIETARY)

PRO	CON
Public now more "drug-conscious." Like ethical, have expanding old-age group and potentials overseas. Low labor costs.	Heavy advertising outlays necessary. Little prospect for dynamic breakthroughs.

| PRO | CON |

DRUGS (PROPRIETARY) (*cont.*)

Products have little obsolescence.
No price-cutting.
Not affected by recessions.

Average P/E Multiple: 20–30

ELECTRICAL EQUIPMENT

PRO	CON
Consumers using more and more electrical appliances, which in turn consume more electricity.	Growing foreign competition for heavy electrical equipment and small appliances.
Benefit from assured expansion of electrical utilities.	Occasional price wars in heavy electrical equipment and so-called "white goods."
Large companies working on atomic energy and countless electronic items.	Appliances sensitive to business cycle; heavy equipment subject to own cycle.

Average P/E Multiple: 18–24

ELECTRONICS

PRO	CON
Countless new discoveries to be achieved in the future.	Heavy research expenditures a necessity.
Fits in with definite trend in missiles, space, automation, miniaturization, etc.	Obsolescence can be rapid.
	Much business depends on government spending.
	Like most young industries, it is flooded with many small companies.
	Large aircraft companies expanding into the field.

(Note: This industry is highly fragmented. A tremendous disparity can exist from company to company.)

Average P/E Multiple: 20–40

PRO   CON

FIBER GLASS

Constantly expanding uses.
Very flexible material with excellent qualities.
Growing use in missiles, space, etc.

Heavy reliance on textile and building industries.
Has been sensitive to business cycle.

Average P/E Multiple: 25

FINANCE AND SMALL LOANS

Buying with credit now an accepted practice in U. S.
Former "luxuries" become "necessities" and people will borrow to buy these.
Unemployment insurance, medical insurance make people better credit risks.
Most companies have shown consistent, although not dynamic, growth over the years.

Amount of consumer credit now very high in relation to historical pattern.
Fluctuating auto and appliance sales represent large part of business.
More competition from banks.
More "captive" companies competing (i.e., auto companies, retailers).
Credit cards taking away business.

Average P/E Multiple: 10–13

FOOD CHAINS

Chains still eliminating smaller, marginal stores.
Taking on more profitable non-food lines.
Recent alliances with discount retail stores hold interesting potentials.

Most areas now have ample supermarkets and thus it will be more difficult for the chains to achieve the rapid penetration they have had in the past five years (many areas over-stored).
Profit margins under pressure.
Independents have more flexibility to compete.
A low margin business.

Average P/E Multiple: 10–15

PRO   CON

FOOD AND LODGING

Restaurant business now being approached in more scientific way to save labor, lower food costs, etc.

Affluent society eating out more; and traveling more.

Low cost travel packages increasing demand for hotels.

Hotels, restaurants going into fewer and stronger hands.

Trend to higher rates (hotels) and menu prices.

Franchising is leading to proliferation of outlets.

Food, lodging should be sensitive to general economy.

High labor factor industries.

Sharply rising supply situation (large expansion in hotel rooms and restaurant outlets).

Average P/E Multiple: 30–40

FOOD PRODUCTS

A stable business—not subject to wide fluctuations.

Trend to convenience foods increasing.

Lower than average labor costs.

Certain companies widening profit margins.

Large advertising outlays necessary.

Sizes of crops vary, which affects prices of raw materials.

Difficult to achieve dynamic product breakthroughs.

Sterilization of food by radiation would alter whole processing and packaging methods.

Growing use of private labels.

Average P/E Multiple: 12–18

INSURANCE (FIRE AND CASUALTY)

Everyone needs insurance.

Companies have large investment income, which is growing steadily.

Investment income has made dividends secure.

Rate relief being granted.

Rates are regulated.

Lag in receiving rate increases harmful.

Profits from insurance underwriting have been cyclical; most often, large losses occur.

Inflation not to their benefit.

Average P/E Multiple:
Top operating companies: 14–18   More marginal companies 10–15

PRO	CON

INSURANCE (LIFE)

Growing recognition of its importance by public.	Large fire and casualty companies and other financial service companies entering field.
Companies have aggressive sales forces.	Trend to group coverage means lower premiums per $1,000 of coverage.
Prospects for broadening product line (i.e., mutual funds, variable annuities).	Trend of higher interest rates hard to duplicate in future.
Longer life expectancy means more premiums and profits.	Security analysts more skeptical of "adjusted" earnings assignments of past.
Investment income growing.	People becoming more conscious of equity (rather than fixed dollars) for their future.
Enjoy favorable tax shelter.	

Average P/E Multiple: 20–25

MACHINE TOOLS

Possibility of more governmental stockpiling.	A function of capital spending; sensitive to business cycle.
More sophisticated equipment a necessity for businesses.	Heavy competition developing as large companies pushing hard to get in N/C business all at once.
U. S. far advanced in producing specialized equipment.	U. S. economy currently operating at low rate of capacity—means less urgency for expansion.
Government spurring plant modernization through tax incentives.	
Numerical control tools revolutionizing industry.	
No developed second-hand market for N/C tools.	

Average P/E Multiple: 15–20

MACHINERY (FARM)

More large farms now. These become mechanized and need more machinery.	Sales have been cyclical—according to farmer's income.
Government subsidies have favored farmers.	Public concern over huge subsidies to farmers.
	Profit margins have varied widely.

PRO   CON

MACHINERY (FARM) (*cont.*)

New kinds of machinery being developed.

Increasing labor costs force farmers to more mechanization.

Average P/E Multiple: 12–14

MACHINERY (INDUSTRIAL)

Local, state and federal projects growing steadily.

Highway programs require large equipment needs.

Tremendous potentials for mass rapid transit—and equipment needs for this.

Foreign nations have huge construction needs (i.e., dams, highways).

Sales subject to strong cycles.

Machinery quite durable and can be made to last (style not important).

Average P/E Multiple: 13–18

MOVIES

Film libraries great asset.

Getting higher prices at box offices.

Large profits from lease of films to television.

Many companies have valuable real estate.

Industry's financial management improving.

Lower theater attendance because of competition from television.

Overseas markets will eventually get widespread television.

Risks of producing high-cost films.

Average P/E Multiple: 15–20

OFFICE EQUIPMENT

Trend to automation.

Machines reduce dependence on

Many items are durable and purchase can be postponed.

PRO   CON

OFFICE EQUIPMENT (*cont.*)

labor, cut costs, are more efficient. Unlimited potentials of new products.

Large research expenditures necessary.

Many companies have steadily growing rental business.

Glamour has attracted new competitors.

Supplies and forms business very profitable.

Average P/E Multiple: 25–40

OIL

Fully integrated companies have shown consistent growth over the years.

Oversupply of crude oil exists. Price structure not firm.

Per capita consumption of energy increasing.

Companies hold large reserves overseas—and there is considerable risk of ownership in foreign countries.

Rapid increase in usage overseas.

Profitable by-products exist (chemicals).

Potential usage of atomic energy and possibility of electric or steam auto.

Favorable tax treatment because of depletion allowances.

Possibility that depletion allowance will be reduced.

Increasing foreign pressure on royalty, tax structure.

Average P/E Multiple:
Fully integrated companies: 12–14   Refinery companies: 10–12
Producing companies: 15–25

PAPER

Consumer paper products showing steady growth.

Ample capacity in most lines.

Companies with extensive timber reserves have a great asset.

Historically a poor "price discipline" industry.

Limited foreign competition.

Industrial uses somewhat sensitive to business cycle.

Paper an expendable item which is used up rapidly.

PRO   CON

PAPER (*cont.*)

Per capita consumption overseas increasing rapidly.
1969–71 supply–demand position favorable.

Average P/E Multiple:
Mainly Consumer Paper Products: 15–20   *Others: 12–20*

PUBLISHING

Expanding "middle class" in U. S. More and more adults with greater education (more "readers").

Good television programming would detract from reading.
Magazine publishing very difficult to make profitable.

Textbook sales should expand fast with assured growth in college enrollments.

Paperback book field crowded and difficult profit-wise.

Firm price structure for successful hard cover books.

Possibility of more paperbacks taking away from hard cover sales.

Growing need for reference books.

Retailers can return unsold copies.

Average P/E Multiple:
Magazine Publishers: 12–16   Textbooks, Business Services: 20–25
Normal Hard Cover Publishers: 15–20

PHOTOGRAPHY

Benefits from increased leisure time activity, expanding middle class.

A luxury item which could be affected by a drastic business depression.

Film an expendable item—rapidly used up.

Profitable processing business being proliferated with local competition.

The more cameras owned the more film sold.

Trend to more easily-operated cameras.

Average P/E Multiple: 25–35

PRO

CON

RADIO AND TELEVISION

More older sets to be replaced. More 2–3–4 set families. Color TV saturation point still low. Prospects for hi-fi, stereo, and home video recorders.

Typical durable goods where purchase can be postponed. Imports a serious threat. Severe price-cutting at close-off of models. After color saturation, industry will be typical cyclical industry.

Average P/E Multiple: 15–20

RAILROADS

Vital part of our country's transportation system. Mergers should eliminate duplication of equipment, facilities, etc. Transportation Act of 1958 beneficial to railroads. Advent of "piggyback," "fishyback," are very helpful to rails. Possibility that unfair labor practices will be reduced. Incentive freight rates have attracted considerable business. Many companies control extremely valuable assets (land, resources). Many companies forming holding companies, which will lead to diversification and better utilization of assets.

Inroads made by trucks and air freight. New pipelines taking part of traffic. Passenger business a drain on earnings. Huge upkeep costs. Need large amount of equipment to remain in business. Companies have large amounts of debt—are heavily leveraged. Business very sensitive to general economy—very cyclical. Burdened by unrealistic labor practices (feather-bedding, etc.). Earnings records quite erratic. Competing forms of transportation get direct and indirect subsidies which railroads do not enjoy. High labor factor industry.

Average P/E Multiple: 10–15

RETAIL TRADE

Government payments make personal income more reliable. Consumer has been a reliable

Sales sensitive to changes in disposable personal income. Stores with large durable goods sales

PRO   CON

RETAIL TRADE (*cont.*)

spender over post World War II period.	subject to wider fluctuations.
Some automation procedures to help industry.	Competition from discount houses.
	Highly seasonal business.
	Hard to increase productivity of its labor.
	Variety chains (5 & 10 cent stores) losing business to supermarkets.
	Many new entrants coming into discount field, which is a low margin business.

Average P/E Multiple: 14–20

RUBBER

Companies have expanded rapidly into non-tire products.	Large sales to auto manufacturers —fluctuate with new car sales.
More cars on road lead to more replacement demand.	Tires now lasting longer.
Synthetic rubber lessens dependence on natural rubber, which fluctuates in price.	Compact cars, light in weight, use smaller tires and do not wear out so fast.
Major companies have own retail outlets.	Have occasional price cuts.

Average P/E Multiple: 11–16

SAVINGS AND LOAN

Companies still attracting growth in deposits.	Have to offer higher interest to depositors to attract savings.
Industry basic to all-important building industry	Banks getting more competitive.
Many companies in fast-growing geographical areas (California in particular).	Possibility of more normal taxation in future.
Prospects for broadening lending areas.	Some companies engage in risky land and construction loans.
Enjoy favorable tax treatment.	Need for more sophisticated management.
Participants in anticipated building boom in 1970's.	

Average P/E Multiple: 13–18

PRO	CON

SOFT DRINKS

Demographic trends very favorable, with expanding young population (who are large consumers of soft drinks).

Very firm price structure on part of syrup manufacturers.

Few firms enjoy exceptional brand loyalty.

Recession-resistant.

Per capita consumption increasing.

Low labor factor.

Increasing use of private labels by food chains.

Need for heavy advertising.

Weather can be a factor (i.e., cool summer a negative).

Expensive to launch new products.

Average P/E Multiple: 20–30

SHIPBUILDING

Eventual conversion to atomic fleet would mean tremendous business for many years.

Continuous fleet replacement program, both in military and commercial (subsidies help this).

Foreign competition for commercial shipbuilding.

High labor costs and continuously rising costs which have hampered margins.

Average P/E Multiple: 8–12

STEEL

Industry investing heavily in plant modernization and improvement.

Operating break-even points trending lower.

Efficiency improvement possibilities large.

Industry has well-disciplined price structure.

Companies financially strong.

Large earnings leverage when business good.

Foreigners now voluntarily restricting shipments to U. S.

Closely tied to autos and construction and other cyclically-sensitive industries. Thus, quite sensitive to economy.

Meeting strong competition from other materials.

Foreign competition.

Small per capita growth in consumption.

Really a mature industry.

Government focusing sharply on industry's pricing practices.

Average P/E Multiple: 10–14

PRO	CON

TEXTILES

A basic industry.	Raw materials vary widely in price.
Companies modernizing plants and getting greater productivity.	Foreign competition is severe.
Industry has gone into fewer, stronger hands.	High labor costs especially with increasing wage rates and minimum wage laws.
Industry trying to get more tariff protection.	Hard to control inventories.
Cotton legislation favorable.	Wide swings in prices.
	Excess capacity exists.
	Shifts in fashion.

Average P/E Multiple: 13–16

TOBACCO

Companies have reduced their costs substantially. Low labor costs.	Product lacks explosive growth potential.
Sales are really depression resistant.	Heavy advertising and promotional expenses necessary.
Disciplined price structure.	Companies introducing many new brands—could lead to inventory problems.
Most companies diversifying into other consumer products.	The health issue.

Average P/E Multiple: 11–14

TRUCKING

Short-haul business cannot be replaced by other means.	Regulated by the I.C.C.
Can depreciate trucks rapidly and usually make capital gains when equipment is sold off.	Continuous labor difficulties in the industry.
Improved highways beneficial.	Long-haul business will eventually be dominated by the railroads (because of piggyback) or shippers (fishyback).
	Most companies heavily leveraged.
	Business very cyclical.

Average P/E Multiple: 12–20

Naturally a discussion such as this cannot be all-inclusive. I have tried to list basic industries as they are normally shown. It is my hope that you will have cause to refer back to this in future years—whenever you are considering a purchase or sale in the market. As you can see, there are arguments for and against *every* industry. The main thing is that this discussion forces you into objective thinking—into the "vacuum" approach I talked about earlier. You will no doubt come up with some positives and negatives which I haven't listed. This is where you will benefit from your own imagination. Then it's merely a matter of determining how much the pros outweigh the cons (or vice versa) and relating this appraisal with the P/E multiple the investing public has assigned to the industry.

Now that you've devoured this "food for thought," it's time for dessert—some further guide as to how you should aim your dollars for investing in the future.

CHAPTER 27

Onward, Ever Onward

Much of your investment success is going to depend on what the future holds for our country. To be a better investor you should know what trends are apparent. Economists differ in their opinions as to the future, but then it's a rare occurrence when economists completely agree on anything. As George Bernard Shaw put it so aptly: "If all economists were laid end to end—they would not reach a conclusion."

Still there are certain developments which appear certain to take place in the United States in the future. I've summarized these for you, with the hope that they will help shape your investments.

Here they are:

1. *The 1970's will witness an explosion in the all-important 25–34 age group.*

No doubt you have heard something about a burgeoning "family formation" group in the United States. Needless to say, this terminology refers to those young people who have reached the age of marriage and parenthood. You might argue with the exact age which signifies the start of all this; but let's be practical and exclude cousin Jimmy who runs off at 16 with the girl next door and let's not count on cousin Frank who thinks that nobody is good enough for him and waits til he is 50 to wed that long-legged beauty who was third from the left in the chorus line at one of Las Vegas' plushiest hotels.

The fact is that people get married and start to raise families when they reach 20–30 years of age—all of which is extremely important to the economy. This is naturally because the newly marrieds suddenly become large consumers of items such as appliances, furniture, new housing and the like. And invariably they have their additions and these little joys necessitate spending on baby clothes, cribs and new housing (again). In a nutshell, family formation costs money—enough to stimulate a great deal of business within the country.

Now why should I emphasize all this—and why did I highlight a prediction of an explosion in the 25–34 age group in the 1970's? Why hasn't this group "exploded" in size before?

The reason, of course, is the depression period of the 1930's and the booming increase in births following World War II. The terrible state of affairs in the depression reduced the birth rate severely, and this had some sort of a restraining influence twenty or so years later. Those who were born during the depression reached family formation age during the 1950–1960 period and this decade therefore had no special impetus from the family-way phenomenon.

Particularly after World War II, however, the birth rate in this nation rose sharply again—and these kids will be banding together and producing offspring *and related spending* in large amounts in the years ahead. (No doubt the war in Vietnam has delayed some of this—but it will, of course, be forthcoming). To place all of this in perspective, let's see just how startling the statistics are. In the 1960–1970 decade just coming to an end, for example, the 25–34-year-olds in the U. S. showed only about a 10% increase; from 1970 to 1980, however, we should witness more than a 45% increase. Incidentally, I emphasize the 25–34 age bracket when approaching this look to the future, rather than the 20–30 group. There are many reasons for this—the most important of which is that a great deal more affluence develops as time goes on and my interpretation of the statistics leads me to believe that the older 25–34-year-olds will provide the economy with an unusual impetus.

2. *The country has a rapidly rising "middle income" group.*

Whereas "the rich" have a strong influence in this country (as in others), there is no doubt but that the affluent society is expanding very rapidly—to include a far greater number of citizens. For example, it wasn't many years ago that less than 10% of the families in the U. S. were earning $10,000 to $15,000 annually. This percentage figure has about doubled in the past ten years and projections show that at least *25%* of all families will be in this income category by 1975. Furthermore, a short ten years ago there were only about one million families earning over $15,000 —a figure which has skyrocketed to about 3½ million today and which could well reach a hefty 10 million by the middle 1970's.

What all of this means, of course, is that people in this country simply have more "discretionary income"—that is, more dollars that can go into goods of their choice. This, in turn, means an increased standard of living, more luxury buying and more time and money spent on leisure-time activities. In short, the United States has a fast-rising "middle income (and above)" group, which should certainly be to the benefit of overall consumption over the years.

3. *Our country is being guided by a new, more stimulative, economic approach—something which is fostered by growing social needs.*

One of the problems which the United States encountered in its drive for economic growth was a basic attitude towards the economy itself. In a nutshell, certain theories had been accepted over the years which were, in some ways, the equivalent of negative thinking. To be more explicit, the economists who had the strongest influence on our administrations were reluctant to take a chance on stimulating the business picture drastically (i.e., through tax cuts and more aggressive governmental spending) for fear that these measures might not bring about the desired results —and that the resultant deficits might be startling. The proponents of the more aggressive attitude, on the other hand, took the positive approach and insisted that the measures would very rapidly bring in additional revenue (i.e., greater prosperity means more tax receipts for the government) and that the deficits would not loom large. Those with this more modern tack, who advocate what is known as "New Economics," were (and are) actually willing to live with consistent deficits—so long as the nation gets back a more-than-compensating growth rate (and greater prosperity). Needless to say, these New Economists believe that our employment picture will benefit accordingly from the aggressive approach—and thus that the social and welfare advantages are greatly enhanced.

Enough of the theory, however. The important thing is the experience. While the war in Vietnam has made an assessment of New Economics more difficult, the initial efforts toward the stimulative way of life were successful—and there is little question but that the approach of the 1970's will be directed in this manner (provided, of course, that war demands do not take precedence). When one adds to this trend the growing recognition of social needs in the U. S., it is obvious that the whole economic attitude today is more positive than it was ten or fifteen years ago.

The bugaboo here is, of course, inflation. If politicians (and/or our administration) continue in a "guns and butter" spending and let the price level jump as it did in 1968, then restriction will be the necessary order of the day instead of stimulation. For the subject at hand of the future, however, I think it is safe to conclude that the dis-inflation moves are more likely to be short term in duration and that the large preponderance of time will be spent in New Economic thinking—and acting.

4. *The United States particularly is in the midst of a new era of discovery.*

Earlier in the book I talked about the importance of research and development in assessing a company's potentials. The same measurement can be used to judge a country's potentials and here is one place the U. S. looks strong. Research expenditures have expanded sharply in this country over the last 20 years. For example, in 1941 an estimated $1 billion was spent on "R & D" (research and development); by 1953, this figure had risen to $3.7 billion; in 1957 it amounted to about $7½ billion and it was running around $21 billion in 1965 and is currently at a level well above this.

As I mentioned previously, R & D is the backbone for successful pursuits in the future. But it doesn't usually provide results overnight. In fact, it has been estimated that it takes as long as *five to seven years for a new product to get from the laboratory stage to market.* You can see that the tremendous expenditures which have been made in recent years and which are now being made should bring a flow of new products to market in the future. This is our greatest hope for solution to the problem of foreign competition. American industry has been pretty ingenious in the past and these large R & D expenditures are our hope for the future.

WHERE TO INVEST?

I've written the above for a reason. Believe me, I am not striking for a job with the Chamber of Commerce. I've tried to show you certain trends which I'm confident will exist over the next 10 to 15 years in the United States. Wherever possible, I urge you to fit your investments into these trends.

For example, I've always felt that investors should have a solid representation in their investments in consumer fields. The consumer is king in our economy—he saved us from a severe jolt in 1957–58 when he continued to buy non-durable goods despite a general slowdown in business and again in 1960, 1962 and 1966 when conditions generally looked shaky. Certain industries came through those periods with flying colors—a tribute to the strength which they possess. For example, cosmetics and proprietary drugs have been almost completely exempt from recessions, but then I have already talked about their advantages.

Another field which withstood the general business decline involves the broad term "services," something which I emphasized in the first edition of the *Primer*. It is important to point out here that a greater and greater portion of the consumer's dollar in this country is going towards the purchase of services. Needless to say, there are countless service industries and companies existing, and there is a considerable divergence in their characteristics. Some have very favorable elements working for them, and some (despite being in the service field) are very *un*attractive. To give you an idea as to correct thought process, let me name four companies which have held fairly unique positions within the service complex and which have done reasonably well for their holders, namely A. C. Nielson (market research and ratings), American Express (travel), Dun & Bradstreet (credit rating) and Commerce Clearing House (tax and law services). At the close of 1967, I "conceptualized" one area which I thought held unique opportunities (and which had not yet been glamorized by the investment community)—that of "protection." Needless to say, I was not referring to the kind of protection which the Mafia used to foist upon unsuspecting citizens. Instead, I was talking about the needs for companies such as Burns Detective and Pinkerton's—especially as the tendency towards civil disturbances threatened to expand.

What other service areas, you might ask, qualify as holding attraction? All-important, which ones have not yet been wildly sought by investors? A few come to my mind, the first of which is that of insurance brokerage. No doubt this will sound strange to most of you, since at this time (early 1969) there is only one major publicly held company in this industry (Marsh & McLennan). While this business is competitive (what isn't?), the characteristics of the industry appear quite favorable. Needless to say, insurance is a necessity, something which is bound to be more and more in demand in the future, and something inflation is bound to lead to higher rates (and corresponding higher premium volume for the brokers). Furthermore, the whole area of financial services (i.e., numerous services being offered by one unit, instead of separately) is obviously a trend for the future. While the purpose of this book is not to make detailed industry analyses, the thesis that a top (and growing) insurance brokerage concern provides the investor with the advantages of the insurance business *without* the disadvantage of both regulation and/or the heavy underwriting losses suffered by the insurance companies themselves over the years appears to be a sound one.

Another service field which looks promising is that of mass-feeding. Unfortunately, this is an area which has been glamorized in the past. Thus, I will direct myself to what looks to be an unusual segment of the industry—that of feeding *and housing* of students in our growing campus population. The business of building and operating school dormitories could well be the next "convalescent-home" type of industry for the market to discover.

(Note: this is no recommendation for convalescent-home stocks, which I feel have become a fad in today's market. I have referred to them only to indicate the pattern of acceptance which school dormitory construction and operation might receive by investors.) At any rate, sophisticated feeding techniques entail a scientific approach—something which is not easily accomplished. Once done, however, the vistas are open for considerable business—and for extension from schools into hospitals and other institutions.

Relating back to our last chapter (26) on "Food for Thought," I should call your attention to the sharp differentiation existing in my discussion of Machine Tools between general purpose equipment and highly specialized machinery. As pointed out, machine tools themselves have been and will be terribly sensitive to overall capital spending by businessmen. Since such spending will fluctuate, it follows that general purpose tools, which can be made to last longer if desired and which are a product of plant expansions, will continue to be erratic in their demand.

But, as mentioned, all is not black and white—and entirely different demand patterns should exist in the future for the highly sophisticated numerical controlled tools. In essence, numerical control (N/C) machine tools may bring about a minor industrial revolution throughout the world; these tools are either computer- or tape-controlled and they bring that all-important factor of automation into what has been a pretty stagnant industry.

What I am pointing to here is the assessment that: 1) those companies which are heavily involved in N/C will have less downward fluctuation in their business as time goes on; and 2) they are, for the first time in centuries, actually operating within a growth demand pattern. Let me repeat that it is strictly the N/C companies which hold some unusual growth attraction. Naturally, most, if not all, of the larger machine tool companies will be getting into this business but the investor will want the maximum exposure for his dollars—and thus a company such as Kearney & Trecker, which is a leader in the N/C field, stands out.

While on the subject of automation, let me comment on one important strategy for an investor to consider. In a way, this approach is no more than an extension of one of man's most desired characteristics—empathy (my definition: the ability to see and feel things as they are seen and felt *by others*). In this case, I urge you to turn any important developments around and project just how they might be affecting those which are the *recipients*. Back to N/C tools, it is obvious that such automation is going to strengthen their users and thus many industries which have been saddled with impossible overhead and labor problems may at last find some alleviation.

On a similar subject, it is my belief that some truly great changes are forthcoming in the area of *materials handling*. Very specifically, I foresee numerous industries saving themselves countless dollars—and achieving unusual efficiency—through modern handling equipment. One prime example will be in the field of lumber and wood. With timber assets becoming more and more valuable (*this is one of the most assured conceptual growth areas I can think of, incidentally*), the forest products companies will be spending large sums to improve the yields from their forests. Thus, it is my belief that demands for handling, sorting, and grading equipment will advance sharply in the years ahead.

Living in the San Francisco Bay Area makes my next area of the future rather easy to see. Several years ago certain counties here voted a billion-dollar rapid transit system for the area. At this moment, unforeseen financial problems have been encountered; despite this, before too many years, the system will be operational. Frankly, the whole nation will be watching this development because, let's face it, almost every metropolitan region in the country is getting clogged with traffic—and those highways are becoming a constant sea of steel (and aggravation).

The conclusion from this is obvious: that countless billions will be spent for mass transit in the years to come. But where and how can the investor take advantage of this trend?

Needless to say, the companies designing the cars will be beneficiaries (i.e., G.E., Westinghouse Electric, and Westinghouse Air Brake); also, a great deal of signaling equipment will be needed (i.e., General Railway Signal). And it could be argued that the makers of cement and steel will get sharply increased business therefrom, although the same argument was made for the huge highway program and yet it hardly helped these participants on an overall basis.

Actually, it is my guess that the companies involved in earth-moving, particularly tunneling, will find extraordinary prospects coming their way. The tunnel contractors are generally not publicly held and of course their business can be fraught with risks, but outfits such as Joy Manufacturing, Ingersoll Rand and Smith Industries could experience unusual demands in relation to their overall size.

Naturally, many new developments will occur which will change the names of the companies to be the most important beneficiaries; the important point is that you should set out to explore this area. Take my word for it: San Francisco will only be the beginning of a huge surge toward mass and rapid transportation in this country (and elsewhere throughout the world, too).

A discussion of the future would hardly be proper without some venture into the "wild blue yonder"—into the kind of science fiction which has so often proved *not* to be fictional at all.

Certainly I do not have to convince you that some very dramatic discoveries and scientific advances will be made both over the near-term and in the more distant future. And certainly I should direct myself to these possibilities.

The trouble with this whole subject—from an investment standpoint—is really twofold, namely: 1) So many of the glamourous areas will *not* be great profit contributors for many years to come —and after all, the secret to success in stocks should come from present and potential earning power (not just hope and publicity); and 2) So many of the possible beneficiaries of scientific breakthroughs have already been "picked over" by investors and speculators in the stock market. Said another way, I do not want to give "sheep-like" opinions and thoughts and thus am going to avoid mention of electronic miniaturization, lasers and the like; and I am going to skip already-conceptualized areas such as oceanography.

What I have in mind instead is not exactly a closely guarded secret from investors, but then neither is it something which has been given the attention it justly deserves. I am referring to one segment of the mighty computer business which really holds a key to the maximizing of the computer itself—that of the input and output devices which are bound to become integral parts of these complicated systems. As of early 1969, the sophistication of the input-output devices is not nearly up to that of the computers themselves. Thus, it stands to reason that some great success stories will be written in the future for those companies which are able to solve the problems and fill this void.

While all of this is, I hope, interesting, it is hardly helpful in that it is so broad and non-specific. Thus, I thought I should be more helpful and pinpoint one area which is already emerging as "Phase II" of computer usage and development—that of computer display terminals. Actually the dominant current trend in computer development is to the use of multiple terminals which are connected to the central processing unit for remote information display and data input and output. As a matter of fact, chances are that display terminals and other peripheral equipment will constitute the largest segment of the multi-billion dollar computer market in the early 1970's.

In other words, the use of computers is bound to be maximized by making them inter-active, which is no more than a fancy way of saying that their users should have the ultimate in communication to and from them (the computers). Thus, a terminal should give the user the ability to "talk" back and forth to the central unit and not have to go through a number of intermediaries, which is just another way of stating that the terminal gives the user his own "private" computer, having the benefit of all the sophisticated programming done at the central station.

Investors should always be conscious of supply-and-demand relationships, both within the stock market itself and within the businesses they are considering. In this area of terminals, volume of business is presently very small in relationship to the number of potential outlets. Therefore, a considerable amount of "catching up" will have to be done. While a number of companies have already shown units to the industry (i.e., Conrac, Raytheon, Sanders, Tally) the one I know best and which may well be worthy of exploration is Tektronix—which has taken its basic know-how in the area of oscilloscopes and applied this technology to computer display terminals.

At any rate, this segment of the computer peripheral equipment industry is close enough at hand where one can envision profitability and not have to wait indefinitely for the "seed" to weather many storms before the "flower" appears.

Lastly, it is certainly no secret that our country is currently under-building residences of all sorts. Whereas the early 1960's witnessed an over-building, the pendulum has obviously swung to the other extreme. A normal supply-demand progression would lead to a boom in this area, but on top of all this the Senate recently passed the so-called Omnibus Housing Act, which calls for a tremendous increase in family dwellings over the next decade.

Within this demand pattern, two significant developments will occur—if I see it correctly. For one thing, automation is inevitable in this field, too, and any companies mastering the art of *modular construction* (modular construction being the modern term for what was once referred to as pre-fabrication) should have some large markets to tap. Secondly, there are many reasons to believe that *apartment construction* has one of the most encouraging demand patterns of all. For one thing, the demographic trends favor them—the assured rise in marriages in this country will simply lead to an increase in apartment residency. In addition, the major metropolitan regions are seeing land and construction costs skyrocket—and let's face it, home construction is a luxury (multi-family dwellings offer much lower cost per square foot than homes). With this in mind, some keen developers of apartments have an unusual market to "hit" in the time ahead—as do companies which market materials which constitute an important part of such construction.

CONCLUSION

I hope all of the above will be helpful to you in going *onward, ever onward* to investment success. I have tried to give you some long-range, objective thinking. Naturally, projections and ideas are subject to change, especially when they are made well in advance of a publication—as these are. In other words, because of the time lapse, my thoughts deserve a check on your part—to see whether they are still valid.

As a summary, I thought you might like a recapitulation of the many industries as they might be viewed in the early part of 1969. To be of greatest help, I have provided you with two groupings: the first in pretty general categories; and the second according to their "strength" characteristics. The combination of the two should give you an excellent "feel" of the industries themselves and should point you to the areas where it seems logical that the best opportunities for the future exist.

1. *A General Approach to Industries for Investment.*

	INDUSTRIES GROWING AT A SOMEWHAT FASTER RATE	
Conservative Industries	Those selling directly to consumers	Those not selling directly to consumers
Banking	"Convenience" Foods	Aluminum
Containers	Drugs	Chemicals
Food Chains	Education	Electrical Equipment
Petroleum	Leisure Time	Electronics
(integrated)	Life Insurance	Fiber Glass
Retail Trade	Photography	Office Equipment
Tobacco	Sanitation and	Rare Metals
Utilities	Personal Adornment	
	Services	
	Soft Drinks	

Cyclical Industries	Other Industries
Automobiles	Aircraft
Automotive Parts	Airlines
Building	Distilling
Copper and Non-Ferrous Metals	Fire and Casualty Insurance
Heavy Machinery	Food & Lodging
Machine Tools	Foreign Securities
Radio and Television and other Appliances	Paper
Railroads	Petroleum (producers and refiners)
Railroad Equipment	Rubber
Steel	Savings and Loan
	Shipbuilding
	Textiles

2. Industries and Their "Strength" Characteristics

To provide you with better perspective, I have separated the industries according to their relative strengths and weaknesses. In doing so, I have used three broad categories: those industries which are directly sensitive to general business cycles; those which are sensitive to cycles which are not necessarily tied to the general economy—but which still experience definite cyclical tendencies; and those which are not sensitive to cycles. Within these three headings, I have gone further and assessed specific strengths and weaknesses. Within each group I have assigned "1," "2," "3" and "4" ratings, with the first evidencing the greatest strength (or least weakness, as the case may be), the number two rating signifying above-average strength, the number three meaning less strength and the bottom (number 4) reflecting the least strength.

Needless to say, P/E multiples should reflect these strengths and weaknesses (if they have been properly assessed). At any rate, I strongly believe that an industry breakdown such as this can be very beneficial to you—now and over the years.

CATEGORY I:
INDUSTRIES DIRECTLY SENSITIVE TO GENERAL BUSINESS CYCLE
Ratings:

(1)	(2)	(3)	(4)
Rubber	Aluminum	Auto parts	Lead, Zinc
	Automotive	Copper	Railroads—
	Chemicals	Machine Tools	(without
	Containers	Radio-TV	other income)
	Fiber glass	Railroads—(with	Trucking
	Paper	other income)	
	Retail Trade	Steel	

CATEGORY II:
INDUSTRIES HAVING CYCLICAL TENDENCIES BUT THEIR OWN SEPARATE AND INDIVIDUAL CYCLES
Ratings:

(1)	(2)	(3)	(4)
Electrical equipment	Airlines	Aerospace	Rail equipment (construction)
Electronics	Air conditioning	Building	Shipbuilding
	Broadcasting	Farm equipment	
	Construction equipment	Food chains	
	Rail equipment (leasing)	Insurance (property)	
		LPG distributors	
		Petroleum (refinery)	
		Savings & Loan	
		Textiles	

CATEGORY III:
INDUSTRIES WITHOUT CYCLICAL TENDENCIES
Ratings:

(1)	(2)	(3)	(4)
Cosmetics	Banks	Distilling	Finance Companies
Drugs	Food & Lodging	Natural gas	Tobacco
Office equipment	Foods		
Photography	Household products		
Services	Leisure time		
Soft drinks	Life insurance		
	Petroleum (producers & integrated companies)		
	Publishing— educational		
	Utilities		

PART IX

UTILITY STOCKS

CHAPTER 28

Back from Vacation (or, Making Money for and from Utilities)

The other day I returned home from a short vacation. On entering my house I activated four conveniences we all take for granted—I turned on the lights, flipped on the heat, turned the water on and picked up the telephone and made a call. All of us spend a sizable amount of money each year on these conveniences which, in investment circles, are lumped together under the title "utilities."

In the last two chapters, I gave you some food for thought about the many industrial fields which exist today. Aside from railroads, which constitute a separate and distinct field, the others are termed "industrial stocks." I didn't include utilities in this section because the utility group deserves a discussion of its own.

Investors probably have more money in utility stocks than in any other group, so I think it important to acquaint you with the characteristics of this field. Some of you may be turning up your noses right now, thinking that utility stocks are only for widows and orphans and what you want are stocks which are going to show some *big* profits over the years. All I can say is—don't go away—you may be surprised.

As you already gathered from the first paragraph, utilities are the companies which supply us with electricity, telephone, natural gas and water.* While there are some basic differences between these four utility services they do have some common characteristics, as follows:

* Telegraph is a fifth utility, but I prefer to discuss it separately.

1. *All are noted for their stability.* Regardless of what happens to the general economy, you and I are going to heat our homes, stay clean, turn on the lights and talk to our friends. In short, we're going to use the utilities and, because of this, these companies can count on having *stable* revenues and profits. Utilities are resistant to business recessions and can be expected to grow consistently—although gradually—over the years.

2. *All the companies are regulated. The rates they charge are set by a regulatory body.* Utilities which operate within one state have their rates set by either their state Public Utilities Commission or a local body; those which cross a border into another state are regulated by federal bodies (gas and electric companies by the Federal Power Commission and telephone companies by the Federal Communications Commission). Naturally, regulation is a negative for any industry.

3. *Utilities are granted franchises, which prohibit identical competition in their operating area.* The electric utility in your area has been granted a franchise to supply electricity to you, and no other company can offer you this service. Your utility may or may not also have the franchise for supplying natural gas, which of course is competitive for the home heating and cooking market. *If the utility supplies both electricity and gas, then it has really no competition at all.*

4. *All utilities have to install expensive equipment to serve you* (huge generating equipment, extensive pipelines and storage facilities, etc.), but *all can finance this through heavy borrowing because of the industry's stability.* It is a rare exception to find a utility that is not heavily leveraged with debt and/or preferred stock, but this leverage is of little risk because the utility's business fluctuates so little.

5. *Utilities don't need as much cash on hand as industrial companies.* I mentioned earlier that utility companies get by with a current ratio of slightly over 1 to 1. This is because the companies have money coming in every month without fail. Their accounts receivable (the monthly bills mailed to you every month) are paid on time; if you avoid the bills

too long, the utility can shut off its service to you—and
then you're really in the dark.

6. *Utilities don't have the problem of carrying inventories.*
Whereas General Motors has a sizable inventory of this
year's cars—which are worth far less if they're not sold this
year, a utility has no such problem. Electricity, for example,
doesn't have to be produced far in advance of its sale and
it never goes out of style.

Now that we know the similarities between the utilities, I think
you'll be interested to know the differences which do exist between
them. These differences may alter your investment decisions and
should help you in deciding where you might put some of your
investment dollars to work.

Electric Utilities—Sales of electricity to industries amount to
almost half of the business. This industrial business can fluctuate, especially in geographical areas which are subject to wide
swings. Residential customers seem destined to consume more
and more electricity, however, because of the wide variety of
electrical appliances which are finding their way into the home.
Because of this residential trend, electrical output is perhaps
the most stable of all businesses and one which promises consistent growth as time goes by. It is estimated that electrical
output will about double each decade through this century.
Growth of air conditioning and the prospect of heating homes
electrically (through use of the "heat pump") are all added
benefits.

Natural Gas Utilities—Natural gas has been accepted everywhere
it has been introduced. As a fuel, it is clean and efficient; it has
almost eliminated the anthracite coal business and has made
great inroads into fuel oil. Residential business predominates
and thus revenues are stable, but the industry has more regulatory problems than electric utilities. The price of natural gas
rises consistently and the utilities have to count on higher rates
to their customers to compensate. Certain areas are not yet
completely covered by natural gas and thus there is not yet a
saturation of the market. Contrary to electric utilities, there is

a question as to whether natural gas reserves will hold out forever.

Telephone—Although American Telephone is regarded as the most secure of all stocks, the telephone business in general would be more sensitive to a severe business recession than the electricity business. A.T.&T. certainly qualifies among the most secure, however, because its business has not fluctuated (it has grown steadily) and because the company's leverage is far less than other utilities. Tremendous strides have been made in the mechanization of the telephone business and there are countless new fields of service which could produce growth in the future (microwave developments, mobile telephone, etc.).

Water—Most cities own their own water facilities and the trend toward taking over private facilities continues. This is one utility which can (but seldom does) suffer from a shortage of its commodity. De-saltification improvements are being made and this could open up unlimited quantities from sea water.

Telegraph—The telegraph business is much more sensitive to changes in general business than other utilities. Competition from long distance telephone has hurt, but a great deal of mechanization of the telegraph business has taken place (Desk-fax, etc.). Labor costs are still much greater than other utilities. New growth prospects stem from microwave systems and from greater use of private wire systems.

What to consider in buying utility stocks—Just as in the analysis of industrial stocks, there are certain keys to investment success in buying utility stocks. I'm sure you'll want to know what makes one utility stock a buy and another not such an attractive purchase. Here are the factors you should consider:

1. *The geographical area in which the utility operates.*
   Needless to say, a utility operating in a fast-growing area has much better opportunity for growth than one in a stagnant or slow-growing region. So look at the recent population trends, which will give you an idea of what kind of growth to expect in the future.
   In addition, it is important to look at the area's "back-

ground." Certain areas are dependent on heavy industry (machinery, steel, etc.) and business is subject to greater fluctuation because of this. For example, during the 1957–1958 recession, Detroit Edison suffered from sharply lower industrial activity and reported reduced earnings in 1958, while the utility in my backyard, Pacific Gas and Electric (not dependent on heavy industry), showed increased profits for the year. Some utilities are very dependent on one industry and this of course entails more risk than a utility which serves a diversified community.

2. *The attitude of the regulatory authorities.*

Public utility regulatory bodies can vary greatly in their philosophy from area to area. Some authorities are tough as nails on granting rate increases while others are extremely liberal. One of the reasons for the great growth of utilities in Florida and Texas has been the attitude of their governing bodies. Utilities in these states have consistently been granted a higher rate of return than in other states; because of this, the operating utility companies have shown higher profits and their stockholders have benefited enormously.* In contrast, a state such as Oregon is well known for its negative attitude towards private utilities. In 1960, for example, Portland General Electric was granted its first rate increase in 11 years. All in all, it's of great benefit to you as a stockholder to have the authorities on your side.

3. *The utility's past record of growth and future projections.*

As with industrial stocks, a utility company's past record of growth can give you a good indication of what the future has in store. It's once again a matter of looking at a company's record of earnings per share over the *past* 3–5 years and asking whether anything has changed to alter this pattern either upward or downward over the *next* 3–5 years.

Needless to say, you should be especially attracted to

---

* Your first reaction might be that these higher profits are at the expense of the population. Liberal authorities claim that in the long run, it is to the existing population's benefit. After all, the area's growth can be fostered by an aggressive utility and a utility which realizes that its expansion will be profitable to it will do everything possible to promote the region.

those utilities which seem sure to report consistent and rapid growth in the future.

4. *Yield.*

In Chapter 20 I pointed out how high yield can limit your risk in a stock and how, in certain cases, high yield will signal that a stock should be bought for at least a temporary rise in price. I concluded, however, that yield is of little use if long term growth of capital is your investment objective.

In the case of utility stocks, yield *is* of major significance in a majority of cases. This is because most utility stocks are bought by investors *who need income* and these people are naturally attracted by high yield. Many utility stock owners are widows or retired people who depend on their dividends to live; *they buy stocks on the basis of yield alone* and thus we have to give this consideration when we analyze utility issues.

For example, in the desk drawer of my office I keep a list of utility stocks and their current yields. Because many utilities are so similar (they all have the same product to sell, all are regulated, etc.), I can make recommendations for those who want above-average income and security *almost solely on the basis of yield.*

Like all stocks, correct timing of your purchases of utility issues can make a good deal of difference. It's true that you're not going to worry how safe the $2.40 dividend on American Telephone and Telegraph is, but it's certainly to your benefit to buy the stock at 50 or 55 instead of 65, if you can. It's hard to generalize as to exactly when utility stocks should be purchased, but there are two important factors you should consider when buying them. These factors are *1) The Level and 2) Trend of Money Rates* (that is, whether interest rates in the country are high or low at the time and whether they are going up or down in the near future).

I know you're aware that interest rates change from time to time. One year you get 4% on your bank savings account and a few years later you get only 3%; one year you can buy U. S. Government Bonds that yield 5% or 6% and a year later you can get only 4% on the same bond. Why should it make so much difference to the utility stock buyer where interest rates are and which way they are trending?

The answer: *because many utility stocks are bought for income, which puts them in competition with other income-producing securities for the investor's dollar.* For example, suppose U. S. Government Bonds are yielding 4% today and utility stocks are yielding 6%. Many investors who might ordinarily put their money into government bonds might well be attracted instead to utility stocks and thus it should be good timing to buy the utilities. Likewise, if the bonds are yielding 6% and the utilities 4%, many investors might switch out of utilities into bonds and this might be an improper time to buy utilities. The *trend* of money rates is equally important. Suppose interest rates in the country are beginning to come down; perhaps business in general in the U. S. is not so good and the federal authorities are trying to stimulate it by lowering money rates. If you buy a utility stock today with a 5% yield and six months from now money rates have come down sharply, chances are that your utility purchase will be up in price. The figures would go something like this:

Buy a $100 Stock paying $5.00 a year, for a yield of 5%, when 5% is the "going rate" for income investors.

Six months later the "going rate" is only 4%. The stock, still paying $5.00 a year, might sell at $125 to yield 4%.

$$(\$5.00 \div \$125 = .04 \text{ or } 4\%)$$

Thus, your $100 Stock has gone to $125—and only because of the change in money rates. The reverse is, of course, true when money rates trend higher instead of lower. Therefore, we can make the following generalization: *Utility stocks are an especially good buy if you think that interest rates in general are going lower,* or if existing yields on industrial stocks are low.*

---

* Low interest rates actually have a double-barrelled effect on utilities. Public utility companies, which rely heavily on raising needed cash through the

5. *Price-Earnings Multiple.*

Earning power is just as important in utility stocks as in industrials and thus it is also important to compare the P/E multiples of utilities you are considering. *Dividends are paid out of a company's earnings and thus the more earnings you have per dollar of market price the more potential dividends you have.*

For example, say you are comparing two utility stocks, both of which sell for $50 per share. Company A pays out $2.50 per share in dividends for a yield of 5% ($2.50 ÷ $50 = .05, or 5%), while Company B only pays out $2.00 per share for a yield of 4% ($2.00 ÷ $50 = .04, or 4%). Is Company A a better buy with a 5% yield than Company B with a 4% yield? Not necessarily so. Let's compare the earnings of these two:

Company A is earning $2.75 per share, which gives a P/E of 18.
    ($50 market price ÷ $2.75 earnings = 18.2)
Company B is earning $3.50 per share, which gives a P/E of 14.
    ($50 market price ÷ $3.50 = 14.3)

On the basis of earnings, Company B is a far better buy than Company A. Company A's yield is much higher because the company is paying out almost all its earnings in dividends to stockholders (over 90% of its $2.75 earnings paid out). In contrast, Company B is paying out only 57% of its $3.50 earnings directly to its stockholders. If Company B were to pay out 90%, its dividend would be increased from $2.00 per share to $3.15, which would give a yield of 6.3%. Company B has chosen *not* to pay out 90%. It is probably retaining the bulk of its earnings for more expansion than Company A, and this expansion will no doubt lead to higher earnings *and higher dividends* to Company B stockholders in the future.

You can see how important earnings are and you can see that, like industrial stocks, *the utility stock with the most potential earning power is the best buy for you.*

---

sale of bonds and other fixed income securities, naturally save money when interest rates are low (their borrowing costs are lowered and this leads to increased profits).

GROWTH UTILITIES

For years Florida Power and Light, Texas Utilities and other "growth utilities" have been recommended to investors seeking capital growth. People are often amazed when a utility stock of any sort is suggested for dynamic gains over the years. They would not be amazed, however, if they had ever looked at the past records of companies such as those just mentioned. To illustrate, here is what happened to these two companies over the 1950–1960 decade:

| | FLORIDA POWER AND LIGHT | | | TEXAS UTILITIES | | |
	Earnings per Share	Dividends per Share	Mean Market Price	Earnings per Share	Dividends per Share	Mean Market Price
1950	$ .61	$.32	5	$ .60	$.24	6⅛
1951	.62	.35	6⅛	.67	.34	7⅜
1952	.71	.37	7½	.78	.43	9⅞
1953	.77	.40	9	.83	.48	10¾
1954	.88	.44	12	.97	.52	14
1955	1.03	.51	16⅞	1.03	.58	17⅜
1956	1.29	.61	21¾	1.17	.64	19⅜
1957	1.49	.665	26	1.28	.72	22
1958	1.75	.76	36½	1.37	.80	27
1959	1.93	.865	49⅜	1.47	.88	34¾
1960	2.11	.97	60	1.56	.96	39¼

Indeed, the growth was both consistent and remarkable. And the performance of these two stocks in the market was equally remarkable. Both companies passed the first three tests I provided for you earlier in this chapter; they both operated in fast-growing regions, they both benefited from liberal regulatory commissions and both anticipated a continuation of their growth in the future.

Let's see how they stacked up, at the beginning of 1961, on tests #4 and #5, namely yield and P/E multiple:

	Present Market Price	Annual Dividend Rate	Yield	Estimated Current Earnings	P/E Multiple
Florida Power & Light	65	$1.00	1.5%	$2.15	30
Texas Utilities	45	1.04	2.3	1.63	28

Naturally, we have the benefit of hindsight here, so let's do a Compounding Growth Guide analysis of these two stocks as they should have been approached in 1961. First of all, let's see what the compound growth rates had been for the two companies.

Without going into the mathematics, here is how the recent past had stacked up:

Company	1955–60 Annual Growth Rate	1957–60 Rate
Florida Pwr & Lt	15½%	12½%
Texas Utilities	8½	7

An important lesson to consider here is the *most recent trend of events*, which in both cases shows some diminution of growth. Whereas, for example, FPL showed a 15½% annual growth rate from 1955–60, the most recent three years was 12½%—and the latest year (1960/1959) had declined further to around 9%; in the case of TU, the five year growth was 8½%, the three year rate was 7% and the latest year was only 6½%. Needless to say, all of this should have had a strong bearing on our all-important projected growth rate for the future. Granting some benefit of the doubt, however, let's assume that FPL qualified at that time as a 10% + growth company, and that TU promised about 7½% +.

Our next step is to categorize the companies according to glamour. Since utilities lack the excitement of the I.B.M.'s, Xerox, Polaroid, etc. (and since we should reserve the Super Glamour category to areas and companies such as these), we think it would be logical to say that the slow growth utilities would qualify as only Average Glamour status and that the more rapid ones would fit in the Above Average niche. Since both FPL and TU were in the latter growth range, we can assume that they deserved Above Average multiples. Looking to our Guide (page 178), we find that FPL (with assumed 10% growth) starts off with a P/E of 18–20 times and that TU (with 7½%) rates around 18 times. Since both companies had decent institutional support, an additional 3–5 multiple would have given you a "buying area" of 21–25 times for FPL and 21–23 for TU.

Both of these assessments indicate that the two stocks were selling way above what our Guide showed they deserved (the table on page 255 shows a current 1961 multiple of 30 times for FPL vs. our Guide's 21–25 and a 28 P/E for TU vs. our assessment of 21–23). Thus, despite the great past record of these growth utilities and despite their acceptance by the investment community, our Guide approach pinpoints their "richness." In short, both were selling way above what their combined growth rate-glamour image deserved.

None of the above refutes the theory behind the purchase of growth stocks generally. In utilities, as well as in industrial stocks, the investor will reap double-barrelled rewards from ownership of the growth vehicle. He will not only end up with vastly superior capital appreciation, but *in the long run he will end up with more annual income from owning growth companies as opposed to those in the non-growth or slow-growth category*.

Incidentally, our Guide approach would have proved to be quite accurate. Some eight years later, in 1969, both FPL and TU are selling very little above what they did then—hardly the kind of performance which you should be striving for, and learning to accomplish, through your reading of this book.

But stocks do have their price, something which our Guide should help us with immensely. At any rate, all of the above should tell you what you need to know about utility stocks and show you how to assess them objectively. I think it only proper to close with the thought that utility companies should show consistent, although generally moderate, growth in earnings over the years— with corresponding dividend increases. Fortunately for the 1969 investor, the stocks are not inflated as they were in 1961. As a matter of fact, many of them are now below what the Compounding Growth Guide indicates is average value. Certainly any "normal growth" portfolios should have representation in this field —and 1969 may well prove a most propitious time to start with such a program.

PART X

SOME TAX ADVICE
FOR INVESTORS

CHAPTER 29

Ugh!!

Perhaps you're wondering whether the letters "UGH" represent a symbol for a secret stock which is going to be the IBM of tomorrow. So sorry! They stand only for Ugh!!, which is just what people say when they start talking about income taxes. And that's just what I'm going to talk about right now.

Not that I am an expert on taxes. "Only a fool is his own attorney," they say, and the same thing goes for a non-C.P.A. or non-accountant who thinks he can handle complicated tax problems by himself.

But I am familiar with certain tax items which concern the average investor and I feel it only fair to relate these "tips" on to you. They are elementary—but they can save you money.

DIVIDENDS

Very little discussion is necessary when we talk about dividends. At the present time, you are completely exempt from income tax on the first $100 in dividends you receive each year. If you are married, you and your spouse are entitled to $100 each, for a total of $200 in dividends tax-free during the year.

Interestingly enough, there are a select number of stocks which pay dividends that are either partially or completely free from taxation. A goodly number of utility stocks are paying out tax-free dividends* but in almost all cases this tax-free status has a limited life. Sierra Pacific Power, Washington Natural Gas, Portland Gen-

---

* Usually only a portion of the dividend is non-taxable.

eral Electric, Pacific Power and Light and Arizona Public Service are but a few in a long list of these utilities. In addition, certain non-utility companies offer the same tax-exempt income: Ogden Corp., United Corporation and Standard Shares are examples here.

Needless to say, don't buy a stock on the basis of non-taxable dividends alone. This status can serve as a little "kicker" for you, however, if you've decided on the basis of other analysis that a stock is a good buy.

TAKING PROFITS

There's an old saying: "No one ever went broke taking profits." But I'm sure you're aware that Uncle Sam's money counter—the Internal Revenue—gets a slice of every profit you take when you sell a stock. It's indeed a pleasure to buy a stock at 10 and sell it at 20 or 30 or 40, but it's important to know how much of your gain belongs to the government.

There are two kinds of gains you can make as an investor:

1. a "short term" gain, which is when you sell a stock at a profit *within* six months of your original purchase date, and
2. a "long term" gain, generally referred to as a "capital gain," when you make a profit on a stock you have held for more than six months (six months and one day is enough).

There is a considerable difference in the tax liability of a short term and long term gain. In the case of the former, *your total profit is taxed as ordinary income*—that is, it is added *in full* to the rest of your income for the year and thus you can be taxed up to 70% on this income. In the latter case—when you have a capital gain—*you only have to declare one-half of the gain* and the most Uncle Sam can take is 50% of this one-half regardless of your tax bracket. Thus, 25% of the total capital gain is the most you will ever have to pay (maximum 50% of 50% of the gain = 25% maximum of the total gain).

Take the case of Mrs. Ima Smart Investor. Ima bought 100 shares of Brooklyn Bridge stock on January 1st at $10 per share. Here it is June 15th and the stock is at $20 per share. Ima sells the stock at $20. Very shrewd! Ima's $1,000 investment has gotten her $2,000—for a profit of $1,000. Comes next April and Ima is stewing over her Form 1040. She arrives at the summary of her stock transactions for the previous year. She proudly puts down the Brooklyn Bridge coup—and suddenly she discovers that she could have saved herself some tax money had she only waited until July 2 (six months and one day) to sell the stock. You see, Ima's in a 50% tax bracket and here's the difference between a short term gain and a capital gain for this $1,000 profit:

Short term: $1,000 profit taxed at 50% = $500 tax to be paid.
Capital Gain: $500 profit (only ½ the profit has to be reported) at
    50% = $250 tax to be paid.*

Thus, there is a $250 difference in tax because Ima didn't wait for July 2nd. Sure, maybe Brooklyn Bridge stock might have gone down between June 15th and July 2nd, but as a matter of fact, it could have declined from $20 to $17 and Ima would have realized about the same after-tax profit. And who knows, maybe the stock would have gone up over that short, two week period, so you can see the importance of watching your acquisition and sales dates and being conscious of how long you have held a stock you are planning to sell. This is especially important to people in the higher tax brackets.

TAKING LOSSES

Stock market losses are things I hope you'll have very few of in your lifetime. Let's be practical, however. In the stock market, as in all forms of investments, even the shrewdest will at some time make mistakes and experience losses. While you never make money by losing money, at least you can learn to take the fullest "advantage" of the losses you incur.

Our government is sympathetic about your losses—but only to a limited extent. Uncle Sam will let you subtract any losses you

---

* If Ima were in a higher tax bracket, the saving would be even greater. If her bracket is 70%, the short term gain would cost her $700 in tax; the long term tax would still only be $250 because, as I've mentioned, the maximum capital gain tax is 25% of the total profit ($1,000 in this case).

take during the year against your gains and thus losses taken will reduce the amount of tax you would have to pay on these gains.

If you haven't taken any gains during the year, a loss can be helpful in reducing the amount of normal income tax you might have to pay. You see, you are allowed to take a $1,000 net loss (over and above gains taken) each year and use this to reduce the amount of income you report to the Internal Revenue. Suppose your yearly taxable income is $7,000. As you know, the tax rate gets higher as your income grows: you pay 20% on income up to $2,000, but on the last $1,000 which hikes your income from $6,000 to $7,000, the rate is 30%. Thus, by taking a $1,000 loss, which in this case lowers your income from $7,000 to $6,000, you are saving the 30% tax you would have had to pay on this last $1,000, for a saving of $300. Incidentally, if you take a loss by selling a stock, you must wait 31 days to re-purchase the same stock—if you wish to deduct the loss on your income tax statement. If you buy it back *within 30 days*, the Internal Revenue calls it a "wash sale" and forbids your utilizing the loss.

BENEFITING FROM OTHERS' LOSSES

People are always thinking ahead to the time when they will have to fill out their tax forms. I'll agree that these forms are a nuisance. If you *don't* fill out your form correctly, you go to *jail*; if you do fill it out right, you go to the poorhouse!

Most of us are procrastinators at heart. We leave our unpleasant tasks and decisions to the very end. This applies to investors, too. They have a loss in a stock early in the year and yet wait till the very end of the year to sell the stock in order to establish a tax loss. Suddenly in November and December people comb through their stock lists to see where they can establish a loss which will "save" them some taxes. The stocks they sell are naturally the ones which are down in price. All of a sudden a great deal of "tax loss selling" occurs in certain depressed stocks. *This concentrated selling further depresses the market prices of these stocks—many times to bargain levels.* Therefore, you should keep your eyes open in December for these artificially depressed issues.

ONE IMPORTANT WORD ABOUT LOSSES

Suppose you bought a stock at $50 and it's now at $45. You have a loss of $5 per share right now. Some people contend there is no such thing as a loss until a stock is sold. They contend that they have no loss on this $45 stock because it hasn't been sold. After all, the stock might go back up to $50 and then they'd be even again. True, indeed. But the stock might never go back to $50—it might instead go down to $40 or $35.

Believe me when I say that if you bought a stock at $50 and it is now at $45, you have a loss of $5 whether you sell the stock or not. Which brings us to the point in mind! So many times I've heard people say, "I can't afford to sell that stock—I'd have to take a loss." This is incorrect investment thinking. If conditions have changed in the company or the industry since you bought the stock and *if the stock has lost its attraction it should be sold regardless of what your cost is.* The smart thing to do is to admit your mistake and buy another stock which does look attractive. I'm sure you've heard that *the most successful investors are those who minimize their losses and maximize their gains.* You can see that this axiom recognizes that losses will have to be taken and if you "wear blinkers" and fail to recognize your mistakes then you cannot abide by this good advice.

SPLITTING YOUR GAINS AND LOSSES

Let's assume we're in the month of December and that you have two stocks you are considering for sale—one in which you have a $1,000 capital gain and the other in which you have a $1,000 loss. At first thought you might conclude that both stocks should be sold *this year* so that you incur no extra taxes (because the $1,000 loss offsets the $1,000 gain, thereby giving you no gain at all to report). While this seems logical, in practice it is not correct tax thinking. Instead you save some important tax dollars by splitting your gain and loss into *separate* tax years. Here's the way it works:

1) Sell the loss stock now. This gives you a net $1,000 loss for the year and reduces your taxable income by this amount. Assuming you're in the 50% tax bracket, the $1,000 loss saves you $500 in taxes.

2) Wait till next year (only a few weeks away) to sell the gain stock. Since it is a long-term gain, you are taxed on only half the gain or on only $500. Your 50% tax rate takes away $250 of the $500.

Thus, by splitting your loss and gain into separate years, you have saved yourself $250 in taxes, as follows:

Tax *saved* by taking $1,000 loss this year:	$500
Capital gain tax to be paid on $1,000 gain next year:	250
Tax Savings	$250

The same thing can be reversed—whereby you take the long term gain *first* (this year) and take your loss the next year, but the above is the most normal.

Incidentally, if you want to establish a capital gain in one year *you have to sell the stock within five business days* (exclude Saturday, Sunday and holidays) of December 31st. In contrast, to establish *a loss you can sell the stock right up to and including the very last day of the year.*

SOME MORE INVESTMENT ADVICE ON TAXES

You can see the importance of knowing something about taxes as they relate to your investments. Despite this, perhaps the best advice I can give you is *not to let taxes influence your investment judgment.* If you think a stock is greatly overpriced, then it is usually better to sell it, regardless of tax considerations. Of course, the case of Ima was an exception—it is seldom you can't afford to wait a few weeks if it is to your tax advantage to do so.

A person who owns a stock with an extremely low cost might be influenced in his investment decision by tax considerations. If, for example, your cost on ABC stock is $1.00 per share and it is now selling for $21.00 per share, you may think you are "locked in" to owning this stock because of taxes. After all, you will have to report a capital gain of $20 per share if you sell it and the taxes on this gain may run up to $5.00 per share—which is a pretty big hunk. In a case like this you have to be convinced that ABC stock is selling way too high at $21 before giving consideration to selling it. Or you have to have a new purchase in mind which looks exceptionally attractive to switch out of ABC.

The case of Ima and ABC are the exceptions rather than the rule, however. Don't be afraid to pay some taxes—if your investment judgment tells you a stock should be sold. Remember that, unless you live your whole life with a stock and die still owning it, you will eventually have to pay tax on your gain. In the ABC example, too often a person will refuse to sell, and argue that "after the $5.00 per share tax I am really receiving not $21.00 but only $16.00 a share for my stock." Experience has shown that, if the stock then proceeds to go down, too often the same person will then sell it at a lower price—and then have to pay a tax which will net him far less than he would have received at the beginning.

PART XI

A HARD LOOK AT SOME STOCK MARKET THEORIES

CHAPTER 30

So You Want to Trade

"What I want is to make some quick profits."

I wish I had a twopence for everytime I've heard this expression over the years. Actually, who doesn't want quick profits? I know I do. But, like everything else in life, *wanting* and *getting* are two different matters.

Perhaps you're disillusioned by my apparent pessimism about achieving quick gains in the stock market. After all, I am a research analyst and stockbroker; as such, I should know when the market is going up or down; and I should know whether or not XYZ stock will go up or down three points over the next few weeks. Or should I?

My reply to people who assume that I know these answers for sure is:

"If I knew for sure, I wouldn't be working—I'd be on the beach at Waikiki right now. And so would all the other research analysts and stock brokers in the world."

Don't misunderstand me. I'm in favor of quick profits. I've seen some fabulous gains made for both my clients and myself in just a very short time. But I think it only fair to say that there is a certain amount of *luck* involved when your price objectives on a stock are achieved in a very short period.

Let's explore this a little deeper! As you know, *stock prices go up when there are more buyers than sellers and they go down when the pressure from sellers exceeds the buying interest.* When you choose an attractive stock *for the future* you are in essence saying, "I believe that this company's earnings will rise over the years" or "I believe the glamour status of this company will improve as time goes on" or a combination of these two statements. You conclude that these favorable developments (increased earnings and/or improved glamour status) will create more buyers for the stock than sellers and that the stock will go up in price.

In contrast, when you are choosing a stock for quick profits (say for a few weeks) it is another matter. Here you are saying, "I believe there will be more buyers than sellers in this stock *in the next few weeks*." How can you know such a thing? How can you know what people all over the country are going to do with XYZ stock over a few weeks? To be truthful, you cannot.

After all, just when you're convinced that a mass of buying interest will build up in a stock over the near term, someone with a very large block of that stock may decide to sell. Perhaps a large estate has a block of 150,000 shares and has to liquidate in these few weeks you are aiming for. There are countless elements similar to this which make it difficult to foretell what will happen to a stock (or the market in general) over a very short period of time.

If you don't think it's difficult to gauge where the market is going, try reading the sage comments made in the periodic market letters published by most of the large brokerage houses in the U. S. It's normal for these letters to hedge some, so that they don't put their feet in their mouths, but some are really absurd. Here's one that really caused me to chuckle one day:

"The market has had a sizable advance, one which indicates investors should take a cautious attitude. On the other hand, stocks appear on firm ground, because of improving earnings. As corporate earnings reports are released investor confidence should be strengthened, but the release of these reports may well invite profit-taking."

You tell me which way the market should go after reading this mumble-jumble. And this is supposedly from the mouth of an expert.

Have you ever been to Harold's Club or to a host of similar gambling casinos in Reno? How would you like to own one of the dice tables at one of these casinos? My guess is that you could retire in peace by owning just one. But suppose someone offered you ownership in one table—not for keeps—but only for one hour. Could you rest in peace with that? Certainly not! That one hour could be disastrous for you. Some lucky fellow might make 20 passes and the table might show a huge loss for this one hour. Over the years this table is certain to show a good profit as the percentages and statistics work to your favor. The same principle applies to stocks. Choose a good stock and the statistics will work to your favor as time goes by, but who knows what will happen to it "in one hour."

I hate to use a gambling casino as an analogy to the stock market. When you talk about trading in and out of stocks *day in and day out*, however, the analogy is not so far-fetched. Trading really is gambling and I don't like to confuse it with investing for gains over a longer period of time.

There are many traders in the market—people who will buy a stock one day and sell it the next for a small profit. This is about the toughest way to make a living I know of. *I wholeheartedly advise you against this kind of gambling*. I feel very strongly about this, so I think it only fair to tell you why:

1. You will pay a fortune in commissions to your broker. I tell people who ask me about day-to-day trading that "it will make *me rich, not you*." I doubt whether your objective is to make your broker rich, so protect yourself.

2. You are trading against professionals. There are hundreds of men on the floor of the exchanges who specialize in trading. They have the advantage of not paying commissions, so they can survive with very small profits every day. By being on the exchange they can get a better "feel" of trends than you can sitting in a brokerage office. In addition, you are at a time disadvantage; the professionals are on the spot and can act instantly. You are a minute or so away and this can make a big difference (in the case of frequent "late tapes" you may be 5, 10 or even 20 minutes behind).

3. Trading involves making many decisions. It takes far more time than long term investing and many times it detracts from a person's everyday vocation.

4. Higher commissions mean you have to count on wider swings in stocks to make a profit. For example, the commission to buy 100 shares of a $30 stock is $36.00; to sell costs you the same amount and thus you have a total round trip cost of $72.00 or almost ¾ of one point—just to break even.

5. All your gains will be subject to ordinary income tax. You will never benefit from the advantageous capital gain rate, because you are not holding stocks for six months.

6. You will *never have big winners*. Traders who are happy to make a few points will never own stocks which will double, triple, quadruple, etc.

Many people envy traders. They hear them brag about their fabulous turns in the market. But I ask you—do you suppose you would actually hear about the losses the traders take? No, sir. Perhaps the best answer to the question of whether people should trade is the following, which was made by a man who had spent his whole working lifetime in the stock market. He said simply:

"I know a lot of millionaire *investors*, but I *don't know one millionaire trader*."

So now you know the way I feel about day-in and day-out trading. Still we have to recognize that there is a middle road between trading and long, long term investing. There are many investors who simply don't want to wait a lifetime to realize some profits on their money. For them I have a special set of rules of my own. I'm going to pass them on to you now and I hope they'll be helpful:

1. Realize that your judgment will not be perfect and that you will have to take losses on occasions.

2. Buy stocks you "can sleep with." Don't buy junk.

3. Do not buy stock for small gains. Set your sights for good-sized profits.

4. Do not concern yourself after "the race is over." If you have decided on an investment philosophy of taking occasional profits, do not consider jumping off the nearest building if a stock goes way up after you have sold. It's part of your game.

5. Do not be impetuous and overanxious to take down profits. Try to let them run.

CONCLUSION

Trading is gambling—not investing. The latter is both the easiest and most profitable way of making money, so concentrate on it. You'll be glad you did! (Note: In our next-to-last chapter (37) on "Common Stock Commandments," I make reference to an important chapter from *The Common Sense Way to Stock Market Profits*—the one entitled "How to Amass Large Amounts of Capital." The philosophy here is diametrically opposed to trading —and I strongly recommend it to all investors, particularly those who are considering, or actively involved in, trading.)

CHAPTER 31

Beating the Market

Human beings are constantly striving for schemes which will make them money. Because the stock market itself is a vehicle for making money you can imagine the number of schemes which have been invented to "beat the market."

In the early days there were plenty of illegal ways of moving stock prices to one's favor through manipulation. Fortunately the Securities Exchange Act of 1934 set up the Securities and Exchange Commission in the United States and most of the illegal practices are now a thing of the past.

The legal schemes, of course, remain and every investor should be conscious of what they have to offer. Let's take a look at a few of the widely-used stock market theories and see what kind of merit they have.

THE DOW THEORY

The most widely publicized theory of all is the "Dow theory." One Charles Henry Dow, who was the first editor of *The Wall Street Journal*, wrote some editorials in that paper from 1900–1902. These editorials were later interpreted by W. P. Hamilton and Robert Rhea and the Dow theory as it now exists was formulated.

Actually the originators of the theory did not contend that it would allow you to "beat the market." Their suggestion was that it would tell you whether the stock market in general was in an over-all upward trend (a bull market) or in an over-all downward slide (a bear market). The originators were confident that their barometer could predict business conditions many months in advance. They were not interested in analyzing any of the economic indicators which I discussed in Chapter 7. Instead, they contended that the action of the stock market itself would tell you where business was headed.

The Dow theory is based strictly on certain interpretations of the Dow Jones Industrial Average and the Dow Jones Railroad Average. This in itself denotes weakness, since the Dow Jones Industrial Average is a very limited one and the railroad stocks do not carry the significance they did years ago when railroad issues were more highly regarded than they are now.

Like all theories, the Dow is subject to all sorts of interpretations and assessments. Also like all theories it is sometimes right and sometimes wrong. It had a wonderful record in "predicting" a downfall in 1929. The above-mentioned W. P. Hamilton published a now-famous editorial on October 25th of 1929—entitled "A Turn in the Tide." In the editorial, Hamilton stated that the action of the averages on October 23rd signaled the end of a long bull market and the beginning of a bear market. Had a person sold everything on October 23rd, he would have saved himself a fortune. He would already have seen the market on industrial stocks drop about 19%, but after October 23rd it was to fall another 70% from its high to its low in 1932.

On the other hand, the Dow theory had not forecast the fantastic bull market which had preceded the 1929 crash: the theory in early 1926 gave very bearish indications and of course the 3½ years which followed were the most profitable in history.

An objective appraisal of Hamilton's work was made by an economist, Alfred Cowles, III, in 1933. Cowles studied Hamilton's editorials for the 26-year period from 1904 to 1929. During this span Hamilton made 90 recommendations for a change in attitude toward the market (55% were bullish, 16% bearish and 29% doubtful). In retrospect it was found that 45 of the 90 forecasts were correct and 45 incorrect—which indicates that you might have done as well by flipping a coin. Cowles also concluded that an investor would have had a better performance from outright ownership over these 26 years than from buying and selling on Hamilton's signals.

CHARTS

In addition to the followers of the Dow theory, there are many stock market students who adhere to the use of charts to predict which way the market is going and the trend of individual issues. There are countless chart systems, but most of them attempt to correlate a relationship between market price action and the volume of trading. The idea is that it is a sign of strength when a stock advances on a large volume of shares traded; conversely, when volume in the market or on one stock enlarges as a stock declines, it shows that the pessimism is mounting and that the trend is for lower prices.

In essence the chartists contend that a study of a stock's behavior not only tells you where a stock has been but also where it is going. Say, for example, a stock has risen to $50 twice in the last few months and each time the stock has backed down from this $50 price. The second time it falls off from $50 the chartists conclude it has formed a "double top," and it is assumed that it will have a very difficult time going up through this price in the near future.

Or perhaps a chartist keeps a trend line on a stock's behavior just like you would on a company's sales trend. You might form a chart on the stock's behavior and try to judge from this just where the stock is going.

Actually chartists have scores of terms to designate price action. "Head-and-shoulders top," "dormant bottom," "scallop and saucer," "rounding top," etc. All of them assume you can predict a stock's future by charts—*with no regard whatsoever for its fundamental values.* Pure chartists couldn't care less about earnings, dividends, industry position, new products, over-all outlook. All they care about is what the charts tell them.

I can't help but think of charts and the position of the market on September 16, 1960. At that time, the market was hovering about the 600 level on the Dow Jones Industrial Average. The market had already retreated to this level three times and each time it had rallied upward—thus, the 600 level was a "triple bottom." Chartists were saying that the market would meet tremendous support at this level. Why? Because business was getting better? Certainly not! Only because the charts told them so. Now I ask you, what should be so magic about 600 on the Dow Jones average? If people were getting more pessimistic, the market would go lower regardless of "triple bottoms." It was only a matter of days until the magic number was pierced. This penetration below 600 caused many chartists to liquidate their holdings and this heavy selling forced the market lower. By October 25, the Average hit 566 and this proved to be the bottom of the decline—from which the market commenced a dramatic upsurge. In other words, the people who were frightened by the penetration of this ridiculous magic number sold out within 5% of what proved to be the market's low. The interesting thing to me is the fact that most of these chartists had no idea what the outlook was for business, earnings, inflation, political climate and all the important considerations which affect and even determine the level of the stock market. All they were concerned with was the Dow Jones Industrial Average—and they were so completely fooled by its action.

Interestingly enough, a sharp decline in just *one* of the 30 stocks comprising the average might have caused the DJIA to go below 600. I ask you—should isolated declines like this speak for the whole market? Of course *not*.

Interpretation of charts is very much of a personal affair. In a way, it's like abstract art. Take an abstract painting and show it to ten people and you'll get at least eight different interpretations of what is seen. Take one set of chart figures and show it to ten chartists and you're liable to get almost as many interpretations of which way the stock is going.

The trouble with most chart patterns is that they cause their followers to change their opinion so frequently. Most chart services change like the wind. One day they put out a strong buy signal; two weeks later, they see a change in the pattern and tell their clients to sell; then two weeks later, they tell them to buy again. The result is that these patterns force their followers in and out of the market time and time again. As I mentioned in the last chapter, this is great for brokers' commissions, but not so great for the investor.

Another disadvantage—and a great one—which exists in charting is that decisions are almost always made on the basis of the *chart alone*. Most buyers under this method have no idea *why* they are buying a company's stock. They rely alone on a stock's action, assuming that the people who have caused or are currently causing this action really know something about the company. This is generally naive thinking—simply because, as more and more chartists are attracted to a stock, there are simply more and more owners who know little or nothing about the company.

As you have no doubt gathered from this discussion, it is the way in which charts are used (I should say "mis-used") that causes my criticism. I will admit that charts *can* be helpful. They can point out to the potential investor that "accumulation" is going on in a security—that some, supposedly knowledgeable people are quietly buying stock for investment purposes. (Or that "distribution," or concentrated selling, is being done by insiders— by people who know best what is really going on.) But, upon discovering such accumulation, should one become a sheep and follow the action blindly? I say *"no!"* Never buy a stock "blind" —ignorant of the important facts I have stressed in this book. It's true that my insistence on sound reasoning may cause you to delay action and you may miss out on some winners, but you will avoid many more losers through this approach—and you will have a much better performance over the years. And you will no doubt sleep better at night—because there is nothing worse than a nervous stockholder who has no idea in the world why his stock is retreating.

Personally I have never bought a stock "blind" and I have *never* regretted it.

I should make one further, and I think important, comment about the use of charts in common stock selection. I already mentioned the major thesis regarding charts, i.e., that they can be useful in pinpointing what "insiders" or other knowledgeable people are doing with their securities. There comes a point, however, when *too many* people are utilizing charts—which is another way of saying that the chart no longer tells the tale. If, for example, a multitude of investors start basing their decisions on chart patterns, they begin to "feed" on one another. A chart may have bullish implications at the beginning, but as more and more chartists follow it, then there are simply more and more owners of the stock who really have *no* special information or reason for owning it. As stated, the buyers (or sellers, as the case may be) are merely feeding on one another and they are perpetuating the chart pattern. What invariably happens is that one day in the future the values start to tell and, when the chart suddenly changes from bullish to bearish (or vice versa), one heck of a rush for the exits commences. Then, with no chartist support existent any longer (as a matter of fact, just the opposite), a truly disastrous result can occur.

Therefore, I implore people to be especially wary of charts when they are widespread in use. The history books are filled with examples similar to that just described. Just for the record, it is my opinion that the heavy charting of 1968 will be in large part responsible for some painful losses in lower quality issues sometime in the 1969–70 period.

"BACK TO FUNDAMENTALS"

Most of the great football coaches in the U. S. have stressed fundamentals. A team which cannot block and tackle cannot be expected to win! After a disappointing loss the top coaches don't run helter-skelter looking for a magic play to beat their next week's opponent—they put their boys to work and cry, "Back to Fundamentals."

The same thing goes for buying stocks. You must be conscious of the fundamentals of potential earning power to achieve success. If you forget your "blocking and tackling" you're asking for trouble. Whenever I think of charts vs. fundamentals, I am reminded of a true story of a woman who was very much involved in charting stocks in the 1920's. She was a master at it, too, and was making a handsome living from it. As she gained confidence in herself, she started selling some of the blue chip stocks she had owned for years and put the proceeds into stocks which looked good on the charts. She had one stock in particular that had the most assuring chart pattern of any she had ever seen. The stock was Kolster Radio, which was then listed on the San Francisco Stock Exchange. Despite the fact Kolster's fundamentals were not enough to warrant it being bought, the stock was zooming upward and it was a chartist's dream. Higher and higher it went and each new high confirmed that it was destined to rise further. By the end of 1928 Kolster was 73¼ and this lady chartist was up to her earrings in the stock. By January of 1929 the trend in Kolster stock reversed itself and suddenly the bottom fell out. By May of the same year, the stock had plummeted to 25½. Then a rally followed in June, but by October it was down to around 11 and by December the same stock was $3. In January of 1930 Kolster announced it was in receivership and went through bankruptcy proceedings. The story is tragic but true and the worst part about it is that the lady had nothing left—no earning power, no dividends, no fundamentals on which she could at least hope for the future.

As you've gathered from both my earlier discussions and this illustration, I believe in buying value. This does not insure you against making an occasional mistake, but if you buy value you will not end up with stock certificates which are only useful as wallpaper. Using charts without reference to fundamentals gives you no such insurance against the wallpaper result.

PART XII

INVESTMENT TRUSTS, PRO AND CON

CHAPTER 32

Putting Your Dollars in Someone Else's Hands

About 35 years ago a number of men decided that many investors wanted *someone else* to make their investment decisions for them. To accomplish this they sold shares in an *investment trust*. The idea was simple: with the money they received they would invest in stocks and bonds and each owner of the trust would share in the profits or losses which the trust incurred.

The idea was indeed sound. The originators found that many people preferred to have experts do their thinking for them and, as a consequence, many dollars rolled in to buy these trusts.

Today investment trusts (or investment *companies* as they are more commonly called), constitute a multi-billion dollar industry. Let's look at some of the characteristics of these trusts, so that we can decide whether they're for you or not.

There are two main advantages of an investment trust, namely *professional management* and *diversification*. The first of these is obvious. The people who run the trusts and make the investment decisions are professionals; in this age of specialization, you know that a person trained in one field should do a lot better than an amateur and thus you expect the person who spends his working life studying investments to do a superior job. In addition, an investment trust does not rely solely on one person; it retains a large staff of experts and you have the advantage of the judgment of many versus the judgment of one (You!).

Diversification is an equally important advantage. When you

buy a share of an investment trust you are buying all the stocks and bonds they own and thus you have your eggs spread around rather than all in one basket. It's interesting to note that there have been about 1,500 automobile manufacturers in the U. S. since 1920—and now there are only 4. If you had all your eggs in any one of the 1,496 which failed to survive, you'd have gone down the drain with them.

Investment trusts are *convenient* to own, too. If you had your own portfolio of 20 or 30 stocks, you'd be deluged with dividend checks from all the companies you owned. In a trust, which may own 50 or more different securities, you receive one check only every three months (they lump all their dividends and interest received together for you).

A few other advantages also exist. First of all, a trust is constantly supervising its investments, whereas you as an individual owner might not have the time or inclination to do this religiously. Secondly, trust management is more flexible than the average individual. They are more inclined to take profits on occasions, whereas individuals often "fall in love" with their stocks and lose their objectivity in appraising them. Thirdly, trust shares are not as volatile—they do not move up and down as wildly—as most individual stocks do. The advantage of this is that their owners are not prone to panic in a declining market, as the trust shares will usually decline rather gradually. Of course this lack of volatility is a two-headed coin. It also means that trust shares may not rise very fast in a good market. Many trusts are so widely diversified that they end up with only mediocre performance; a trust with 50 stocks, for example, may see only 25 go up, 10 go down and 15 remain the same even in a strong day in the stock market.

Now for the *dis*advantages. Aside from the criticism of mediocre performance, which you may or may not be able to make, depending on the specific trust, the *major drawbacks of investment trusts involve their costs of ownership*. All trusts charge a *management fee* which generally runs around ½ of 1% of the trust assets per year. Now ½ of 1% doesn't sound like much, but this management fee is charged against the income received by the trust (the dividends and interest earned on the stocks and bonds held) and this reduces the ordinary income paid to shareholders to the point where *trusts generally pay lower yields than can be obtained from owning individual stocks outright.*

The most valid and glaring criticism of the trusts involves the large sales commission charged to buy them, but this criticism has to be confined to one type of investment trust—the "open-end trust," more commonly known as the "mutual fund." I'll discuss this in a minute, when I talk about the mutuals separately.

Another drawback of the trusts involves their size. Most trusts (especially the mutual funds, which continue to grow in size) accumulate large blocks of stocks. When these stocks are going *up* in price, the trusts have no problem in disposing of them, if they seek to do so. But what happens if the market is tumbling or if a company's business turns sour and its stock is being actively sold by the public? How can a trust with 400,000 or 500,000 or more shares get rid of them without driving the price down unmercifully? This is a problem which was encountered in 1929. While we can't compare anything to 1929, the principle remains and this is one hidden, little-publicized risk which could exist in a large trust.

Aside from the advantages and disadvantages, there are just two more facts you should know about investment trusts. The first involves a special kind of dividend usually distributed once a year—a *capital gain dividend*. This distribution comes from profits the trust takes during the year. Suppose, for example, your trust bought IBM a number of years ago and this year sells off some of the stock for a large gain. These profits are lumped together with others taken during the year and are paid out to you. Like any other capital gain, you will only have to pay tax on half the profit, with a maximum rate of 25%. These capital gain dividends are bound to fluctuate, depending on how good the market is each year. They can be sizable and they can be nothing. Some investors get very excited about the high yield they receive when they add their regular investment income (the ordinary dividends from the trust) and the capital gain income together. Say you get a 3% yield from the regular dividends and then you get a capital gain dividend which, when related to the market price of the trust, amounts to another 5% yield. Total yield for the year looks like 8%. The Securities and Exchange Commission wisely prohibits security salesmen from combining these yields and quoting prospective customers on this combined basis—because of the variable nature of the capital gain distribution, and because this payout may be termed simply a return of your own capital —and thus not "true yield."

A second question should also be answered for you, namely: "How does one judge management's performance in an investment trust?" In an individual company you judge performance by the company's earnings record. *In an investment trust, you judge performance by its growth in net asset value per share.*

Don't worry, you don't have to figure this net asset value; the trusts figure it for you and usually compute it once or twice a day. What they do is add together the market values of all the securities held and divide this by the number of trust shares outstanding. This net asset value per share tells you how much each share would be worth if the trust were to liquidate completely. If management does a good job and buys stocks which go up in price then the net asset value per share will go up. By noting the trend in net asset value per share (plus the capital gain dividends they pay out) you can judge management's performance. Incidentally, some investment services summarize the performance records of the trusts for you. The best known of these is the Wiesenberger service.

Time now to distinguish between the two basic types of investment trusts—the closed-end and the open-end.

CLOSED-END INVESTMENT TRUSTS

These are called "closed-end" because the *number of shares of the trust outstanding is limited.* Let's say a new closed-end trust is brought to market today. One million shares are to be sold at $10 per share. This one million shares is the total amount the trust is planning to issue. A year from today you want to buy shares in this trust. It may be listed on one of the exchanges or it may be traded over-the-counter. Its price will depend on its net asset value per share at that time, but it may sell a little above this value (at a premium) or a little below it (at a discount). Whether the trust shares are selling at a premium or at a discount will depend strictly on what people think of management; in other words, like other stocks, it will sell at a price determined by supply and demand.

The same thing applies if and when you want to sell the trust stock. You have to depend on the market to sell your holding—you cannot require the trust to redeem the shares for you (as you will see, a stockholder in an open-end trust does redeem his shares with the trust).

Closed-end trusts may differ in their philosophy and/or approach from open-end trusts. Closed-end trusts often can leverage themselves—they can borrow money to buy stocks. Likewise, they may or may not be limited in what kind of investments they can make (some are permitted to own large interests in companies which have no public market for their stock).

Two prominent examples of closed-end trusts are Lehman Corporation and Madison Fund, both listed on the New York Stock exchange, and Standard Shares, which is listed on the American exchange.

OPEN-END TRUSTS—MUTUAL FUNDS

The number and size of mutual funds in this country has grown like Topsy. In 1950, for example, investors had $2½ billion invested in the funds; by 1961 this figure exceeded $20 billion and this had skyrocketed to over $52 billion by 1968. This mushrooming can be attributed to a growing awareness on the part of the public to get their dollars to work, to a rising stock market, to some spectacular performances of growth investing and to some imaginative and aggressive sales efforts. This brings us to the *major disadvantage of the mutual fund—the high selling commission involved*. Whereas the commission you pay to buy a stock on the New York Stock exchange might be 1–2%, most mutuals have a "sales load" ranging from 6–8¾%. A person can buy $1,000 worth of a stock on the exchange for a commission of $15.00 (you could buy a closed-end trust for this amount, too), while a similar purchase of a mutual fund would cost you $60–$87.50. You can see why security salesmen eagerly seek mutual fund purchases.

There are a few redeeming factors to consider, though. Of real importance is the fact that the sales load on a mutual fund takes care of your cost for *both buying and selling*. In other words, you pay the 6–8¾% commission when you buy, but you *pay no commission* (or, in some cases, only ½ of 1%) *if and when you sell the fund*. This is, of course, *not* true in the commission you pay to buy and sell an individual security on the exchange. You pay your 1–2% when you buy and another 1–2% when you sell. To be completely objective then, you should cut the mutual sales load in half to 3–4⅜% in comparing it with other investments. Therefore, on average you pay 2 to 3 times as much to buy the mutual fund and there is no question but that this is quite a premium to pay. And, if you are the type of investor who almost never sells a stock (one who "buys and dies" with an issue), then you are probably paying about five times as much to purchase the mutual fund as opposed to buying a security on the stock exchange.

Commission rates on funds, however, do drop sharply as the amount of purchase increases. Whereas the sales load might be 8½% on purchases up to $25,000, the rate might be about 7% over $25,000, 5% over $50,000—and gradually working down to 1% on purchases over $500,000.

A minor consideration is that you pay no odd lot fee when you buy a mutual fund, whereas if you buy or sell less than 100 shares of a stock on the exchange you will have to pay the ⅛ and ¼ point differentials (Chapter 4).

In the financial section of your newspaper you will see a long list of prices quoted on mutual funds. These prices show like those of the over-the-counter (unlisted) stocks—with a bid and an ask price shown. Here is a typical quotation as it might appear in the paper:

	Bid	Ask
XYZ Mutual Fund	$10.00	$10.75

In all cases the bid price represents the net asset value per share of the fund. The ask price is merely the *net asset value plus the sales load*. In this case, the sales load is 7½%, or 75 cents, on a $10.00 net asset value for a total of $10.75. You buy mutual fund shares at the ask price and, if and when you sell, you do so at the bid price.

You can see that it's going to take time for you to break even after your purchase. It may be a year or so before XYZ net asset value rises to $10.75 per share—where you can get out without any loss. Thus, *mutual funds should only be bought by long term investors*. If you're investing money you think you might need in a year or two or even three, don't put the money into the funds.

Before I give you some other conclusions, and my opinion of mutuals, let me point out a few more characteristics. You remember in the discussion of closed-end trusts I said that the latter has a limited number of shares outstanding and that a buyer or seller has to contend with market conditions of supply and demand. This is *not* the case in open-end trusts. They are called open-end because they have no limit as to the number of shares they will sell. Mutual funds want to sell as many shares as possible and they stand ready to do so at the asset value plus sales commission. By the same token, mutuals must stand by to redeem their shares in cash at the asset value in unlimited amounts. Here you have a little protection. Even if the market goes down sharply you know you can get the asset value as it stands on the day you redeem; in a closed-end trust a sharply declining market might take the stock to a substantial discount from its asset value and you might have to settle for this if you want out.

You might be thinking now—"Suppose a large number of mutual fund stockholders decided to redeem all at once. The mutual might have to sell a lot of stocks very suddenly to get the cash for redemption and these forced sales would tend to lower the asset value very sharply. Or perhaps the mutual wouldn't be able to raise the cash right away." This is a legitimate thought. Fortunately, redemptions over the post World War II period have been negligible, even in depressed markets. But the risk, although not probable, does exist.

TYPES OF MUTUAL FUNDS

There are many types of mutual funds. Some seek very aggressive capital gains and invest in growth stocks and some of the smaller companies which, while more speculative, could become the "Polaroids of tomorrow." Dreyfus, Diversified Growth, Enterprise, Fidelity Capital, Putnam Growth are representative of these. Some funds have growth as their major objective, but take a more conservative approach—they concentrate mainly in already-proven companies. Typical of these are Investment Company of America, Massachusetts Investors Trust, Affiliated, etc. Then you have the very conservative funds, whose major objective is to provide good income and very gradual gains over the years; these are usually "balanced funds," which means that they own a large amount of bonds and preferred stocks in addition to their somewhat conservative common stocks. Eaton and Howard Balanced Fund, Boston Fund and Wellington are good examples.

In addition, there are certain funds which concentrate in one or two industry groups, such as Chemical Fund. If you are enthusiastic about one segment of our economy but have a hard time making a choice of one stock in the group you can solve your problem by purchasing an industry fund.

HOW HAVE THE FUNDS PERFORMED?

The test of theory is in performance. There were countless inventors who knew the theory behind flying before the Wright brothers. The latter were heroes because their airplane performed and didn't do a dipsy-doo and end up in a heap.

The same thing goes for mutual funds. The theory behind professional management, diversification, constant supervision, flexibility, etc. is fine, but has it proved itself or has it ended up "in a heap?" The answer cannot be generalized because of the many funds doing business; some have been quite successful and others unsuccessful. Just like choosing individual stocks, you have to analyze the performance of the individual funds to determine whether they're worth considering.

Let's see, however, how an average of the funds have performed over the past ten years. Using the Wiesenberger compilation of mutual fund management results, which incidentally allows for both dividends and capital gain distributions made to shareholders but which does *not* account for the sales charge made at the initial time of purchase, here is how a $1,000 investment would have grown from January 1, 1959 to December 31, 1968. I will present four broad categories of funds, as follows: 1) the large growth funds; 2) the smaller growth funds which have generally high volatility; 3) the middle-of-the-road "growth and income" trusts; and 4) the very conservative balanced funds, which hold decent amounts of fixed income securities along with common stocks. Repeating the fact that the sales load has not been deducted and thus that the figures should be somewhat *lower*, here is how the mythical $1,000 would have looked after its ten-year life:

Categories:	(1)	(2)	(3)	(4)
	$3,399	$3,707	$2,398	$2,106

Certainly this is acceptable, if not exceptional, performance— especially in the funds which are devoted to capital growth (the balanced fund's objective is more for income and just enough appreciation to keep ahead of inflation). I would guess that most investors would have been satisfied to have seen their 1959 dollars up 3 to 4 times their initial investment.

Of course, the past ten years have been excellent ones for the stock market in general. It is questionable whether the next ten will be as good, but the idea is to buy fund management which will outperform the market.

You might—or might not—have outperformed the statistics I've shown above by buying certain individual stocks. If you had put your money in certain big winners, you probably would have had far better success in much less time. But would you have been smart enough to buy these "stars"? And, just as important, would you have been smart enough to stay with them, or would you have sold out for small gains?

All of this brings us to my conclusions about mutual funds.

CONCLUSIONS ON FUNDS

People occasionally ask me whether I put any of my own money into the mutual funds. I have not. Nor will I. I guess it would be an admission of defeat if I did. My training and my experience are all pointed to helping people make money and I would be a poor broker if I thought that somebody else could do a better job than I can. But the average investor does not have a great deal of time to study his investments; or he doesn't have enough money to afford some diversification of stocks; or he doesn't have a broker who can guide him correctly; or he doesn't have a broker who has his (the investor's) best interests at heart.

If you are in one of these categories, then you should consider investment trusts. Naturally, you should concentrate on superior management—to offset the aforementioned sales costs—but the right kind of "stewardship" can mean a lot to you and can overcome the costs fairly fast under the right conditions.

Actually, the mutual funds are ideal for periodic investment programs (i.e., monthly investment plan), but I will discuss this in detail later in Chapter 34.

PART XIII

SOME SPECIFIC HELP
IN PLANNING
FOR THE FUTURE

CHAPTER 33

The Four W's

All newspaper writers are taught to emphasize certain facts in the first paragraph of a story. For one thing, they are taught to answer at least the "Four W's" of:

WHO (is involved in the story)?
WHAT (was the action which took place)?
WHERE (did the action occur)?
and
WHEN (did it happen)?

In the field of investments we have our own Four W's. Just as a journalist has to ask his basic W's to make an article complete and successful, an investment adviser has to answer these:

WHO should invest in the stock market?
WHEN is a person ready to make the plunge?
WHAT is the investor's objective?
and
WHERE should the money be invested?

Let's look at the W's one by one:

WHO SHOULD INVEST IN THE STOCK MARKET?

I'd be a poor stock broker if I didn't tell you that there's room for *every* investor in the stock market. After all, there are as many types of stocks as there are types of investors, ranging from the most conservative to the most speculative.

Even though the market has a potential for everyone, there

294

remains an important question of just *when* a person is ready to make the plunge. Therefore we have to tie in the next W of *when* in deciding just *who* is suited for stocks.

WHEN ARE YOU READY TO INVEST?

A good investment adviser should be able to tell you when you are ready to buy stocks. It goes without saying that you should have all your necessities and a lot of the luxuries you desire before you think of investing. After all, our basic purpose is to live and enjoy life and we should be doing this before we start thinking of fortune-building.

Please don't forget two necessities which you should certainly have before investing. First of all, be sure you have adequate *health insurance* for you and your family. If you've spent a few days in a hospital of late, you'll know the tremendous costs involved. I'm especially strong on so-called "catastrophe" health insurance, where you protect yourself against the big expenses. Most families can afford the bills which run up to a *few hundred* dollars, but it is the *few thousand* dollar expenses that can create insurmountable problems. If a person has normal health insurance *plus* the protection against catastrophe, he can relax more with his investments and this is important.

A second necessity involves *life insurance*. Some people call life insurance "death insurance" and that's really a more apropos title. Life insurance is best bought for what it can do for your heirs *after* you're dead. But since we're all certain to die someday, "death insurance" is a basic part of our future planning.

I've been asked many times, "How much life insurance should I carry?" There is no one answer to this question. If you knew you were going to die tomorrow you'd put all your dollars into life insurance and not one penny into stocks, real estate and other investments. On the other hand, if you knew you were certain to live to be 80, you'd put all your money into investments and not a penny into insurance. Some insurance salesmen present the very pleasant assumption that you could be snuffed out tomorrow and that you should carry $200,000 or $300,000 worth of insurance to provide an adequate income for your family. To carry these amounts would of course cost you a small fortune in annual premiums and you'd be "insurance poor." As they say—life insurance is a plan which keeps you poor all your life so you can die rich.

Like many other things in life, you are probably better off striking a happy medium in your life insurance buying. Have a program whereby you increase your coverage as time goes by and as you can better afford the premiums. Life is somewhat of a gamble throughout and you have to gamble that you will enjoy some years of good health ahead and that you can buy insurance progressively over the years.

Let me repeat the fact that *no one* should think of investing in the market or real estate until he has adequate health and life insurance. In addition almost every family should have a cash reserve—an emergency fund—before investing. Most home economists say you should set aside at least three months' salary into a savings account and never touch it. I heartily agree.

All of the above means different things to different people. For example, if you're a bachelor or a career girl, you have little use for life insurance. Or if you know you're going to inherit a lot of money in ten or twenty years you should protect yourself for now (through cheap term life insurance) instead of for the distant future. Or if your business will carry on regardless of your state of health you will require less life insurance and less of an emergency fund than the next fellow.

WHAT IS YOUR OBJECTIVE IN INVESTING?

People invest their money for different reasons. Some want to get a higher return than from bank interest so that they can live better. Some want to see their money grow so that they can drive Cadillacs instead of Chevrolets. And some (a large percentage) are investing for the future. They are looking ahead to retirement and want to have security and comfort in their later years. In Chapter 34 I'll show you in black and white how to plan for the future, but for the sake of this discussion, it's important for your investment adviser to know what your objectives are.

Actually there are two basic questions you should ask yourself and answer honestly. Then make sure your adviser knows the answers, too:

1. *How important is current income to you?*

Some people get a fixation about receiving a certain yield on their money and yet they never spend or use this income. As we've already seen, some of the most successful stock investments have been the growth companies, which pay a low yield.

On the other hand, you may need additional income to live and higher dividends may be of great importance to you.

Determine under which category you qualify and let your broker (or counselor) know whether high dividends are necessary.

2. *How many years ahead are you looking for the major benefits of your investments?*

If you're looking 10 or 20 years ahead you can buy the growth companies. If, instead, you're already 70 years old, you're interested in today and you should buy stocks which give you safety, security and income now.

WHERE SHOULD YOUR MONEY BE INVESTED?

Now we're ready to pull the trigger! You've satisfied yourself that you have adequate health and life insurance and an emergency fund; you've set your investment objectives and determined how important current income is to you and how far in the future you are looking for the real fruits of your investments. Now to specifics:

Where should you put your money? Here again there are a few questions you should ask yourself and you should relate the answers to the person who's helping you with your stock decisions.

1. *When will you be investing again?*

If the capital you now have is all you expect to invest for quite a while, you're safer to stagger your purchases over a period of time—perhaps a few years. If, instead, you plan to invest sums consistently over the years then you don't have to worry about automatically spacing your investments.

2. *What is your personal temperament?*

Your investments are beamed to making you money, but it is extremely important that they also make you happy. Some people are poor gamblers by nature. They can't "take" losses—they upset them greatly. It goes without saying that people who fall into this category should avoid gambling stocks, or stocks which fluctuate wildly in the market. By the same token, aggressive investors who are looking for quick gains are not generally going to be happy with Consolidated Edison or American Snuff.

I recall a client of my firm who owned conservative stocks, but who decided she wanted more growth. She had become unhappy with her stable holdings and decided to put her next investment dollars into a growth stock. She did—and she bought a good one. A few days after she purchased her growth stock it had risen from 64 to 71. We didn't hear from her. Then one day the stock dropped sharply from 71 back to 68½—a loss of 2½ points. That day the phone did ring. She was concerned over the drop, even though she still had a 4½ point profit after only owning the stock 10 days. This went on for a few days more—till we finally advised her to sell the stock—on the basis that it was making her unhappy. She simply wasn't temperamentally equipped to buy volatile stocks (even though she could afford losses) and the wide price movements were disturbing her. Living with a stock that bothers you is like living with a mate who makes you unhappy. So it's best to analyze a stock's "personality" before you "marry" it.

In conclusion, decide how much risk you are willing to take when investing. I usually put it this way: "Decide whether you want to *sleep well* or *eat well*." The "sleep well" stocks should never hurt you; they will provide you—not with spectacular gains, but with peace of mind. Your "eat well" stocks are intended to put steak and caviar on the table. So take this advice—

> *Don't try for steak*
> *If it keeps you awake.*

Or

> *Caviar's indeed a delicate dish,*
> *But the worrisome type should settle for fish.*

CHAPTER 34

Stocks for People

I don't mean to imply by this title that there are stocks for animals as well as for human beings. But there have been certain stocks which have consistently met the different objectives of investors over the years. Every investment adviser has his own favorites. I have compiled a list of stocks which have proved rewarding for my clients in the past and *which I believe will continue to do the job for them in the future.*

In presenting these securities I have separated them according to the individual's status in life. Determine under which category you fall and concentrate on these comments. I hope they will be helpful to you in shaping your investment decisions now and over the years (remember, of course, that we are living in a changing society and in a changing stock market and that these stocks have to be re-assessed according to outlook and according to market price at the time of your reading).

Just one comment before starting. You will notice that I make reference in each case to the amount of fixed income securities (bonds and preferred stocks) which appear suitable in each port-folio. In our business we call this apportionment of fixed income securities the amount of *balance* we wish to achieve. The more conservative the investor's objectives are the more balance we strive for. A widow, for example, might have 50% of her money in fixed income securities (the other 50% in common stocks) and we would say she has a 50–50 balance. On the other hand, a young professional man, who has no need for immediate income and is looking 20 or 30 years away for the benefits of his invest-ment program, might have *no* bonds or preferred stocks—and have *no balance* in his portfolio. *Balance refers solely to how the capital is divided between fixed income securities and common stocks.*

We've talked about not having all your eggs in one stock; it is safer to have them spread around into different stocks. When we talk about *diversification* we *are* talking about *how the common stocks are divided.* A certain percentage of the common stock portion of a portfolio might go into chemical stocks, a certain percentage into electrical equipment, foods, oils, utilities, etc. This is diversification by industries. In addition, an investor will generally have some geographical diversification; in a large portfolio, for example, it is wise to have utility stocks from a few geographical locations.

While we're on the subject, let me warn you against *over*-diversification. This is a common ill among investors. Too often I've seen a person with $20,000 or $30,000 with a list of stocks as long as your arm. Many people think it is safer to keep diversifying and adding new companies to their portfolio. This is untrue and can actually lead to dangerous consequences, because:

1. There are only so many companies which are truly deserving of investment and too often a person ends up lowering his standards to achieve diversification.
2. A long list of stocks is difficult to supervise. It's hard enough to keep current with ten or fifteen stocks, much less to have to keep up with 20 or 30 or more.
3. It's a nuisance to receive small dividend checks from a multitude of companies.
4. Your brokerage commissions to buy many securities are more than concentrating in a lesser number.
5. You'll no doubt end up with very mediocre performance with too long a list. Even on a strong day in the market, you might see, say, 20 stocks go up, 10 go down and 10 remain unchanged.
6. Too much diversification can lead to laziness. When you're concentrating on fewer issues, you really take the time to analyze correctly. There's usually a slightly different attitude

when you're choosing ten stocks instead of three. In the case of ten, you know both consciously and subconsciously that you can afford a mistake or two; in the case of three, you know you can't chance this and you take greater pains to reach the decision.

The most successful portfolios have been those which have concentrated to a degree, rather than to "buy the board" and own everything. If you really want complete diversification, perhaps you're better off putting your money into someone else's hands—into an investment trust.

Now—on to stocks for people:

STOCKS FOR THE ULTRA-CONSERVATIVE (WIDOWS, ETC.)

Like all the categories to be covered, much will depend on just how much *current* income is needed. Fixed income securities might account for as much as 50% of the list; 50% is terribly conservative, however, and most advisers will put between 25–40% in bonds and place the remaining 60–75% in conservative common stocks such as the following:

Utilities (might represent 25% of the *common stock* portion), including American Telephone and Telegraph, Boston Edison, Consumers Power, Southern California Edison, etc.
Paper, with Crown Zellerbach.
Foods, such as National Biscuit.
Proprietary Drugs, such as Sterling Drug.
Food Chains, such as Safeway.
Building, with Otis Elevator.
Banking, such as Chase Manhattan, Chemical Bank, Wells Fargo.
Finance—Beneficial.
Tobacco, like American Tobacco.
Oil, such as Standard Oil of New Jersey.
Retail Trade, like J. C. Penney.
Also, a moderate amount in solid, high yielding industrial companies such as General Motors.

MIDDLE-OF-THE-ROAD OBJECTIVES OF GRADUAL GROWTH WITH GOOD SAFETY (SALARIED WORKER, CAREER WOMAN LOOKING TO RETIREMENT)

Here's the person who really has enough money to live on, but wants a moderate current income to supplement his or her needs —and who needs a feeling of security while planning for the future. If he or she won't retire for 10 or 20 years, then I suggest little if any balance. Instead, I would choose the following common stocks:

Utilities (perhaps 15–25% of the common stocks), including American Telephone, Commonwealth Edison, Pacific Gas and Electric, Middle South Utilities.

Foods, such as General Foods.

Household Items, such as Procter and Gamble, Gillette.

Proprietary Drugs, such as Bristol-Myers.

Services, like Dun & Bradstreet, American Express, Marsh & McLennan.

Ethical Drugs, such as Pfizer.

Oil, like Texaco.

Electrical Equipment, such as General Electric.

Insurance—CNA Financial.

Chemicals and Photography, such as Eastman Kodak, du Pont.

Forest Products, like Weyerhaeuser.

Banking, including Chemical Bank, Wells Fargo.

AGGRESSIVE GROWTH (BUSINESSMAN, PROFESSIONAL MAN)

Here are the people who are investing to build up capital. They have ample income and, as a matter of fact, would prefer not to add any more direct income; instead, they want capital gains. They want their money in common stocks and are not attracted by fixed income securities. First of all, these people should build up a foundation of growth stocks, such as:

Forest Products: Boise Cascade, Weyerhaeuser.

Growth Utilities, like Sierra Pacific Power.

Office Equipment: IBM, Xerox.

Services, such as American Express, Marsh & McLennan.
Drugs, like Bristol-Myers, Johnson & Johnson, Merck.
Electronics, with Hewlett-Packard, Tektronix.
Photography, such as Eastman and Polaroid.
Other established growth companies like MMM.

In addition, these aggressive growth investors can afford some speculations—companies which are in their early stages, but which stand a chance to be the big winners of tomorrow (like the "bikini" stocks discussed in Chapter 36).

HOW ABOUT THE KIDDIES?

Before we leave the subject of how to invest for different people, let's pause to consider what to do for our children, grandchildren, nephews, etc. Anyone making a gift to a child or having the decision of investing a child's money has good intentions, yet this is perhaps the least understood area of investment. Many grave errors have been made here.

Think, for example, of all the dollars which have flowed into annuities for children. Take little Junior, age three months. You don't want him to get his little mitts on any substantial money for 18 or 21 years, lest he squander it on a souped-up racing car with mink cushions. You want the money to grow so that it will pay for college or for furniture when he marries. Putting money into an annuity is like putting the money in the bank at 2½% or 3% interest. You wouldn't consider that a good investment, I'm sure, and thus I subscribe to the belief that money for children should be placed into stocks.

But which stocks? Amazingly, the first reaction of most parents is to put the money into the safest stock they can think of—with little regard for growth. My contention is that you should look instead to the solid growth companies. After all, even if the child is ten years of age, you are looking about ten years ahead and you want growth over this period. A child is an ideal growth investor, because he has time and because he doesn't watch the ups and downs of the market. If you believe in the growth of our country, then you must believe that a ten-year investment in a solid company in a good industry will achieve excellent results for your child. For this reason, I suggest you consult the stocks of either the middle-of-the-road or aggressive growth investor and put them in the safe deposit box for Junior.

CHAPTER 35

How to Reach That Pot of Gold

There are very few of us who don't dream a little. Our dreams of course take different patterns. Some of us still see ourselves scoring the winning touchdown for dear Peduka Sub Normal; others of us picture relaxing by the ole fishing hole with not a care in the world; and still others dream of building mansions and owning yachts, etc. Aside from scoring the touchdown— which is impossible to do at the age of 40 anyway—most of our personal dreams have one thing in common: *they all take money.*

Please don't misunderstand me. I know that money can't buy happiness and that there are countless joys and dreams which are void of materialism. Yet the fact remains that it takes capital to live and it takes capital to retire later in life. Regardless of what you want for yourself now, it is important to build yourself a pot of gold at the end of your working years so that you can enjoy retirement. This involves *planning for the future* and I hope to be able to help you do this.

"Planning for the future," I had a man growl to me, "is frustrating. You work and work and save your money all your life so that when you're old you can have the things *that only the young can enjoy.*" He had a good point, but it doesn't rule out the necessity for looking ahead and determining just what you will need when you do retire.

Ask yourself how much *income you will need* when you stop working. Then look at how you will get this income. More times than not, people find that they haven't provided enough for themselves. And more times than not, they find out *too late* that they're short on capital.

Pick a monthly income figure out of the air. Assume you and your wife will need a minimum of $400.00 per month to retire 20 years from now and live the way you want. But will $400.00 per month in 1989 buy you what $400.00 per month will buy you today? Not if inflation continues. Thus, you'd better account for inflation in your figuring. There's no way of estimating what the increasing cost of living might be over 20 years. From 1958–1966 it was a little under 1½ % per year; since then it has been on the upswing and the present rate is a frightening 3½–4%. Disinflationary measures are being administered, however, so let's hope for a return to at least 2–3%—but let's be conservative and count on the high part of this range. Three percent a year over 20 years is 60% and thus we should add on 60% of $400, or $240, to bring our monthly living expenses (requirements) to $640 for 1989.

Now that we've decided how much you'll need, we'd better see *where the money's going to come from.* Most of us are entitled to Social Security and this might provide about $240 per month —which will no doubt be raised as time goes by. Let's assume that it is raised to about $300 per month by 1989. Actually, it will probably be much higher by then—but then the $400 "requirement" we started with is no doubt too low to begin with.

Next we should figure any other income you will be receiving at that time. Let's assume you will receive a pension from your company of about $150 per month when you retire.

Here's the way you stand right now:

In 1989, you will get:	$300 from Social Security
	150 from Pension
	———————————————
	$450 Total
In 1989, you will need:	$640
You are lacking:	$190 (let's round it out to $200)

You have to count on some form of investments to bring you that extra $200 per month in 1989. The logical question which follows is:

How much capital will you need in 1989 to give you an income of $200 per month, or $2,400 per year?

This is hard to answer because we don't know what kind of return we can count on from stocks or real estate 20 years from now. But assuming an average return of 5% on your money, you will need $48,000 in stocks and bonds to give you this $2,400 per year (5% of $48,000 = $2,400). Or you can turn over about $33,000 in cash to a life insurance company and they'll guarantee to pay you $2,400 a year for the rest of your life (in this case, you will have no capital to leave to your heirs, however—the $33,000 is no longer yours). Or you might find a piece of property which will net you 8% on your money and you'll need $30,000 (8% of $30,000 = $2,400).

Thus, depending on how you want to do it, you will need between $30,000 and $48,000 in 1989 to bring your income up to what you want. Let's split this around the middle and say that you need about $40,000 to live in the style to which you're accustomed 20 years from now.

Now the big question. How are you going to accumulate $40,000 in the next 20 years? The answer: through *saving*. Now don't run away. I, too, know that the number of people who are able to save $40,000 during their lives is but a very small minority. But I also know that the reason that so few are able to is *because they don't start early enough.*

You know that money compounds as it sits collecting a return. Take a hundred dollars and invest it at 6%; the first year your $100 will grow to $106; the next year the $106 will grow to $112.36. By the 12th year the $100 will be $201.22—it will have doubled. Thus, the secret to accumulating capital is to start early and let your money compound itself.

Even though I know the figures, I never cease to be amazed at *how little a person has to save every year to accumulate a huge amount of money later in life.* To illustrate the point, here's a table which shows you *how much money you have to save each year to end up with $10,000 in 15, 20, 25, 30, 35 and 40 years.*

The 4% column could represent money put in a bank savings account; the 6% column could represent return from corporate bonds; and the 8% column should be achieved by putting your dollars into stocks. Naturally it's hard to generalize and predict just what rate of return (including both dividends and capital

Number of Years To Save	Yearly Saving Which Will Produce $10,000— If Money Is Invested at a Compounding Rate of Return of		
	4%	6%	8%
40 Years	$105	$65	$40
35 Years	135	90	60
30 Years	180	133	90
25 Years	240	182	135
20 Years	335	272	220
15 Years	500	430	370

gains) you will get in stocks, but I think 8% is pretty conservative over a long period of time. As a matter of fact, we saw in our discussion of investment trusts how $1,000 in a normal growth trust in 1959 grew to about $3,000 in 1968. Going from $1,000 to $3,000 in 10 years amounts to a compound return of about 11½% per year. Thus, I don't think I'm being unreasonable to expect a return of 8% in the future from stocks; it's apparent that I'm being conservative.

Now let's go back to your problem of amassing $40,000 in 20 years. Here (from the table) is how much you'll have to invest to accumulate *$10,000* in 20 years:

At 4%—$335 per year
At 6%—$272 per year
At 8%—$220 per year

Since we need $40,000, we have to multiply these figures by 4, as follows:

At 4%—$1,340
At 6%—$1,088
At 8%—$ 880

As you can see, even if you take the most conservative course and just put your money in the bank, you will have to save $112 *per month* ($1,344 per year) to amass $40,000 in 20 years.

If stocks perform at the 8% rate, *you will only have to put aside $73 per month ($876 per year) to achieve your pot of gold.* Chances are you can save at least a portion of this amount and can count on a pretty good hunk of investment capital in 1989. The main thing is *to get started* and let the snowball grow for you as time goes by.

If you're fortunate enough to have 40 productive, saving years ahead of you, your pot of gold should be a cinch to reach. The table shows that you need set aside only $40 *per year* to accumulate $10,000 over 40 years at the 8% rate of return. To amass $40,000, you will need 4 times as much, or $160 per year ($13.30 per month). I ask you—how many people cannot afford to do this? Very few!

The idea of investing money regularly in stocks has been widely publicized by both the New York Stock Exchange and by the many mutual funds. The idea is of course simple. You send in your money periodically just as you would deposit money in a Christmas Club savings account in your local bank. Investing small amounts is "painless;" just as in Christmas Club saving, people don't miss the small amounts they invest. As I explained before, these small amounts can grow to large proportions over the years.

Whereas many people used to consider that stocks were only for the very rich, the Exchange and the mutual funds have made a strong play for the small investor in recent years. The Exchange has the monthly investment plan (monthly is really a misnomer because the investor can invest every two months, every quarter, or however often he chooses). The procedure is simple. The investor chooses a stock and indicates on a form how much he intends to invest and how often in this issue. An Exchange member firm signs the form and from then on out the investor sends his check directly to the Exchange in the amount of his choice. He has the option to receive his dividends in cash or to have them re-invested in the same stock. The money is invested in both full and fractional shares (out to four decimal places) and the shares are held for him by the Exchange in New York. He can get his stock certificates anytime he wishes—they are held in escrow for him for convenience sake.

The mutual funds have similar plans, which they usually call "periodic" or "cumulative" investment plans (rather than "monthly investment plan"). The fund plans operate just as the Exchange, except in most cases the funds require slightly more capital to be invested. For example, many funds require that at least $300 per year be invested in order to keep the plan going and some require that an initial investment of $250 or $500 be made to start the program. The fund plans do not give the investor the option of taking dividends out or having them reinvested—they are automatically reinvested (regular dividends at the fund's price with commission, capital gain dividends at net asset value, without commission).

I mentioned in Chapter 32 that I heartily recommend the fund periodic investment programs. I do, because they are generally cheaper to buy than by participating in the Exchange's monthly investment plan. Investing up to $100 at one time on the exchange costs 6% commission; $200 at one time costs 3%—and these are all "one-way" commissions (you have to pay another commission if and when you sell the stock). In contrast, you pay commission generally only when you buy a fund and thus the 8½% commission covers both buying and selling. *Unless you are investing over $200 at one time it is as cheap or cheaper to buy the funds than it is to buy a stock on the New York Stock Exchange.* If you are investing less than $200 you might as well avail yourself of both the lower cost and of the professional management provided by the fund—and this is where I believe the funds are most useful. They are really ideal for a long term periodic savings program and I strongly recommend them to anyone wanting to build a pot of gold.

"DOLLAR AVERAGING"

There are many advantages to periodic investment programs. When you buy a stock at different intervals over a period of years, you will of course buy some at very low prices, some at high levels and some in-between. When you buy on a consistent basis, you are not trying to outguess the market—you are only trying to establish a reasonable average cost for yourself. As a matter of fact, a person engaged in systematic investing *actually benefits from declining prices* along the way. Say, for example, you have decided to invest $100 per month in a stock or an investment trust which sells at $10.00 per share. The first month your $100 buys you 10 shares. By the next month the stock has declined to $9.00, but is this drop cause to shed tears? Absolutely not. Just the opposite. Why? Because now your $100 buys you $1\frac{1}{10}$ shares of the same stock. You are getting more shares for the same amount of money. If the stock eventually sinks to $5.00, your $100 will buy you 20 shares. Now you are getting even more for your money. This is great—*provided of course that the stock eventually recovers and goes way up in price*. In other words, the problem of *timing is eliminated*—the only problem is selection of the right stock.

Many large investors, such as insurance companies, colleges, etc., adhere to investing fixed amounts on a periodic program. In essence, they are saying, "We believe in the future of this company. We want to own the stock and, rather than try to pick out the low points (and maybe never get them) we aim for a reasonable average cost." They practice what we call "dollar averaging" and this is a wise policy for individuals, as well as institutions. Dollar averaging forces you to buy your stock or stocks just when you might hesitate to do so—when the outlook for the market is gloomy and stock prices are low. Needless to say, this is just the time you should be buying.

PART XIV

AN EXPLOSIVE AREA
FOR PROFITS

CHAPTER 36

"Bikini" Stocks

Bikini bathing suits have become the rage of the beaches throughout the world in recent years. Naturally there's only one reason for their popularity, namely that these small suits provide the male population with maximum exposure to feminine pulchritude. The more curvaceous a woman is the more she benefits from the small bathing suit.

It stands to reason that common stocks which provide maximum exposure to pleasant things will be popular, too. The more curvaceous a company is (with exciting products and developments) the more it benefits from "a small bathing suit"—which in this case means having a *small amount of common stock outstanding*.

Take, for example, a company which has a new product with dynamic possibilities. Assume this product has a sales potential of $10 million, on which the company should show a profit of $1 million. This $1 million sounds big, but everything is relative: to a very large company with 100 million shares outstanding, the $1 million is peanuts (only one cent per share) whereas to a small organization with only 100,000 shares, the $1 million amounts to a gigantic $10.00 per share.

Thus, you can see the possibilities which exist in a growing company with only a small number of shares on which to compute its earnings (a "small capitalization," as they say in investment circles). A company like General Electric, which has over 90 million shares, *has* to come up with *countless* new discoveries which will bring a large volume of sales and profits to keep earnings per share growing, while companies with only a few hundred

314

thousand shares can grow rapidly with only one or two new developments. The experience of Mead Johnson & Co. with its weight-reducing formula "Metrecal" was a perfect example, although it was short-lived. Mead Johnson had a little over 1¾ million shares outstanding (this is still a relatively small capitalization) when it introduced Metrecal, and this one product was primarily responsible for the company's earnings ballooning from $3.02 per share in 1959 to $7.25 per share in 1960. This magnified effect was in turn responsible for Mead Johnson stock going from as low as 60 to as high as 164¾ during this one year.

Of course, there are two sides to the coin. Just as gains are magnified, so are losses. A small company which spends a great deal of money on a new development—only to see it flop—will experience large losses on a per share basis.

Still, because of the dramatic results which can be shown by small capitalization companies, investors should be willing to pay somewhat of a premium in price to own the promising ones. But you do have to be particular about which bikini stocks you buy.

RESULTS OF FIRST EDITION BIKINIS

In the first printing of *Stock Market Primer* (1962), I compiled a list of eight bikini companies which had proved successful for me in the preceding years. For the sake of example, I summed up the potential developments to which an investor had what I considered maximum exposure in each stock. Following is an *exact* reprint from the 1962 edition, showing my chosen "bikini" companies, the number of shares they had outstanding at that time and the major developments which looked to be the source of potential future excitement.

"BIKINI" STOCKS

Company	Shares Outstanding (Number)	Developments Which Could Be Magnified
American District Telegraph	651,000	ADT, approximately 80%-owned by Grinnell Corp., is the nation's largest factor in the field of burglar and fire alarm protection. Rising costs of employing round-the-clock watchmen plus constantly rising insurance rates (large discounts come from having efficient alarm systems) invite growing use of ADT services. Government has anti-trust suit against Grinnell; if ADT were spun off and became a completely separate entity, its stock would become popular. True earnings hidden by heavy depreciation charges.
Dymo Industries	442,000	Company has a unique labeling tape (used in conjunction with its own machines) which could have wide application by both consumers and by industry.
Heli-Coil	698,000	Has patented fastening device with increased strength, which could open up unlimited markets for a wide variety of uses.
Interstate Hosts (now Host International)	841,000	Provides participation in the future of air travel without being subject to regulation of C.A.B. Provides restaurant, beverage, snack bar, gift shop and newsstand services in many airports. Los Angeles airport

Company	Shares Outstanding (Number)	Developments Which Could Be Magnified
		(a major installation for Interstate) to be open completely in 1962.
Masco Corp.	734,000	Masco manufactures the "Delta" faucet, one of the top selling one-lever faucets in the U. S. Delta has only one moving part and has been strongly merchandised by management. Trend in bathroom construction and modernization is towards the single lever faucet.
Paddington Corp.	1,191,000	Exclusive distributor of J&B liquors, which have not yet been introduced into certain geographical areas (low saturation point).
Raychem Corporation	1,001,000	One of the few companies in the U. S. well advanced in the treatment of wire insulation and tubing by radiation. This method imparts certain qualities to materials (rubber, plastics, etc.) which adds to temperature resistance, strength, etc.
Howard W. Sams	501,000	Leader in supplying technical diagrams of electronic equipment to repair and maintenance people. Recently bought Bobbs-Merrill, book publishers.

Just for the record, here is how these eight companies performed over the ensuing years (all prices adjusted for subsequent splits, stock dividends, etc.):

Company	Sept. '62 Price	Subsequent High	% Gain to High	1968 Year End Price	% Gain to Present
A.D.T.	12½	42	237%	39¾	218%
Dymo	18⅝	52⅛	180	26½	43
Heli-Coil	11½	39⅜	251	23⅜	103
Host Int.	3½	48	1270	39	1015
Masco	5½	48⅜	780	41¼	650
Paddington	23¾	45⅝	84	40[a]	68
Raychem	29½	323	995	299	915
Sams (Howard)	20	62	210	58¼[b]	190

[a] Now merged into Charing Cross Importers, Ltd.
[b] Merged into International Telephone; price reflects current value of ITT stock.

As you can see, the overall performance of these bikini equities was pretty dramatic. The eight stocks showed an *average gain of 400%—which, of course, means that they quintupled in value.* Within the group, we find *two* situations which multiplied *over ten times their September, 1962 levels* (Host International and Raychem), one (Masco) which went up 7½ times and two more (ADT and Sams) which about tripled. In addition, their owners would have had the opportunity to derive an even higher return if they had been able to come close to selling near interim high points.

One further point should be stressed here—something which spells out the philosophy of many investors who seek out high reward situations. Successful venture capitalists and special situation stock buyers take the approach that a few big winners will achieve their goal. Realizing that it is difficult to predict just which individual stocks will succeed famously, they take a package approach and buy a handful (or so) of situations. Within the package, they hope to have selected a few like Hosts, Masco and Raychem which will appreciate sufficiently so as to bring about a very high return. *Most important, this philosophy dictates holding on for the huge returns those several situations might produce.* As I hope you have already gleaned from your reading, the secret to success is in thinking *BIG* and not being satisfied with small profits (if amassing large amounts of capital is your goal). Without this philosophy, this chapter—or any other on common stock selection—is of limited value.

Certainly the performance of these bikini stocks has been dynamic and yet, in many cases, the experience shown constitutes but a part of the story. So that you can understand the approaches necessary to bikini selection and so that you can see just how large the potential rewards really are, let me trace the reasoning and the results of four of these companies—ones which I uncovered and recommended strongly to people at one time in the past.

Dymo was first brought to market in June, 1960 at $9.00 per share. I knew absolutely nothing of this company at that time, but a few weeks later I saw its product in action and was immediately attracted by it. I proceeded to study Dymo and found that it had many growth company characteristics: management was aggressive, honest, able and hard-working ("hungry" as we say in our business); its labeling machine was well-engineered and the specialized Dymo tape had patent protection; the tape was expendable, meaning that repeat sales would be large; and competition was almost non-existent.

Equally important was the fact that Dymo had less than 450,000 shares outstanding. At that time Dymo stock was selling for $14 per share, and I had only to ask the following question to conclude the stock was a great buy: "Can Dymo some day soon earn $1 million?" This question was so important to answer because, with less than 450,000 shares outstanding, a net profit of $1 million meant per share earnings of over $2.00. Obviously these $2.00 per share earnings would guarantee far higher prices for Dymo stock than the existing $14 per share.

My analysis concluded that Dymo had at least this earning potential in the near future and it was on this basis that I became enthusiastic about this stock.

Before long the company reached the $1 million level in earning power—and Dymo common stock soared to $120 per share. In a span of a few years, the stock appreciated over 8 times. The combination of a growing and profitable product and a small capitalization had indeed brought spectacular results. Incidentally, Dymo is an example of a bikini company which required real flexibility. The company did not capitalize on its success as it should have; it failed to develop new products to complement its line—and as was to be expected, competition soon appeared on the scene. Because of this, I changed my position on the stock (very luckily, near its highs).

Another successful bikini stock of mine was Masco Corporation. Contrary to Dymo, which had just come on the market as a new issue and was trading over-the-counter, Masco had been publicly held for many years and was listed on the Detroit Stock Exchange. Like Dymo, I was attracted to Masco through my recognition of its product—in this case, the "Delta" one-lever faucet. It had come to my attention that one-lever faucets were becoming the trend in certain types of new residential construction and modernization, and I soon discovered that Masco's Delta faucet was increasing in acceptance and popularity. Masco had engineered a quality product—one that had only one moving part (an important sales feature); and the company had developed strong merchandising and had become one of the top two in its field.

I was amazed when I learned of Masco's growth record since it had introduced the Delta product in 1954 (the company had previously concentrated on serving the major auto manufacturers with auto parts—basically an unattractive business). Here's how the company's record looked in January, 1961, when I first became interested:

Year	Earnings Per Share
1956	$.06
1957	.15
1958	.17
1959	.48

You can imagine how amazed I was to find that Masco stock was selling at only $3.50 per share. Here again was an ideal bikini stock—a well-managed company with a fine product line, increasing business and only (*not* adjusted for splits) 367,000 shares outstanding. And—selling for less than 7 times 1959 earnings (more than a year before).

My analysis (which, as in the case of Dymo, included contact with management) led me to believe that profits in the year just completed (1960) were above those of 1959, and that 1961 would show even higher results. Some months later, Masco reported 1960 net income of $.65 per share. Yet the stock was still relatively unknown and was selling for a very reasonable $6.00 per share.

The rest of the story is certainly gratifying to me, because Thanksgiving Day of 1961 (less than a year after my discovery of Masco) found Masco stock at (adjusted) $27.00 per share— or almost 8 times its worth in January. A little over four years later, Masco had doubled again in price and was thus up about 16 times over its original "discovery" price. And today—in 1969 —the stock is selling for about 40 times our entry price.

The attraction of Host International should have been fairly obvious. As the description on page 316 indicates, the company had successful service operations located in airports which were certain to see increasing traffic over the years. In short, the thesis behind this bikini company was that it offered participation in the growth of air traffic without the vagaries of Federal regulation.

Typical of so many bikini situations, Host International took a number of years to blossom and become fully accepted for what it was. As a matter of fact, I lived with this stock for several years without finding any acceptance of its real worth. Once accepted, however, the stock found higher and higher evaluation by the investment community, which of course meant a higher and higher P/E multiple. At any rate, the stock multiplied more than eleven-fold over the period from 1962 to 1968.

Lastly, Raychem was a company which had an unusual technological know-how in an area which held startling possibilities. It held a tremendous lead time on potential competitors—something which is hard to come by and which is especially important if it exists within a bikini capitalization. Like Host International, Raychem took some time to develop. As a matter of fact, my Research Department at J. Barth published the "bible" on Raychem in July of 1963 (some 18 months after I completed the writing of *Primer*'s first edition) and the stock was actually lower then than before. A few years later, significant profits started to show at the company and the combination of these figures and a real acceptance of Raychem by investors took the stock up to the $300 level. Once again, concept + earnings + small number of shares outstanding brought unusual happiness to those who recognized bikini thinking.

BIKINIS, 1969 STYLE

Needless to say, selectivity in the bikini world is all-important. And since this book is devoted to more than theory, I suppose it is only right that I place my neck on the proverbial chopping block as I did in 1962. With a natural preface to you that both company progress and market prices can change sharply between writing time and your reading, following is a 1969 bikini edition. You will notice that most of those selected have more than one million shares outstanding—contrary to my 1962 list, which had but two stocks in this category. The main reason for this emanates from the position of the stock market in Spring of 1969. In short, the market has had excessive speculation and has witnessed a "picking over" of small companies—especially those trading over-the-counter and on the American Exchange. Said another way, you cannot "force" things in this business of stock selection. You either have the right situations or you do not—and if the values are not there in many of the smaller situations, you simply have to search for others. In no case, however, do I believe that the size of the capitalization restricts what should be well above-average growth. The potentials in relation to shares outstanding are still, in my opinion, sizable.

"BIKINI" STOCKS, 1969

Company	No. of Shares Outstanding	Developments Which Could Lead to Exceptional Growth
Bekins	1,698,000	Top mover in nation, yet not well-known in investment circles. Business not as cyclical as current P/E suggests. Management now diversifying into interesting service areas.

Company	No. of Shares Outstanding	Developments Which Could Lead to Exceptional Growth
Coldwell, Banker	1,707,000	The first publicly-owned real estate brokerage company, C-B is heavily involved in fast-growing California; engages in many aspects of real estate activity, including property management, appraisal, mortgage loan brokerage. Will no doubt use public vehicle to purchase related companies, which should add to earnings. Interesting exposure to assured real estate activity following Vietnam War.
Data Technology	1,184,000	Company with excellent digital voltmeter products. Kicker, however, exists in plastics division where unusual expertise exists. New venture in plastics could provide best investment exposure to fascinating growth of cassette recordings.
Everest & Jennings	1,325,000	The world's leading manufacturer of wheelchairs and related ambulatory equipment, the demand for which ties in to greater longevity of population, Medicare, encouragement to the sick to "get around." Strong product development and marketing. Will be expanding into other "rehabilitation" products.
Honolulu Gas	426,000	Manufactures gas for utility consumption in fast-growing Honolulu. Now planning additional refinery operation to service large energy users in area. Has plans for other energy ventures in Pacific Basin.

"BIKINI" STOCKS, 1969 (*cont.*)

Company	No. of Shares Outstanding	Developments Which Could Lead to Exceptional Growth
Informatics	1,474,000	While computer service area due for consolidation, this company has unusual position with proprietary programs. Large potential exists for AltarCSI computer reservation system for airlines (direct to travel agents).
John Roberts	526,000	Relatively new entry into field of high school and college jewelry (rings, pins, etc.) and into "graduation products." Very aggressive small company with unusual marketing know-how. Fact that students today more affluent, plus steadily rising educated population, give a broadened market to tap.
Maul Bros. Inc.	1,597,000	One of two leading producers of bottle-making machinery and parts. Has developed revolutionary equipment and benefits from significant parts and repair business. Furthermore, machinery operates under constant wear and has limited (2–4 years) life—which leads to steadily growing demand. Growing acceptance of non-returnable bottles is taxing industry's capacity, which is creating unusual demands for new machinery.
Rogers Corporation	867,000	Company has unusual technological know-how in plastics-related materials many of which are proprietary to Rogers. "Poron" breath-

Company	No. of Shares Outstanding	Developments Which Could Lead to Exceptional Growth
		able plastic finding growing use by shoe manufacturers; exclusive rights to unique concept for fastest growing segment of printing industry—offset printing; unusual know-how in high temperature materials and in flexible circuits necessary in office equipment and computers.
Saga Administrative	1,616,000	Largest independent factor in feeding educational institutions. Also engaged in actual development of school dormitories—and in providing food services for same. Fairly undiluted vehicle for exposure to the coming concept of mass-feeding, with emphasis on a fast-growing segment of business.

PART XV

DO'S AND DON'TS
IN THE STOCK MARKET

CHAPTER 37

Common Stock Commandments

The preceding pages have given you some basic facts and fundamentals about investments and the stock market. In addition, I have provided rules in each chapter which I believe will guarantee you greater success in your ventures. I won't bore you by repeating all these rules, but I have some further comments which should be equally helpful to you. I call these "common stock commandments" and here they are:

1. *Do not make hasty, emotional decisions about buying and selling stocks.* When you do what your emotions tell you to—on the spur of the moment—you are doing exactly what the "masses" are doing, and this is not generally profitable. It is better to wait until your emotions have returned to normal, so that you can weigh the pros and cons objectively as we did in Chapter 35. In line with this thinking, do not be pressured to buy or sell securities by anyone. Hard-selling techniques hint there may be "stale merchandise on the shelf," and that's not what you want. If you're in doubt about buying, my advice is to *do nothing.*

2. *If you are convinced that a company has dynamic growth prospects, do not sell it just because it looks temporarily too high.* You may never be able to buy it back lower in price and you stand to miss a potential *big winner*—which is just what you should be looking for. Perhaps the gravest error I've seen made over the years is selling great companies with bright future prospects just because they temporarily looked a few points too high. While on the subject of big winners, let me suggest the chapter on "How to

Amass Large Amounts of Capital" from the aforementioned *The Common Sense Way to Stock Market Profits.* The philosophy and the approach are a must for growth-oriented investors.

3. *Do not fall in love with stocks to the point where you can no longer be objective in your appraisal of them.* Stocks are different than women. You'd be a fool to think of your wife all day the way she looks first thing in the morning —maybe best that you think of her as she appears all dressed up. But you do have to scrutinize stocks and think of their worst points; you have to re-assess your love constantly and you have to be brutal and unemotional in your appraisal.

4. *Do not concern yourself as much with the market in general as with the outlook for individual stocks.* Often times you will see a fine stock come down in price to an unquestionable bargain price, only to let your feeling about the general market sway you away from buying it. As they say, it is not a stock market, but instead a market for (individual) stocks. Buy a good value as it appears and do not let the general market sentiment alter your decision.

5. *Forget about stock market "tips."* Use your good judgment and you won't have to rely on unreliable information. I realize that this point shows no world-shattering brilliance on my part, but so often I've seen this advice ignored. I'll never forget the day I was visited by a certain client of mine at my office. He wanted a recommendation on a good stock and I suggested he buy American Photocopy Equipment, which looked very attractive to me. I related my reasoning to him about the industry, the company, etc., and I showed him all the facts and figures I had on the stock. I spent 10 or 15 minutes on the glowing outlook of this company, and then my client told me he would think about it and let me know. The next morning he called me and placed an order—for an entirely different stock, one of the "Happyjack Uranium" type. He explained he "had heard some very good things" about this stock and he wanted to own it. A year or so later his purchase

was about half of his cost and he visited me again. This time he told me the "source" of his information: he had spent an hour at a very fancy cocktail lounge the evening of our original meeting and he had overheard a very confidential conversation about this stock. A fine thing, I thought (and my client agreed). Here I had spent hours researching American Photocopy and had given him the benefits of these hours—and he turned around and disregarded this in favor of a hot tip he overheard between two unknown people who had consumed an ample supply of martinis. So you see why I couldn't resist warning you against following tips in the stock market.

6. *You get what you pay for in the stock market (like everything else in life).* Some people consider a $5.00 stock good just because it's low in price. Nothing could be further from the truth. Most often, high-priced stocks provide far better value than low-priced stocks, in that the former generally have more earnings, dividends, etc. behind them than the low-priced issues. Likewise, high-priced stocks go into "better hands" (many are purchased by large institutional investors and others who are long term holders), while the low-priced issues most often go into the hands of the public and speculators and gamblers, all of whom are less-informed and subject to occasional panic selling. Also, remember that high-priced stocks carry one potential which cheap stocks do not—they are all potential split candidates.

7. *Remember that stocks always look worst at the bottom of a bear market (when an air of gloom prevails) and always look best at the top of a bull market (when everybody is optimistic).* Have strength and buy when things do look bleak and sell when they look too good to be true.

8. *Remember, too, that you'll seldom—if ever—buy stocks right at the bottom or sell them right at the top.* The stock market generally goes to extremes: when pessimism dominates, stocks go lower than they really should, based on their fundamentals, and when optimism runs rampant, stocks go higher than they really deserve to. Knowing this,

don't expect your stocks to go up in price immediately after you buy them or to go down after you sell them, even though you are convinced that your analysis of their value is correct.

9. *Do not buy stocks as you might store merchandise on sale.* No doubt you've seen people scrapping and clamoring for goods on sale at stores like Macy's, Penney, etc. They fight to buy this merchandise because the goods are reduced in price and because there is a limited supply of the merchandise. Too often people buy things they really don't need or really don't like and they find that they really haven't made a "good buy" at all. *But they simply couldn't resist the urge to join others in competing for something of which there was a limited supply.*

There is not a limited supply of actively-traded common stocks, thus I advise you not to rush to buy as though the supply is going to dry up. If you've ever sat in a stock brokerage office and watched the "tape" (which shows the stock transactions as they take place), you'll know what I mean. A certain stock might suddenly get active and start rising in price: one minute you see it at 35, a few seconds later it's 35½, then 36, 36¼, 36½, 37. By the time it has hit 37, it is human nature to feel an almost irresistible urge to buy the stock (regardless of its fundamentals of earnings, dividends, future outlook, etc.)—to get in on the gravy train, to join the rest of the flock who are clamoring to buy the stock as though it is "sale merchandise." Resist this urge—only buy "goods" which you're sure you'll like and which meet your objectives.

10. *There is no reason always to be in the stock market.* After the stock market has had a long and sizable advance, it is prudent to take a few profits. Too often, after selling, the money from the sale "burns a hole in the pocket" of the investor. It's like working in a candy shop: no matter how much will power you have, after a few weeks the bonbons look awfully good and it's hard to resist other "bonbon" stocks. Go slowly—there are times when cash can be a valuable asset.

11. *Seek professional advice for your investments.* Find a broker who is honest and who you are convinced will have *your* best interests at heart. Make sure he knows your financial status, your objectives and your temperament. If you don't know the right broker, consult your bank or your friends and then go in and meet the man who is recommended to you. Take the same pains to find the best broker as you would to find the best doctor for yourself. Relative to this, I strongly recommend your reading pages 185–204 of *The Common Sense Way to Stock Market Profits,* which deal with the subject of establishing a *profitable* relationship with a broker.

12. *Take advantage of the research facilities your broker has to offer.* Certainly you'll agree that *Analysis is a better market tool than a Pin.* The top brokerage firms spend hundreds of thousands of dollars every year to find the most attractive investments for their customers. Read the reports which are published—they will give you insight into the investment firm with whom you are dealing. Keep track of their performance over a period of years (performance over a few months may be deceiving, both because the general market may be against them and because you can't expect recommendations to bloom overnight). (Note: Part of the section of *Common Sense* referred to in our #11 above discusses research reports—their functions, advantages *and dangers.*)

13. *Remember that the public is generally wrong.* The masses are not well informed about investments and the stock market. They have not disciplined themselves correctly to make the right choices in the right industries at the right prices. They are moved mainly by their emotions, and history has proved them to be wrong consistently. If you don't believe this I recommend that you get hold of a book entitled *Extraordinary Popular Delusions and the Madness of Crowds,* written by Dr. Charles Mackay and published in 1841. The book totals over 700 pages and is filled with concrete examples of the irrational behavior of human beings. Dr. Mackay's descriptions of the famous

tulip mania in Holland in the 1630's and the famous South Sea bubble about a century later are eye-opening, to say the least. Just in case your high school or college history is not vivid in your mind, let me tell you what happened in these two historical events.

Tulip bulbs in Holland in the early 17th Century were originally sought by collectors and horticulturists just as orchids and other rare flowers are sought today. As the prices of tulip bulbs rose in the 1630's people commenced speculating in them. One thing led to another, prices rose further and suddenly everyone from the downstairs maid to the chimney sweep was speculating in markets which had sprung up solely for trading in tulips. Higher and higher went the prices of tulips—till there was absolutely no relationship between price and the tulips' intrinsic value. As is normal when a wide discrepancy exists between price and value, this situation was short-lived and it was not long before prices came tumbling down. Fortunes which had been made were quickly wiped out and the great majority suffered miserably from their emotional speculation.

In the 18th Century, similar speculation and failure occurred in shares of the English South Seas Company and thereafter there were bursting "bubbles" in all types of stock companies set up for every conceivable venture. To illustrate how emotional and irrational people became, the records show that one company was able to sell its own shares to the public even though it stated that its objective was "to carry on an undertaking of great advantage but nobody is to know what it is."

Dr. Mackay wasn't alive to describe similar events which took place after 1841. It is almost unbelievable, for example, to consider what came over otherwise sensible people in our country in the late 1920's. In this generation, we have witnessed boom-and-bust experience in uranium, boats, bowling, titanium, small business investment companies and an absolute host of others which resulted in large losses for their emotional followers.

A wise investor should be wary of public over-enthusiasm for anything. Don't *you* be "one of the herd" and be led to slaughter as have so many who have tossed sound thinking to the wind.

14. *Beware of following stock market "fads."*

Along the same line of reasoning discussed in commandments 9 and 13, I want to emphasize separately this idea of following fads in the market. Remember the "sack" dresses that became the fad a decade ago? This fashion was ill-conceived from the very beginning (it didn't make sense in such a vanity-conscious nation as ours). Women who rushed to buy the sack outfits found themselves with a useless wardrobe a short time later; and the retail stores which cluttered their racks with this merchandise suddenly found that their inventory was worth very little. But this is but one of many examples of fads in our country. Seven or eight years ago it was hula-hoops; five years ago it was trampoline centers; last year it was "Batman" and next year it will be something else. As a general rule, if you get in early in a fad you stand to make money. But if you come along after it is in full swing you are asking for trouble.

The same thing goes for the stock market. Just like sack dresses, hula-hoops, trampolines, tulip bulbs, etc., the stock market occasionally develops fads for certain industries. In almost all cases a sudden rush to buy the fad stocks pushes them to price levels which are truly unwarranted. *When you buy at the height of popularity you almost always pay prices which have little relationship to value.* As I have emphasized so often in this book, you are only asking for trouble when this situation exists, so remember to do some vacuum thinking and pay prices which correspond to earnings, growth rate, etc.

15. *Do not be so concerned with where a stock has already been—be instead concerned with where it is going.* Many times I've heard people say, "It must be a bargain now— it's down 20 points from its high." Where a stock *has been* is history, it's "spilt milk." Investors may have bid up ABC stock to $100 last year, but the outlook for the

company may have changed entirely since then. Or it may have been emotional speculation (fad-buying) which put it up to an unreasonable price. *The important thing is what lies ahead, not what has already transpired,* and previous market prices have no bearing on the future.

16. *Take the time to supervise your stocks periodically.* Needless to say, conditions are subject to constant change. Don't shut yourself off from the outside world; take an objective look at your holdings periodically, with the thought of weeding out the "weak sisters" and adding stocks which have more potential. Your broker should be willing to make an analysis of your portfolio for you on a regular basis and I encourage you to take advantage of this service.

17. *Concentrate on quality.* While big profits are often made through buying and selling poor quality common stocks, your success in the stock market is far, far more assured if you emphasize quality in your stock selections. Too many investors shy away from the top-notch companies in search of rags-to-riches performers. This, of course, is fine for a certain portion of your investment dollars, since most people can afford an *occasional* "flyer." But a person who starts out looking for flyers usually ends up, not with just one or two, but with a host of poor quality stocks— most of which turn out unsuccessful. These low grade issues are certainly no foundation for a good portfolio; instead, the fine, well-managed companies should form the backbone. And don't for a minute think you can't make money without wild speculation—fabulous fortunes have been made over the years in such high quality, *non*-speculative stocks as Carnation, Coca-Cola, Procter & Gamble, and others. In other words, place your stress on the elite, not on the so-called "cats and dogs" of the marketplace. "Remember," said one wise stock market philosopher, "if you sleep with dogs, you're bound to get fleas."

CHAPTER 38

Final Financial Formulae

At the beginning of this book I discussed finding an effective formula for successful investing in the stock market. Unfortunately you can't have a pure mathematical formula which will solve all the problems of investing. You can't do as the mathematicians do and say that $X = Y + Z^2$ (4 x Y^3) and be sure that X will be correct 100% of the time. But you should strive for a high batting average and the preceding pages have instructed you on how to lead the league in making successful purchases and sales of stocks.

Sometimes the simplest rules are the best and I can summarize all the sage advice that successful speculators and investors have passed down to us over the years. This summary would read simply:

> *Here's the money-making lullaby:*
> *Buy stocks* low *and sell them* high.

But I'm afraid that's over-simplification. Anyway, there is one bit of sincere advice that will bring all that we have covered so far to a conclusion. This important advice can be stated in one significant word:

PATIENCE

Actually, patience is often times the secret to success in any form of investment. Whether you own stock or real estate or your own business, you cannot expect success to come overnight. Obviously, there may be times in your investment life when some of

336

the stocks you own are not moving up the way you would like. But remember—"Rome wasn't built in a day." And patience is indeed an investment virtue. So, don't be fidgety with your stocks. Don't be concerned with the day-to-day fluctuations which occur in the stock market. I always think of a statement made by one very successful investor. He contended that he "made more money *by the seat of his pants than by his agile brain.*" In other words:

Believe in the growth of this country;

Buy the companies which will lead and share in this growth;

Concentrate on quality stocks with top management and buy value;

Have patience and "sit" on the good stocks.

The result should be: real success in the stock market!

The preceding pages have given you all the tools you will need. I have given you the background and the hindsight necessary for success. I've given you food for thought which prepares you to add foresight to hindsight. And I've supplied you with many basic rules which should keep you from making mistakes and a Compounding Growth Guide which enables you to judge a stock's fundamental value. In short, I think we've covered the bases and have both a solid defense against unnecessary losses and a potent offense for making sizable gains. Once again, let me suggest your progression from here—in reading *The Common Sense Way to Stock Market Profits*, which will add to your skills and sophistication in this business of making money in the market.

How to Arrive at a Company's Annual Compound Growth Rate

The basis of our Compounding Growth Guide lies with the investors' appraisal of a company's future yearly rate of growth. The procedure involves:

1) determination of a company's annual compound rate of growth over the *past* 3–5 years;

2) an analysis of whether this growth rate will increase or decrease over the *next* 3–5 years;

3) allowance for the kind of institutional support a stock commands;

4) conclusion of the "proper P/E," according to our Guide.

Because the annual compound growth rate in the *past* and in the *future* is so important, I want to make it easy for you to be able to figure this rate. The mathematical formula for doing this is rather complicated, so I have done all the figuring for you (that is, I had an electronic computer do it). The result is a very simple table for you to use.

All *you* have to do is figure what a company's *total increase in earnings per share* has been (or is going to be) over a 3–5 year period and then the table will tell you what the company's annual compound growth rate has been (or is going to be). Your computation is very simple but, just for review, here is how total increase over a period of time (on a percentage basis) is computed:

First of all, subtract the earnings per share for the first year you are using (your base year) from the *last* year you are using.

Example: You are analyzing ABC Company, which has had the following record over the last four years:

1960	$1.50
1959	1.37
1958	1.10
1957	1.15
1956	1.00

In this case, subtract the first year (the 1956 base year) from the last year (1960):

$$\$1.50 - \$1.00 = \$.50$$

Next divide this answer ($.50) by the base year figure ($1.00):

$$\$ .50 \div \$1.00 = .50 \text{ or } 50\%$$

This is the total percentage increase in earnings per share over the period you have chosen. ABC's total growth from 1956–1960 was 50%.

Once you have arrived at this simple calculation of the percentage increase, it becomes only a matter of consulting the following table to determine the *yearly compound growth rate.* Simply:

1) glance down Column A till you come to the closest corresponding figure to your answer above (percentage increase in earnings);
2) follow this figure to your right—and stop at Column B, C *or* D, depending on whether your calculation is based on a 3, 4 *or* 5 year period. This number designates the company's annual compound growth rate. (In the case of ABC, the 50% line on Column C— four years—is 11%; this 11% is ABC's yearly compound growth rate).

Incidentally, I have given you 3, 4 and 5 year figures for the important reason that you will want to use different periods for different companies. You have to be careful which base year you start with in computing a company's earnings growth. It is naturally wrong to start with a year which is either greatly depressed or greatly inflated. Instead, choose a year which is more normal as a base, or use the average of a few years as a base and compute growth from this.

TABLE GIVING ANNUAL COMPOUND GROWTH RATES

COLUMN A			
If the Company's Percentage growth has been (or will be) a total of	Then the Company's Annual Compounded Growth Rate is* as follows, if the period of years used is:		
	COLUMN B	COLUMN C	COLUMN D
	3 Years*	4 Years*	5 Years*
5%	1½ %	1%	1%
10	3	2½	2
15	5	3½	3
20	6	5	4
25	8	6	4½
30	9	7	5½
35	10½	8	6
40	12	9	7
45	13	10	8
50	14½	11	8½
55	16	11½	9
60	17	12½	10
65	18	13	10½
70	19	14	11
75	20½	15	12
80	21½	16	12½
85	23	17	13
90	24	17½	14
95	25	18	14½
100	26	19	15
105	27	20	15½
110	28	20½	16
115	29	21	16½
120	30	22	17
125	31	22½	17½
130	32	23	18
135	33	24	18½
140	34	24½	19
145	35	25	19½

* Figures rounded out to nearest one-half percent.

Annual Compound Growth Rates (*continued*)

COLUMN A Percentage growth	COLUMN B 3 Years*	COLUMN C 4 Years*	COLUMN D 5 Years*
150	36	26	20
155	37	26½	20½
160	37½	27	21
165	38½	27½	21½
170	39	28	22
175	40	29	22½
180	41	29½	23
185	42	30	23½
190	42½	30½	24
195	43½	31	24
200	44	31½	24½
225	48	34½	26½
250	52	37	28½
275	55½	39	30
300	59	41½	32
325	62	43½	33½
350	65	45½	35
375	68	47½	36½
400	71	49½	38

* Figures rounded out to nearest one-half percent.

INDEX

About the Author

Claude N. Rosenberg, Jr., is one of the country's leading investment experts. His approach to investments emphasizes low-risk, high-reward situations—and his unusual success has stemmed from his ability to uncover many stocks which have multiplied ten-, twenty-, and thirtyfold. Most important, his philosophy is one that discourages an investor from selling good stocks too soon.

Mr. Rosenberg is a general partner in the investment firm of J. Barth & Co. in San Francisco. His Research Department there, which is the largest in the western part of the United States, is one of the most respected in the world. Mr. Rosenberg's stock market comments and ideas are widely read and quoted both nationally and internationally.